William Horatio Barnes

History of Congress. The Fortieth Congress of the United States.

1867-1869

Vol. 1

William Horatio Barnes

History of Congress. The Fortieth Congress of the United States. 1867-1869
Vol. 1

ISBN/EAN: 9783337185305

Printed in Europe, USA, Canada, Australia, Japan

Cover: Foto ©ninafisch / pixelio.de

More available books at **www.hansebooks.com**

THE FORTIETH CONGRESS OF THE UNITED STATES

BY

William H. Barnes

PORTRAITS ON STEEL,

BY

George E. Perine

<⊙•⊙>

NEW YORK:

HISTORY OF CONGRESS.

THE

FORTIETH CONGRESS

OF THE

UNITED STATES.

1867–1869.
VOLUME I.

By WILLIAM HORATIO BARNES, A.M.,

WITH PORTRAITS ON STEEL.

NEW YORK:
W. H. BARNES & CO., PUBLISHERS,
37 PARK ROW.
1871.

Entered according to Act of Congress, in the year 1870, by

WILLIAM H. BARNES,

in the Office of the Librarian of Congress at Washington.

PREFACE.

THESE volumes delineate the men composing the greatest legislative body in the world. No similar assembly is convened from such extended territory, represents so great a constituency, or possesses powers so immense, as the Congress of the United States.

The Fortieth Congress will not suffer in comparison with any of its predecessors. It exhibited more practical statesmanship, sound wisdom, and effective eloquence than had been displayed by the legislative department in any previous period of American history. It is a popular error to assert that earlier Congresses were composed of men superior to those whose names adorn contemporary annals. With a propensity to revere antiquity, we look backward through a golden haze which magnifies the statesmen of remoter times; but observed carefully with critical eyes, and accurately measured by a modern standard, they lose their gigantic proportions. Thirty years ago but few statesmen exhibited such abilities as many living legislators are now devoting to the public service.

In the preparation of this work it has not been the author's task to single out the Eminent Americans and Men of the Times whose portraits and biographies should adorn these pages. The people themselves made the choice. Out of thirty millions they selected those whom they regarded as best fitted for their highest Legislative labors, and thus designated the men of all others most worthy of biographical and artistical illustration.

In presenting this portraiture we hold the mirror up to the people that they may see themselves reflected in their Representative men. They may well be proud to belong to a nation which produces such men, and feel confident of the high destiny of a country whose interests are confided to such statesmen. Youth who admire the portraits will be spurred to emulative activity when they learn from the biographies that the subjects were the architects of their own fortunes. Nearly all in early life walked the stony path of poverty, and arose to eminence by their unaided energy and talent.

The biographies are plain, unvarnished narratives of facts, unbiased by political attractions or repulsions. They will be found to embody much of national as well as personal history. Concise war-histories of New York, Illinois, Indiana, and Michigan are to be found in the sketches of the late Governors of those States who were members of the Fortieth Congress. A history of the war itself may be gleaned from the military exploits of men who were as valiant in the field as they have since shown themselves wise in council.

The material for the biographical portion of the work has been obtained from sources so numerous and varied that they cannot be particularly designated. Hundreds of letters from persons in public and private life have furnished the author with numerous important facts never before published. Biographical books of reference, State Histories of the Rebellion, numerous pamphlets and newspapers, have afforded valuable material. The sketches generally end abruptly and are necessarily incomplete, from the fact that their subjects, with a single exception, are still living to perform other distinguished and useful services.

No body of men ever before received so full and elaborate illustration by means of engraving. The time necessary for the production of finished engravings, as well as the necessary limits of the work, have prevented the presentation of the portraits of all. No previously published book has contained so many first-class engravings. The portraits are as accurate as could be secured by the combined arts of photography and engraving. The work, produced at an immense expense, is submitted with the confident expectation that it will be duly appreciated by an intelligent public.

NEW YORK, September 1, 1869.

LIST OF PORTRAITS.

VOLUME I.

ANTHONY, HENRY B.,	185
ASHLEY, JAMES M.,	255
BARNES, DEMAS,	229
BINGHAM, JOHN A.,	199
BUCKALEW, CHARLES R.,	47
BUCKLAND, RALPH P.,	235
CAMERON, SIMON,	157
CATTELL, ALEXANDER G.,	43
CHANDLER, ZACHARIAH,	81
CLARKE, READER W.,	221
CLARKE, SIDNEY,	205
COLE, CORNELIUS,	99
COLFAX, SCHUYLER,	193
CONNESS, JOHN,	51
CORBETT, HENRY W.,	115
COVODE, JOHN,	215
CRAGIN, AARON H.,	61
CULLOM, SHELBY M.,	235
DIXON, JAMES,	181
DOOLITTLE, JAMES R.,	55
DRAKE, CHARLES D.,	109
DRIGGS, JOHN F.,	217
FESSENDEN, WILLIAM P.,	75
HARDING, ABNER C.,	223
HARLAN, JAMES,	35
HENDRICKS, THOMAS A.,	95
HOWARD, JACOB M.,	139
HOWE, TIMOTHY O.,	147
HUBBARD, CHESTER D.,	275
HULBURD, CALVIN T.,	231
JOHNSON, REVERDY,	119
LYNCH, JOHN,	243

LIST OF PORTRAITS.

MALLORY, RUFUS,	265
MORGAN, EDWIN D.,	85
MORRELL, DANIEL J.,	251
MORRILL, LOT M.,	177
MORTON, OLIVER P.,	167
MYERS, LEONARD,	261
NYE, JAMES W.,	163
PATTERSON, JAMES W.,	127
PILE, WILLIAM A.,	279
POMEROY, SAMUEL C.,	80
ROBERTSON, WILLIAM H.,	229
SCOFIELD, GLENNI W.,	247
SHERMAN, JOHN,	153
SPRAGUE, WILLIAM,	161
STEWART, WILLIAM M.,	159
STOKES, WILLIAM B.,	209
SUMNER, CHARLES,	29
THAYER, JOHN M.,	125
TRUMBULL, LYMAN,	165
VAN AERNAM, HENRY,	213
WADE, BENJAMIN F.,	23
WASHBURNE, ELIHU B.,	203
WASHBURN, HENRY D.,	271
WELKER, MARTIN,	267
WILLEY, WAITMAN T.,	63
WILLIAMS, GEORGE H.,	189
WILSON, HENRY,	133
WILSON, JOHN T.,	259
YATES, RICHARD,	108

THE FORTIETH CONGRESS.

THE Fortieth Congress ranks among the most remarkable legislative bodies of ancient or modern times. The men who composed it, the emergencies in which it was placed, and the measures which it enacted, all contribute to its distinction. It must ever occupy a high historical position by reason of its achievements in completing the work of Reconstruction begun by its predecessor, and the great struggle which it maintained with the Executive branch of the Government.

The Thirty-ninth Congress closed its labors and its existence at noon, on the 4th of March, 1867. At the same hour, in accordance with a recently enacted law, the Fortieth Congress convened, and proceeded to organize for business. So large a proportion of the members had been re-elected, that the new Congress formed essentially the same body as its predecessor. The membership, however, was not complete, since the States of New Hampshire, Rhode Island, Connecticut, Tennessee, Kentucky, California, and Nebraska, had not yet held their elections, and were not represented in the House. The States of Virginia, North Carolina, South Carolina, Georgia, Florida, Alabama, Mississippi, Louisiana, Texas, and Arkansas were unrepresented, by reason of their failure hitherto to comply with the terms of reconstruction.

Before the House entered upon the regular routine of business, the Democratic members took occasion to enter their "most solemn protest against the organization of the House, until the absent States should be more fully represented."

The Senate was called to order by Hon. Benjamin F. Wade, who had been elected its President *pro tempore* before the close of the

THE FORTIETH CONGRESS.

previous Congress. The House of Representatives was organized by the election to the speakership of Hon. Schuyler Colfax, now for the third time the recipient of that high honor.

Congress at once addressed itself to the duty of perfecting the work of Reconstruction. The bill which had been passed over the President's veto, March 2d, was incomplete in not having all the provisions necessary for carrying it into effect in accordance with the purposes of its framers.

Supplementary Reconstruction bills were proposed by Mr. Wilson in the House, and Mr. Trumbull in the Senate. The best features of both having been combined and fully discussed, the perfected bill was finally passed over the President's veto on the 23d of March. In this supplementary bill, directions were given for the due registration of voters, the method of conducting elections, and the mode of calling conventions.

Before the close of the preceding Congress, a conviction had taken possession of many minds that the President, in his career of opposition to the legislative branch of the Government, had been guilty of crimes and misdemeanors which laid him liable to impeachment. On the 7th of January, 1867, Mr. Ashley, of Ohio, offered a resolution, which passed by a vote of 108 to 38, instructing the Judiciary Committee to "inquire into the official conduct of Andrew Johnson," and report whether he had been guilty of "high crimes and misdemeanors, requiring the interposition of the Constitutional power of the House." The Committee to which this question was referred, was unable to complete its investigations before the close of the Thirty-ninth Congress, and the undetermined question of impeachment was handed over to the discussion and action of the Fortieth Congress. In the first session of this Congress its Judiciary Committee was charged with the duty of continuing the investigations, with instructions to report at the second session. Congress adjourned on the 30th of March, making provision for re-assembling on the 3d of July, if the exigencies of Reconstruction or the conduct of the President should make a meeting necessary.

The President manifested extreme unwillingness to execute the Reconstruction laws. He was sustained in his position of hostility to Congress by the opinion of his Attorney-General, which justified him in disregarding the laws recently enacted for the government of the Rebel States. Alarmed by this attitude of the President and his subordinate, Congress re-assembled in full force on the 3d of July, prepared to meet the exigencies of the hour. "The peculiar views," said Mr. Howard in the Senate, "taken by the Attorney-General of the United States of the reconstruction acts of Congress, and the apprehension of the members of this body, at least the majority, that the President of the United States, in the execution of those acts, may or will be governed by the conclusions to which his legal advisers have arrived, have doubtless been the great causes for the re-assembling of Congress."

An additional Reconstruction act was passed over the President's veto on the 19th of July. A practical feature of this bill, which distinguished it from previous acts, was a provision devolving many of the details of the execution of the laws upon the General of the Army, in whose abilities and integrity Congress and the country placed full reliance. That nothing might be left undone to aid in the full restoration of the South, Congress appropriated one million six hundred and seventy-five thousand dollars to defray the necessary expenses of Reconstruction.

The President, in a communication relating to the cost of carrying out the provisions of the Reconstruction bills, stated that if the Federal Government should abolish the existing State governments of the ten States, the United States would be justly responsible for the debts incurred by those States for other purposes than in aid of the rebellion; those debts amounted to at least $100,000,000. He thought it worthy the consideration of Congress whether the assumption of so great an obligation would not seriously impair the national credit; whether, on the other hand, "the refusal of Congress to guarantee the payment of the debts of those States, after having displaced or abolished their State governments, would not be viewed as a violation of good faith, and a repudiation by the National Legislature of liabilities which those States had jointly and legally incurred. The House, by a vote of 100 to 18, resolved that this intimation of the liability of the United States for those debts, "is at war with the principles of international law, a deliberate stab at the national credit, abhorrent to every sentiment of loyalty, and well-pleasing only to the traitors by whose agency alone the Governments of said States were overthrown."

When the Fortieth Congress convened for its second session on the 21st of November, 1867, its first important business was to hear a report from the Committee charged with the work of investigating the conduct of the President, with a view to his impeachment. On the 25th of November, Mr. Boutwell presented to the House the report of that Committee, recommending that Andrew Johnson be impeached for high crimes and misdemeanors. On the same day, a minority of the Committee presented a dissenting report recommending that the whole subject be laid on the table, and that the Committee be discharged. Both reports were ordered to be printed, and the subject was made the special order for Wednesday, the 4th of December. On that day the subject was resumed, and after a discussion of three days, was determined against impeachment, fifty-seven voting in the affirmative, and one hundred and eight in the negative. Of those voting in the negative, thirty-nine were Democrats, and sixty-nine were Republicans. The "overt act" was yet to be committed which would consolidate the Republicans to form the Constitutional two-thirds required for the impeachment of the President.

The character of Mr. Johnson's message, delivered to Congress on the 3d of December, was such as to indicate his unmitigated hostility to Congress, and was calculated to fan the unhappy strife between the co-ordinate branches of the Government. There had been some hope that Mr. Johnson, taught by observation and experience that the Congressional plan of reconstruction was that upon which the country had determined, would relax his opposition, and apply himself to the duty of executing the laws. His December message dispelled this hope. From the moment this paper was made public, it was evident that a fiercer conflict was impending between the Legislative and Executive branches of the Government.

On the 12th of December, President Johnson transmitted to the Senate a communication setting forth his reasons for suspending Mr. Stanton from the exercise of the functions of Secretary of War. The general ground upon which Mr. Johnson justified his suspension of Mr. Stanton, was, that upon grave and important questions the views of the Secretary of War differed from those of the President. Mr. Johnson, in the case of the Secretary of War, did not admit that he was bound by the Tenure of Office Act, since before he had vetoed it, every member of his Cabinet, including Mr. Stanton, had agreed that it was unconstitutional. So soon as it had been discovered that the differences of policy could not be reconciled, those members of the Cabinet who did not coincide with the President, save Mr. Stanton, had resigned. By Mr. Stanton's continuance in office, "that unity of opinion which, upon great questions of public policy or administration, is so essential to the Executive, was gone." Since Mr. Stanton would not resign to produce this desired unity, Mr. Johnson had been induced to resort to his suspension.

This message was referred to the Military Committee of the Senate, a majority of whom, on the 8th of January, presented an elaborate report controverting the statements and assumptions of the President. The design of the Tenure of Office Act was to prevent the President from making any removals except for mental or moral incapacity, or for some legal disqualification; and then, facts must be proved prior to removals. The constitutionality of the Tenure of Office Bill was maintained. The President had himself recognized it by his action in every case. The Report declared that if the purposes of Mr. Johnson, for which he required the unanimous support of his Cabinet, had been carried out, "the plain intention of Congress in regard to reconstruction in rebel States would have been defeated." The Military Committee said of Mr. Johnson, that "his whole course of conduct was notoriously in open and violent antagonism to the will of the nation as expressed by the two Houses of Congress. Mr. Stanton, on the other hand, had favored the execution of these laws. He had good reason to believe, and did believe, that if he resigned his post, Mr. Johnson would fill the vacancy by the appointment of some person in accord with himself in his plans of obstruction and resistance to the will of Congress." With reference to the statement by the President that Mr. Stanton had considered the Tenure of Office Bill unconstitutional, and was opposed to its becoming a law, it was said in the report, "It does not follow because a public officer has entertained such an opinion of a proposed measure, he is to carry his notions so far as to treat it as void when formally enacted into a law by a two-thirds vote of each House of Congress." The Committee eulogized Mr. Stanton's conduct in refusing to resign, declaring that "in so doing he consulted both his own duty and the best interests of the country." They recommended the passage of a Resolution by the Senate non-concurring in the suspension of Mr. Stanton. The resolution was adopted by a majority of thirty-five to six. In consequence of this action of the Senate, General Grant ceased to exercise the functions of Secretary of War *ad interim*, and Mr. Stanton resumed the duties of his office.

General Grant incurred the displeasure of the President because he did not resign the Secretaryship into his hands, that he might appoint another, who would prevent Mr. Stanton from resuming the office. The voluminous correspondence which followed, attracted much attention, and revealed in a clear light the characters of the two distinguished disputants. The letters of the President showed that it was his determination to control the Department of War, despite the Tenure of Office Act and the will of the Senate.

In view of the state of things brought to light in this correspondence, Mr. Stevens, on the 13th of February, proposed to the House Committee on Reconstruction, a resolution to impeach the President for high crimes and misdemeanors. The resolution was laid on the table, Messrs. Bingham, Paine, Beaman, Brooks, and Beck, voting in the affirmative, and Stevens, Boutwell, and Farnsworth, in the negative.

On the twenty-first of February, the President issued an order to Mr. Stanton, removing him from the office of Secretary of War, directing him to surrender all books, papers, and public property of the Department to General Lorenzo Thomas, whom he had appointed Secretary of War *ad interim*. General Thomas immediately presented himself at the War Department and demanded possession. Mr. Stanton refused to surrender the office, and ordered General Thomas to proceed to the apartment which belonged to him as Adjutant-General. This order was not obeyed. Mr. Stanton remained in possession of the War Department, and continued to discharge the functions of the office. At the same time General Thomas was recognized as Secretary by the President, and in that capacity attended the meetings of the Cabinet.

On the 22d of February, Mr. Stevens, as Chairman of the House Committee on Reconstruction, presented a brief report, presenting the fact of the attempted removal of Mr. Stanton by the President, and recommending the passage of a resolution that Andrew Johnson be impeached for high crimes and misdemeanors. An earnest debate ensued, which was closed with a speech written by Mr. Stevens, but read by the Clerk of the House. The veteran Chairman of the Committee and former leader of the House, with a mind still vigorous, found his physical strength insufficient for personal participation in debate. After two days' discussion, on the 24th of February, the Resolution to impeach the President passed the House by a vote of one hundred and twenty-six to forty-seven.

The House also appointed a committee to prepare Articles of Impeachment, consisting of seven members: Messrs. Boutwell, Stevens, Bingham, Wilson, Logan, Julian, and Ward. A committee of two members, Messrs. Stevens and Boutwell, was appointed to notify the Senate of the action of the House—a duty which was performed on the following day. Thereupon the Senate, by a unanimous vote, resolved that the message from the House should be referred to a committee of seven, to be appointed by the chair. This committee subsequently made a report, laying down the rules of procedure to be observed in the trial.

On the 29th of February, Articles of Impeachment were presented to the House by the Committee which had been charged with that duty. After slight modification, these, with two additional articles, were adopted, on the 4th of March. The votes on the different articles slightly varied, the average being 125 yeas to 40 nays. The House then elected the following members to be Managers to conduct the Impeachment before the Senate: Messrs. Bingham, Boutwell, Wilson, Butler, Williams, Logan, and Stevens.

The Democratic members abstained from voting in the election of Managers. They entered a formal protest against the whole course of proceedings involved in the impeachment of the President. While taking this step, they claimed to represent, "directly or in principles, more than one-half of the people of the United States." On the fifth of March the Articles of Impeachment were presented to the Senate by the Managers, who were accompanied by the House of Representatives, the grand inquest of the nation. Mr. Bingham, the Chairman of the Managers, read the Articles of Impeachment.

The Court, consisting of fifty-four Senators, presided over by the Chief-Justice, was organized on Thursday, the 5th of March. The oath was administered to Chief-Justice Chase by Associate-Justice Nelson. The Chief-Justice then administered the oath to the Senators present, except Mr. Wade, whose eligibility as a member of the court was challenged on the ground that he was a party interested, since in the event of the impeachment being sustained, he, as President of the Senate, would succeed to the Presidency of the United States. After a discussion of several hours, the objection was withdrawn, and Mr. Wade was sworn as a member of the Court. On the 7th, Mr. Brown, the Sergeant-at-Arms of the Senate, served upon the President the summons to appear before the bar of the High Court of Impeachment, and answer to the Articles of Impeachment.

The trial commenced on Friday, the 13th of March, the President appearing by his counsel, Henry Stanberry, Benjamin R. Curtis, William M. Evarts, Thomas A. R. Nelson, and William S. Groesbeck. Application was made by the President, through his counsel, for forty days in which to prepare his answer to the indictment. The Senate refused so much time, and granted ten days, ordering that the trial should be resumed on the 23d. Upon that day the President appeared by his counsel, and presented his answer to the Articles of Impeachment. His answer was a general denial of each and every criminal act charged in the Articles of Impeachment. The counsel for the President then asked for a further delay of the trial for thirty days after the replication of the Managers of the Impeachment should be rendered. This was refused, and the Managers, indicating their purpose to present their replication on the following day, it was ordered that the trial should be suspended only until Monday, the 30th of March, and then proceed "with all dispatch." The replication presented by the Managers was a simple denial of each and every averment in the answer of the President.

On the 30th of March, the opening speech on the part of the House of Representatives was made by Mr. Butler. The remainder of the week was occupied by the presentation of documentary and oral testimony on the part of the prosecution. On Saturday, April 4th, the Managers announced that the case on their part was substantially closed. The counsel for the President then asked for three working days in which to prepare for the defense. The Senate granted their request, and adjourned to meet as a Court of Impeachment on Thursday, April 9th. The trial being resumed on the day appointed, Mr. Curtis delivered the opening speech for the defense. At the conclusion of this address, the testimony for the President, both oral and documentary, was presented.

The testimony in the case having closed on Monday, April 20, the Court adjourned until the following Wednesday, when the final arguments were commenced. Oral arguments were presented by each of the President's counsel, and all of the Managers for the prosecution except Mr. Logan, who filed his in writing. The argument was closed for the defense by Mr. Evarts, and for the prosecution by Mr. Bingham, each of whom occupied three days in his address. The delivery of the arguments occupied a fortnight, ending on the 6th of May. On the following day, the mode of procedure having been determined, the Court adjourned until the 11th, when it re-assembled with closed doors for deliberation. Two days were occupied with these deliberations, during the course of which several Senators delivered elaborate opinions upon the case.

Saturday, May 6th, was fixed upon as the day when the vote should be taken. It was ordered by the Senate that the vote should be taken on the eleventh article first. The name of each Senator being called in alphabetical order, thirty-five voted "guilty," and nineteen "not guilty." The former were Messrs. Anthony, Cameron, Cattell, Chandler, Cole, Conkling, Conness, Corbett, Cragin, Drake, Edmunds, Ferry, Frelinghuysen, Harlan, Howard, Howe, Morgan, Morrill (of Maine), Morrill (of Vermont), Morton, Nye, Patterson (of New Hampshire), Pomeroy, Ramsey, Sherman, Sprague, Stewart, Sumner, Thayer, Tipton, Wade, Willey, Williams, Wilson, Yates.

Those voting "not guilty" were Messrs. Bayard, Buckalew, Davis, Dixon, Doolittle, Fessenden, Fowler, Grimes, Henderson, Hendricks, Johnson, M'Creery, Norton, Patterson (of Tennessee), Ross, Saulsbury, Trumbull, Van Winkle, Vickers.

Two-thirds of the Senate having failed to vote in favor of conviction, the Chief-Justice formally announced that the President was acquitted on the eleventh article. The Court was then adjourned until Tuesday, the 26th of May. On that day votes were taken on the second and third articles, on which the President was acquitted by the same vote which had been given on the eleventh article. The Senate sitting as a High Court of Impeachment then adjourned *sine die*.

During the trial of the Impeachment, but little was done in the way of general legislation. The House was officially present in the Chamber of the Senate while that body was sitting as a Court of Impeachment. Although it usually convened after the adjournment of the Court, it was understood to be for the purpose of debate rather than of action. During the days when the court was adjourned or in private session, some important measures were acted upon in the House. Among them were bills relating to certain of the late rebel States. Alabama, Arkansas, Georgia, Louisiana, North Carolina, South Carolina, and Florida, had formed Constitutions in accordance with the Act for the more efficient government of the rebel States, passed March 2, 1867. Bills passed the House in May, and the Senate in June, admitting these States to representation, so soon as they should respectively have ratified the Fourteenth Amendment of the Constitution, upon the fundamental condition that these States should never discriminate in favor of, or against, any class of citizens now entitled to vote, except as punishment for such crimes as are now felonies at common law; and no person shall be held to service or labor as punishment for crime, except by public officers charged with the custody of convicts. The bills admitting these States on such conditions to representation were returned by the President without his signature, and were promptly passed over the veto by more than the required two-thirds.

On the 22d of June, Messrs. McDonald and Rice, Senators elect from Arkansas, appeared at the bar of the Senate and were sworn in. On the day following, Messrs. Boles, Hinds, and Root were admitted to the House as representatives from Arkansas. Senators and Representatives from the other reconstructed States were sworn in at later dates.

All the Democratic members of the House, forty-five in number, entered a solemn protest against "the recognized presence of these persons on the floor of the House from the State of Arkansas, sent here by military force acting under a brigadier-general of the army, but nevertheless claiming to be members of this Congress, and to share with us, the representatives of free States, in the imposition of taxes, and customs, and other laws upon our people. We protest against the now proposed co-partnership of military dictators and negroes in the administration of this Government."

A concurrent resolution was adopted by both Houses on the 21st of July, stating that the Fourteenth Amendment of the Constitution, which had been proposed by the Thirty-ninth Congress, had been adopted by more than three-fourths of the States, and had thus become a part of the Constitution. On the 28th of July the Secretary of State issued his official declaration that the said Amendment had become valid to all intents and purposes as a part of the Constitution of the United States.

That the political status of the colored man might be for ever settled, another Amendment to the Constitution was proposed by the Fortieth Congress providing that "The right of the citizens of the United States to vote, shall not be denied or abridged by the United States or any State on account of race, color, or previous condition of servitude." This crowning act of the Fortieth Congress was passed in the House, February 25, 1869, by one hundred and forty-three to forty-three, and in the Senate on the following day by thirty-nine to twelve.

The labors of the Fortieth Congress were not only devoted to the restoration of the original States, but to extending the Government over new regions. A bill was passed organizing the Territory of Wyoming. Another act appropriated $7,200,000 to pay for Alaska, and extend the laws of the United States all over that country.

Circumstances seeming to demand legislation for the protection of American citizens abroad, the House of Representatives instructed its Committee on Foreign Affairs to inquire and report whether any American citizens had been arrested, tried, and convicted in Great Britain or Ireland, for words spoken or acts done in the United States. Mr. Banks, Chairman of the Committee on Foreign Affairs, presented a report upon the general question of the rights of naturalized American citizens, and proposed a bill, which after amendment by the Senate became a law. It provides that all naturalized citizens of the United States, while in foreign states, shall be entitled to, and shall receive from this Government, the same protection of persons and property that is accorded to native-born citizens in like situation and circumstances. That whenever it shall be made known to the President that any citizen of the United States has been unjustly deprived of his liberty by or under the authority of any foreign Government, it shall be the duty of the President forthwith to demand of that Government the reasons for such imprisonment; and if it appears to be wrongful and in violation of the rights of American citizenship, the President shall forthwith demand the release of such citizen; and if the release so demanded is unreasonably delayed or refused, it shall be the duty of the President to use such means, not amounting to acts of war, as he may think necessary and proper to obtain or effectuate such release, and all the facts and proceedings relative thereto shall as soon as practicable be communicated by the President to Congress.

In the attempt to better the condition of citizens at home, Congress passed a bill providing that "Eight hours shall constitute a day's work for all laborers, mechanics, and workmen now employed, or who may hereafter be employed by, or in behalf of the Government of the United States."

The Fortieth Congress was not deficient in the performance of its duty to legislate in behalf of races long deprived of civil and political rights. Early in the existence of the Fortieth Congress, a law was enacted providing that in the District of Columbia no person should be disqualified from holding office on account of race or color.

Congress ordered that the Freedman's Bureau be continued until July 16, 1869, and ordered the Secretary of War to re-establish the Bureau where it had been discontinued, if the personal safety of the freedmen required it, and to discontinue it where its necessity no longer existed, and providing that the educational division should not be interfered with until a State made suitable provision for the education of the children of the freedmen within the State.

A bill was passed to establish peace with Indian tribes, providing that commissioners should be appointed to select a district sufficient to receive all the tribes east of the Rocky Mountains, not living peacefully on reservations; that the district should contain sufficient arable and grazing land to enable them to support themselves by agricultural and pastoral pursuits; the district to remain a permanent home for the tribes exclusively, and to be so located as not to interfere with the travel on highways located by authority of the United States, nor with the routes of the Pacific Railroads.

The Fortieth Congress exempted all cotton grown in the United States after 1867 from Internal Revenue tax, and reduced the tax on manufactures to such an extent as to diminish the Revenue $60,000,000. The tax on whiskey was reduced to fifty cents per gallon. Illicit distilleries were made liable to forfeit, their owners being subject to fine and imprisonment.

Inharmonious relations continued to exist between President Johnson and Congress to the last. The President sent in numerous nominations to the Senate that were immediately rejected. The most remarkable instance was that of the mission to Austria, which had been resigned by Mr. Motley. The President successively nominated ex-Senator Cowan of Pennsylvania, General Frank P. Blair, ex-Senator Nesmith of Oregon, and Henry J. Raymond, who were all rejected by the Senate. Reverdy Johnson, Senator from Maryland, was confirmed by a unanimous vote as Minister to England. Mr. Stanberry, who had resigned the position of Attorney-General for the purpose of defending the President in the Impeachment Trial, was renominated and was rejected. Mr. Evarts of the President's counsel was subsequently nominated for the same office, and was confirmed. Near the close of the Fortieth Congress the Senate informally resolved that, except in cases of urgent necessity, no nomination to office made by President Johnson would be acted upon.

The President's message, transmitted at the beginning of the last session of the Fortieth Congress, was more hostile in its tone than any that had preceded it. He made severe charges against Congress and its legislation. "The various laws," said he, "which have been passed upon the subject of reconstruction, after a fair trial, have substantially failed, and proved pernicious in their results." He charged that, "one hundred million dollars were annually expended for the military force, a large portion of which is employed in the execution of laws both unnecessary and unconstitutional." He proposed a plan for paying the public debt by repudiating the principal. His message was denounced in both Houses as a disrespectful and offensive document. In the Senate its reading was interrupted by adjournment, but was resumed the following day. That portion relating to the National Debt was made the subject of special animadversion, and resolutions disapproving and condemning it were passed in both branches.

Many propositions were brought before the Fortieth Congress, from first to last, relating to the National Finances. At the very outset Mr. Edmunds proposed in the Senate a joint resolution, to the effect that, except in the cases when other provision was expressly made, the public debt is owing in coin or its equivalent.

Another prominent financial scheme was presented by Senator Morrill, providing that, after the 4th of July, 1869, the Secretary of the Treasury should pay in coin all United States legal tender notes not bearing interest, and that after the same date all National Banks should be required to pay in coin all their circulating notes of $5, and under, and all of a higher denomination in coin or legal tender notes. In July, 1868, a bill was proposed for funding the National Securities, providing that the holders of bonds paying 7.30 may exchange them for new bonds at 3.65 running forty years, principal and interest payable in gold, the bonds and interest to be free from all taxation. This bill passed both Houses, but at so late a day that it was held by the President until after the adjournment, and thus failed to become a law. A bill was proposed by Mr. Sumner, providing for a return to specie payments July 4, 1869, and for funding the National Debt at a lower rate of interest. A bill was proposed by Mr. Morton, designed to render at as early a date as possible the currency convertible into, and therefore of equal value with, gold. A directly opposite plan was proposed by General Butler in the House, looking to the indefinite prolongation of paper currency. No definite and final action was reached upon any of the financial plans proposed. It was thought proper to defer action upon these important questions until such time as the Legislative and Executive Departments of the Government should be in harmony.

BENJAMIN F. WADE.

PRESIDENT OF THE SENATE.

IN Feeding Hills Parish, Massachusetts, on the 27th of October, 1800, was born Benjamin F. Wade, the youngest of ten children. His father was a soldier of the Revolution, and fought in every battle from Bunker Hill to Yorktown. His mother was the daughter of a Presbyterian clergyman, and was a woman of vigorous intellect and great force of character.

The family was one of the poorest in New England. They had, however, among their scanty property a few books, which eventually came into Benjamin's possession. He never enjoyed more than seven days' schooling, yet under the tuition of his mother he soon learned to read and write. He read and re-read the few books of the family library, and as a boy became better informed than most of his age.

He was for a time employed as a farm hand on very meagre wages. When eighteen years old, thinking he might find something better in the West, with a bundle of clothing on his back, and seven dollars in his pocket, he started on foot for Illinois. He walked as far as Ashtabula County, Ohio, when a fall of snow having impeded his progress, he determined to wait for spring to finish his journey. He hired out to cut wood in the forest at fifty cents per cord. He spent his evenings reading the Bible by the light of the fire on the hearth of the log cabin, and in a single winter read through both Old and New Testaments.

When spring came, he was persuaded to further suspend his journey to Illinois, by engaging in a summer's work at chopping, logging, and grubbing. This was followed by a winter at school-teaching. After two years of such employment, he engaged in driving herds of cattle from Ohio to New York. He thus made six trips, the last one leaving him in Albany, New York. Here he taught a winter school, and in the spring hired himself to shovel on the Erie Canal, in which employment he spent the summer.—"The only American I know," said Governor Seward, in a speech in the Senate, "who worked with a spade and wheel-barrow on that great improvement."

Having occupied the summer in work on the canal, he taught school another winter in Ohio. In the following spring he commenced the study of law with Hon. Elisha Whittlesey. He was soon after elected a justice of the peace. After two years he was admitted to the bar. He waited another year for his first suit, and from that time his success was steady. He was elected Prosecuting Attorney for Ashtabula County, a position of great advantage to a young man just rising in his profession.

But Mr. Wade's destined field was politics. He was elected to the State Senate, where he took the lead of the Whig minority. He aided in abolishing the law for imprisonment for debt. He inaugurated a war against the "Black Laws" of Ohio. He took a bold stand against the admission of Texas into the Union. "So help me, God!" he declared, "I will never assist in adding another rod of slave territory to this country."

Mr. Wade having attempted to bring about a repeal of the State laws that oppressed the negroes and gave security to slavery in the neighboring States, incurred the displeasure of his party friends, who left him at home at the next election.

Time and events having at length brought the people up to Wade's position, they again sent him to the Senate against his will. There he procured the passage of a bill which founded the Oberlin College, "for the education of persons without regard to race or color." He led the resistance of Ohio to the resolution adopted by Congress, denying the people the right to petition concerning the abolition of slavery. He labored to bring the Legislature and the State up to the support of John Quincy Adams in his fight for the sacred right of petition.

In 1847, Mr. Wade was elected President Judge of the Third Judicial District. After the session of his court was over for the day, Judge Wade sometimes went to the neighboring school-houses and made speeches in favor of General Taylor, then a candidate for the Presidency. Since Wade was known far and near as a strong anti-slavery man, it was thought strange that he did not support Mr. Van Buren, the candidate of the Liberty party. Some of his friends remonstrated with him for supporting Taylor, a slaveholder. "Taylor is a good old Whig," he replied, "and I am not going to stand by and see him crucified between two such thieves as Cass and Van Buren." For four years he occupied the bench, and obtained with the bar and the people the reputation of a wise and just judge.

In March, 1851, as he was hearing a cause in court, the firing of a cannon in the streets of Akron announced to the public that Mr. Wade had been elected United States Senator by the Legislature of Ohio. The office had not been sought for by him, nor canvassed for by his friends. The arrangements of politicians and the selfishness of aspirants were over-ruled by the people in their desire to have one who would represent the manhood, the conscience, the *progress* of the State.

When Mr. Wade entered the Senate, he found but few opposed to the aggressions of slavery. In 1856, when the great Kansas controversy came up, the advocates of slavery were thirty-two against thirteen in favor of freedom. Wade showed himself brave against all odds and every influence. "I come before the Senate to-day," said he, "as a Republican, or, as some prefer to call me, a Black Republican, for I do not object to the term. I care nothing about the name; I come here especially as the advocate of liberty, instead of slavery."

Mr. Wade has continued a member of the United States Senate, by successive re-election, for eighteen years. His Senatorial career has been marked by indomitable energy, unfailing courage, and invariable consistency. It has been marked by some acts which cannot fail to cause his name to be remembered. He reported from the Committee on Territories the first provision prohibiting slavery in all the Territories of the United States to be henceforth acquired. He proposed in the Senate the bill for Negro Suffrage in the District of Columbia.

It was in the days when Republicans in Congress were few, and the champions of Slavery were dominant in the councils of the Republic, that Mr. Wade rendered services for the struggling cause of liberty that are never to be forgotten. He met the arrogant leaders of the South with a bravery that secured their respect, and gained friends for his cause. Toombs, the fierce fire-eater of Georgia, once said in the Senate, " My friend from Ohio puts the matter squarely. He is always honest, outspoken, and straightforward; and I wish to God the rest of you would imitate him. He speaks out like a man. He says what is the difference, and it is. He means what he says; you don't. He and I can agree about everything on earth except our sable population."

It was the custom in those days for Northern Senators to yield submissively to the insolence of the slaveholders. Mr. Wade had too much nerve and independence meekly to accept the situation. Soon after he took his seat, a Southerner in debate grossly insulted a Free State Senator. As no allusion was made to himself or his State, Wade sat still; but when the Senate adjourned, he said openly, if ever a Southern Senator made such an attack on him or Ohio while he sat on that floor, he would brand him as a liar. This coming to the ears of the Southern men, a Senator took occasion to pointedly speak, a few days afterward, of Ohio and her people as negro thieves. Instantly Mr. Wade sprang to his feet and pronounced the Senator a liar. The Southern Senators were astounded, and gathered round their champion; while the Northern men grouped about Wade. A feeler was put out from the Southern side, looking to retraction; but Mr. Wade retorted in his peculiar style, and demanded an apology for the insult offered himself and the people he represented. The matter thus closed, and a fight was looked upon as certain. The next day a gentleman called on the Senator from Ohio, and asked the usual question touching his acknowledgment of the code.

"I am here," he responded, "in a double capacity. I represent the State of Ohio, and I represent Ben. Wade. As a Senator, I am opposed to dueling. As Ben. Wade, I recognize the code."

"My friend feels aggrieved," said the gentleman, "at what you said in the Senate yesterday, and will ask for an apology or satisfaction."

"I was somewhat embarrassed," continued Senator Wade, "by my position yesterday, as I have some respect for the Chamber. I now take this opportunity to say what I then thought; and you will, if you please, repeat it. Your friend is a foul-mouthed old blackguard."

"Certainly, Senator Wade, you do not wish me to convey such a message as that?"

"Most undoubtedly I do; and will tell you, for your own benefit, this friend of yours will never notice it. I will not be asked for either retraction, explanation, or a fight."

Next morning Mr. Wade came into the Senate, and proceeding to his seat, deliberately drew from under his coat two large pistols, and, unlocking his desk, laid them inside. The Southern men looked on in silence, while the Northern members enjoyed the fire-eaters' surprise at the proceeding of the plucky Ohio Senator. No further notice was taken of the affair of the day before. Wade was not challenged, but ever afterward was treated with politeness and consideration by the Senator who had so insultingly attacked him.

Mr. Wade's fierce retorts sometimes fell with terrible effect upon his adversaries. When he was speaking against the Kansas-Nebraska bill, Mr. Douglas interrupted him with an inquiry designed at once to rebuke and embarrass him: "You, Sir, continually compliment Southern men who support this bill, but bitterly denounce Northern men who support it. Why is this? You say it is a moral wrong; you say it is a crime. If that be so, is it, not as much a crime for a Southern man to support it, as for a Northern man to do so?"

Mr. WADE.—" No, sir, I say not!"

Mr. DOUGLAS.—" The Senator says not. Then he entertains a different code of morals from myself and —"

Mr. WADE (breaking in, and pointing at Douglas with extended arm and forefinger, his face wrinkling with scorn, and contempt and rage flashing out of his eyes)—" *Your* code of morals! YOUR *morals!* My God, I hope so, sir!"

A witness of the scene says that the "Giant" was hit in the forehead, and, after standing for a moment, his cheeks as red as scarlet, he sank silent into his chair.

Mr. Wade gained enduring fame by the unanswerable reasoning, the powerful oratory, and the undaunted courage with which he resisted the extension of slavery against the united might of the propogandists of the South and North.

Near the close of the Thirty-ninth Congress, Mr. Wade was elected President *pro tempore* of the Senate. He was chosen to that office at a time when it seemed probable that his election would soon become an elevation to the Presidential Chair by virtue of the impeachment and removal of Mr. Johnson. The narrowness of Mr. Johnson's escape, and the nearness of Mr. Wade's approach to the Presidency, are among the most curious scenes in recent history.

As an orator, Senator Wade has little polish, but great force, directness, and effect. He is an original thinker, and has much learning for one whose advantages were so few. His manners are plain and unaffected, his tastes are simple as in his humbler years. At home, in Ohio, he lives in a style undistinguished from the substantial citizens about him. His residence is a plain white frame house, hid among the trees and surrounded by ample grounds.

"There is," says one, " a Puritan grimness in his face, which melts into sweetness and tenderness when his sympathies are touched, and which is softened away by the humor which wells from his mirthfulness in broad, rich, and original streams."

CHARLES SUMNER.

THE ancestors of Charles Sumner were among the early emigrants to New England. His father's cousin, Increase Sumner, was one of the early governors of the State of Massachusetts, and was regarded as a worthy successor of Hancock and Adams. The father of Charles Sumner was a successful lawyer, and for many years held the office of High Sheriff of the County of Suffolk.

Charles Sumner was born in Boston, January 6th, 1811. Having received a preparatory training in the Boston Latin School, and the Phillips Academy, he became a student in Harvard College, where he graduated in 1830. He subsequently entered the Cambridge Law School, where he pursued his studies three years under the direction of Judge Story, with whom he formed an intimate and lasting friendship.

In 1836 he was admitted to the bar, and rose rapidly in his profession. He was appointed Reporter of the Circuit Court of the United States; and, while holding this office, published three volumes of decisions, known as "Sumner's Reports." At the same time he edited the "American Jurist," a law paper of high reputation.

During three winters following his admission to the bar, Mr. Sumner lectured to the students of the Cambridge Law School. Then, as in after life, his favorite subjects were those relating to constitutional law and the law of nations. In 1836 he was offered a professorship in the Law School, and in Harvard College, both of which he declined.

In 1837 he visited Europe, where he remained till 1840, traveling in Italy, Germany, and France, and residing a year in England. His time was improved in adding to his previous literary and legal attainments an extensive knowledge of the languages and literature of modern Europe.

After three years spent abroad, Mr. Sumner returned to his native city, and resumed the practice of law. In addition to his professional duties, he was occupied from 1844 to 1846 in editing and publishing an elaborately annotated edition of "Vesey's Reports," in twenty volumes.

Mr. Sumner was recognized as belonging to the Whig party, yet for several years after his return from Europe he took but little part in politics. He made his first appearance on the political stage on the 4th of July, 1845, when he pronounced an oration before the municipal authorities of Boston on "The True Grandeur of Nations." This utterance was made in view of the aspect of affairs which portended war between the United States and Mexico. This oration attracted great attention, and was widely circulated both in Europe and America. Cobden pronounced it "the most noble contribution made by any modern writer to the cause of peace."

At a popular meeting in Faneuil Hall, November 4, 1845, Mr. Sumner made an eloquent and able argument in opposition to the annexation of Texas, on the ground of slavery. In the following year he delivered an address before the Whig State Convention of Massachusetts on "The Anti-Slavery Duties of the Whig Party." In this address, Mr. Sumner avowed himself the uncompromising enemy of slavery. He announced his purpose to pursue his opposition to that great evil, under the Constitution, which he maintained was an instrument designed to secure liberty and equal rights. Provisions in the Constitution conferring privileges on slaveholders were compromises with what the framers of that instrument expected would prove but a temporary thing.

In 1846 Mr. Sumner addressed a public letter to Hon. Robert C. Winthrop, who then represented Boston in Congress, rebuking him for his vote in favor of war with Mexico. In this letter the Mexican war was characterized as an unjust, dishonorable, and cowardly attack on a sister republic, having its origin in a purpose to promote the extension of slavery.

The position of Mr. Sumner was too far in advance of the Whig party to admit of his remaining in full fellowship. In 1848 he sundered his old political ties, and aided in the organization of the Free Soil party, whose platform was composed of principles which he had distinctively announced in his public addresses. Van Buren and Adams, candidates of the new party, were earnestly supported by Mr. Sumner in the Presidential contest of 1848.

The passage of the Fugitive Slave Act tended to obliterate old party lines and overshadow former political issues. A vacancy in the United States Senate occurring by the accession of Daniel Webster to the cabinet of Mr. Fillmore, the duty of electing his successor devolved upon the Legislature of Massachusetts. By a coalition of Free-Soilers and Democrats in the Legislature, Mr. Sumner was nominated for the office, and was elected after an earnest and protracted contest. The result was regarded as a signal triumph of the anti-slavery party.

In the Senate of the United States, Mr. Sumner's first important speech was against the Fugitive Slave Law. He then announced his great political formula, " Freedom is national, and slavery sectional," which furnished the clue to his subsequent career. He argued that Congress had no power, under the Constitution, to legislate for the rendition of fugitive slaves, and that the act was not only in conflict with the Constitution, but was cruel and tyrannical.

The great debate on the Missouri Compromise and the contest in Kansas elicited all of Mr. Sumner's powers of eloquence and argument. His great speech, published under the title of " The Crime against Kansas," occupied two days in its delivery. Southern Senators and Representatives were greatly incensed by this speech, and it was determined to meet argument by blows. Two days after the delivery of the speech, Preston S. Brooks, a Representative from South Carolina, assaulted Mr. Sumner while writing at his desk in the Senate Chamber. Mr. Sumner, unarmed and powerless behind his desk, was beaten on the head until he fell insensible on the floor. A Committee of the House of Representatives reported in favor of Brooks's expulsion. The resolution then reported received a little less than the two-thirds vote necessary to its adoption. Mr. Brooks, however, resigned his seat, pleaded guilty before the court at Washington upon an indictment for assault, and was sentenced to a fine of three hundred dollars. Having returned to his constituents to receive their verdict on his conduct, he was re-elected to Congress by a unanimous vote. A few days after resuming his seat in Congress, he died suddenly of acute inflammation of the throat.

On the other hand, Mr. Sumner did not fail to receive the endorsement of his constituents. In the following January, while still disabled with his wounds, he was re-elected by an almost unanimous vote, in a Legislature consisting of several hundred members. In the spring of 1857 he went to Europe, by the advice of his physicians, to seek a restoration of his health, and returned in the following autumn to resume his seat in the Senate. His health being still impaired, he again went abroad in May, 1858, and submitted to a course of medical treatment of extraordinary severity. After an absence of eighteen months, he returned in the autumn of 1859, with health restored, again to enter upon his Senatorial duties.

It was highly appropriate that the first serious effort of Mr. Sumner, after his return to the Senate, should be a delineation of "The Barbarism of Slavery." In an elaborate and eloquent speech, which was published under that title, he denounced slavery in its influence on character, society, and civilization.

In the Presidential contest of 1860, which resulted in the election of Abraham Lincoln, Mr. Sumner took an active part, and was gratified in seeing the signal triumph of principles which he had long maintained. On the secession of the rebel States, he earnestly opposed all compromise with slavery as a means of restoring the Union. He early proposed and advocated emancipation as the speediest mode of bringing the war to a close.

In March, 1861, he entered upon the responsible position of Chairman of the Committee on Foreign Relations. In this position he has rendered great service to the country by his vigilant attention to our interests as affected by our relations with European powers. His influence has always been exerted to promote peace and mutual understanding. On the 9th of January, 1862, he delivered an elaborate speech, arguing that the seizure of Mason and Slidell, on board the steamer *Trent*, was unjustifiable on the principles of international law which had always been maintained by the United States.

In March, 1863, Mr. Sumner entered upon his third Senatorial term. He advocated with zeal and eloquence all the great Congressional measures which promoted the successful prosecution of the war. The Constitutional Amendment abolishing slavery, which was the great act of the Thirty-Eighth Congress, was a triumph of the principles long advocated by Mr. Sumner, and forms a crowning glory of his statesmanship.

On the first day of the Thirty-Ninth Congress Mr. Sumner introduced a bill looking to the reconstruction of the rebel States under a Republican form of government, and a measure to confer suffrage on the colored people of the District of Columbia.

He took the high ground that it was the right and duty of Congress, under the Constitution, to guarantee impartial suffrage in all the States. He was bold and eloquent in advocating the securing, by Congressional enactment, of equal civil and political rights to all men without regard to color.

He earnestly opposed the reconstruction policy of President Johnson, and shuddered to see his disposition to leave the freedmen in the hands of their late masters. On the 20th of December, 1865, Mr. Sumner denounced the President's "attempt to white wash the unhappy condition of the rebel States, and throw the mantle of official oblivion over sickening and heart-rending outrages where human rights are sacrificed, and rebel barbarism receives a new letter of license."

From first to last Mr. Sumner was one of the boldest of the opponents of President Johnson's usurpations. In the great trial of Impeachment he voted to convict the President, and sustained his verdict in the case by a learned and able opinion concerning the law and the evidence.

Amid all his official and public labors, Mr. Sumner has been constant in his devotion to literature. He published in 1850 two volumes of "Orations;" in 1853, a work on "White Slavery in the Barbary States;" and in 1856, a volume of "Speeches and Addresses." Some of his recent speeches in the Senate are as exhaustive in their treatment of their subjects, as elaborate in finish, as abundant in facts, and as copious in details, as ordinary volumes. Such, for example, is the great speech in the Senate on "The Cession of Russian America to the United States," in which the geography, history, and resources of our newly acquired territory are set forth more accurately and fully than in any accessible treatise on the subject.

Mr. Sumner is tall and robust in person. He has regular features, which bear the impress of thought and culture. His head is surmounted by an abundance of black hair, which is but slightly tinged with gray. As a speaker he is solemn and impressive in his manner, graceful in gesticulation, and deliberate in utterance. The varied stores of learning are so much at his command that he draws upon them with a frequency which sometimes brings upon him a charge of pedantry. By many he is regarded as too theoretical and too little practical for a successful statesman. It is his happiness, however, to have lived to see many of his theories, once unpopular, adopted as the practical principles of the most powerful party in the nation.

JAMES HARLAN.

JAMES HARLAN was born in Illinois, August 26, 1820. At the age of three years, his parents removed with him to Indiana, where he was employed, during his minority, with his father in agricultural pursuits. In the year 1841 he entered the Preparatory Department of Asbury University, then under the presidency of the present Bishop Simpson. Upon meager means obtained by teaching at intervals, he managed to graduate at that institution with honor in 1845.

In the winter of 1845, being elected to the Professorship of Languages in Iowa City College, he removed to that city. Here, among strangers, he early won for himself an enviable reputation for industry, ability, and an unswerving integrity.

In 1847 he was elected by the people Superintendent of Public Instruction of the State of Iowa. This was no ordinary compliment to a young man who had resided in the State less than two years when the election occurred, especially when taken in connection with the fact that his opponent was the Hon. Charles Mason, who graduated at the head of his class at the Military Academy at West Point, had served as Chief-Justice of the Federal Court of the Territory during the entire period of its existence, was conceded by all parties to be a gentleman of ability and unblemished reputation, and who, as a candidate, was the choice of the party which had, up to this election, been uniformly triumphant in the State and Territory, and continued so until the Kansas-Nebraska issue, except when Mr. Harlan was a candidate.

In 1848, Mr. Harlan was superseded by Hon. Thomas H. Benton.

Jr., the officials insisting that the latter was elected by a majority of seventeen votes. The count, however, is now universally conceded to have been fraudulent. In this year he was admitted to the bar, and commenced the practice of law in Iowa City. In this profession, while he remained in it, he was eminently successful; but his friends were unwilling to leave him at the bar, however agreeable to him, or however brilliant his prospects for a distinguished career in the profession.

In 1850, the people, eager to trust and honor the young man who in every public position had proved himself worthy of their confidence, nominated him for Governor; but, not being of constitutional age for that office, he was compelled to disappoint them by declining the proffered honor.

Continuing in the practice of law until 1853, he was then, by the Annual Conference of the Methodist Church, elected President of the Mount Pleasant Collegiate Institute, which during the winter following was re-organized with an amended Charter, under the name of the "Iowa Wesleyan University." His industry and energy, with his varied learning and strong sense, compelled the same success here that had attended all his undertakings thus far, and which has never since deserted him.

After two years of service at the head of the University, on the 6th of January, 1855, he was elected by the Iowa Legislature a United States Senator for the term commencing on the 4th of March, 1855, and was admitted to his seat Dec. 3d following. Upon this election he resigned the presidency of the University, and was elected Professor of Political Economy and International Law.

His first formal speech in the Senate was made March 27th, 1856, on the admission of Kansas, and was regarded then, and must be held by the student of history hereafter, as one of the ablest arguments on the right and finally successful side of that great contest. Such men as Butler of South Carolina, Cass, Benjamin, Toucey, and Douglas soon learned to respect the sturdy logic of the young debater from the West. His speech upon the occasion of presenting the memorial of James H. Lane, praying the acceptance of the memorial of the members of the Kansas Territorial Legislature for the admission of their Territory into the Union as a State, was a terrible denunciation of the great wrongs which the dominant party was inflicting on Kansas.

By a party vote, stimulated by this recent arraignment of the Democracy, it was, January 12th, 1857, resolved by the Senate, "That James Harlan is not entitled to his seat as a Senator from Iowa." The character of this decision may be understood from the following brief statement of facts: The Senate and House of Representatives of Iowa agreed to go into joint session to elect a Senator and Judges. After the joint session had met and adjourned from day to day for some time, it was discovered that the Whigs were about to be successful, and the Democratic Senators absented themselves for the purpose of preventing an election. A quorum of the joint session met, however, and a clear majority of both houses elected Mr. Harlan. Two years after, the matter was brought up on the protest of the Democratic members of the State Senate, and Mr. Harlan ousted as above stated. During these two years of peaceful occupation of his seat, a Presidential campaign was passed quietly, which might have been endangered by such party tyranny in the Senate, and Fremont made President—hence, no doubt, the delay.

But Mr. Harlan repaired immediately to Iowa City, where the State Legislature was in session. He arrived on Friday evening, and was re-elected on the day following. He spent a day or two at his home in Mount Pleasant, returned to Washington, was re-sworn, and resumed his seat on the 29th of the same month, only seventeen days after his expulsion.

In 1861 he was re-elected for a second Senatorial term without a dissenting voice among his party. During his entire service in the Senate, he has acted in harmony with the Republican party, which for four or five years was in a meager minority. He, however, commanded the respect of his political opponents by his modest and yet fearless and able support of the measures which his judgment and conscience approved, by his unwearied industry in the examination of every subject of practical legislation, and by his evident honesty of purpose and integrity of character. The leading measures supported by the Republican party had few, if any, more able advocates, and none more efficient or successful either in the Senate or before the people. The published debates of Congress show that he argued and elucidated with great clearness and conclusiveness every phase of the question of slavery and emancipation, in all their social, legal, and economic ramifications.

He was the earnest advocate of the early construction of the Pacific Railroad, had made himself, by a careful examination, master of the whole subject, and was consequently appointed a member of the Senate Committee on the Pacific Railroad.

As Chairman of the Committee on Public Lands he exerted a controlling influence in shaping the policy of the Government in the disposition of the public domain, so as to aid in the construction of railroads and the improvement of other avenues of intercourse, as well as to advance the individual interests of the frontier settler by facilitating his acquisition of a landed estate, and also by securing a permanent fund for the support of common schools for the masses, and other institutions of learning. Under his guidance the laws for the survey, sale, and pre-emption of the public lands were harmonized, and the Homestead Bill so modified as to render it a practical and beneficent measure for the indigent settlers, and at the same time but slightly detrimental to the public treasury.

Immediately after he was placed upon the Senate Committee upon Indian Affairs, it became manifest that he had made himself master of that whole subject in all its details. He consequently exercised a leading influence on the legislation of Congress affecting our intercourse with these children of the forest; humanity and justice to them, as well as the safety of the frontier settlements from savage warfare, being with him cardinal elements to guide him in shaping the policy of the Government. The effect of the repeal, over Mr. Harlan's earnest protest, of the beneficent features of the Indian Intercourse laws, under the lead of Senator Hunter, which all admit laid the foundation for our recent Indian wars, furnishes a marked illustration of the safety of his counsels in these affairs.

As a member of the Senate Committee on Agriculture, he was the earnest advocate of every measure calculated to develop and advance that great national interest, and prepared the only report marked by scientific research made on that subject by the Senate Committee during the last ten years. He gave his earnest support to the Agricultural College Bill, though in conflict with his views of the proper policy for the disposition of the public lands, because he regarded it as the only opportunity for laying firmly the foundation for these nurseries of scientific agriculture, which must prove of vast consequence for good to the whole people of this continent and the toiling millions of the Old World.

It is impossible in this brief narrative to reproduce even the substance of the many elaborate speeches made by him in the Senate and before the people. Among them may be mentioned as a sample of the whole, his speech in reply to Senator Hunter of Virginia, during the winter of 1860-61, immediately preceding the breaking out of the rebellion. This speech was characteristic in clearness, method, directness, force, and conclusiveness, and was regarded by his associates in the Senate as the great speech of the session. In the commencement he examines and exposes in their order every pretext for secession, and proceeds to charge upon the authors of the then incipient rebellion, with unsurpassed vigor and force, that the loss of political power was their real grievance. He indicated the impossibility of any compromise on the terms proposed by the Southern leaders without dishonor, and pointed out the means of an adjustment alike honorable to the South and North, requiring no retraction of principle on the part of any one, by admitting the Territories into the Union as States. He warned the South against a resort to an arbitrament of the sword; predicted the impossibility of their securing a division of the States of the Northwest from the Middle and New England States; the certainty and comparative dispatch with which an armed rebellion would be crushed, and concluded with a most powerful appeal to these conspirators not to plunge the country into such a sea of blood. Upon the conclusion of this speech, four-fifths of the Union Senators crowded around to congratulate him, and a state of excitement prevailed on the floor of the Senate for some moments such as had seldom before been witnessed in that body.

He was a member of the Peace Congress; but after seeing the members sent from the slave States, and witnessing the election of Ex-President John Tyler presiding officer, he predicted that its deliberations would end in a miserable failure.

He was also selected by the Union members of the House and Senate as a member of the Union Congressional Committee for the management of the Presidential campaign of 1864. Being the only member of the committee on the part of the Senate who devoted his whole time to this work, he became the active organ of the committee—organized an immense working force, regulated its finances with ability and unimpeachable fidelity, employed a large number of presses in Washington, Baltimore, Philadelphia, and New York in printing reading matter for the masses, which resulted in the distribution of many millions of documents among the people at home, and in all our great armies. To his labors, therefore, the country is doubtless largely indebted for the triumphant success of the Republican candidate.

In the month of March, 1865, Mr. Harlan was nominated by President Lincoln for the office of Secretary of the Interior, and the nomination was unanimously confirmed by the Senate without reference to a committee. Resigning his seat in the Senate, he accepted the office, and on the 15th of May, entered upon the discharge of his duties as a member of President Johnson's cabinet.

His short administration of the Department of the Interior was characterized by untiring industry and earnest devotion to the public service. The gradual divergence of the line of policy adopted by the President from the principles of the Republican party, led Mr.

Harlan to sever his connection with the cabinet, by his resignation, which took effect September 1, 1866. Mr. Harlan left the office with the approval of the public for the course he had pursued, and the sincerely expressed regrets of the President himself.

Previous to his resignation of the office of Secretary of the Interior, Mr. Harlan had been re-elected by the Legislature of Iowa to a seat in the Senate of the United States, for the term commencing March 4, 1867.

On resuming his seat in the Senate, he was assigned to service in that body, on the Committees on the District of Columbia, Union Pacific Railroad, Post-Offices and Post Roads, and Foreign Relations, of the first of which he is Chairman. This Committee is one of the most laborious belonging to the Senate, having in charge all the public interests of the District; and in addition to the ordinary duties of the Committee, Mr. Harlan is now engaged, under the authority of a resolution of the Senate, in codifying the local laws of the District, a work that requires care, precision, and legal learning of no common order.

While Mr. Harlan, since his return to the Senate, has spoken on a variety of subjects, his principal efforts have been his speech on reconstruction, delivered on the 10th of February, 1868, and his opinion as a Senator in the Impeachment Trial of President Johnson. Of the former, it is not unjust to others to say, that no speech made during that long debate, presented the questions at issue in a clearer light, or in language better suited to the comprehension of the masses of the people. It received the warmest encomiums of Mr. Harlan's political associates in the Senate, and thousands of copies were subscribed for and circulated as a campaign document, by the members of the two houses of Congress. Of the opinion, it is sufficient to say, that it is a strictly legal document, applying the law to the facts as established by the evidence, and so clear and convincing that none can doubt the sincerity and uprightness of the vote which followed it.

Mr. Harlan is a man of strong political convictions. This is shown by the whole tenor of his political life. Early in life, long before he occupied official station, he was identified, in feeling and principles, with the anti-slavery party of the nation. Almost at the outset of our late civil war, with the eye of a statesman, he foresaw that the rebellion could only result in the enfranchisement of the slaves of the South, and their elevation to the dignity of American citizens. So believing, he always acted consistently with that belief. He was among the first—if not *the* first—to advocate in the Senate the organization of the colored men everywhere in defense of the Union; and since the close of the war, he has uniformly spoken and voted in favor of conferring upon them those rights of citizenship which they have honorably won by their endurance and bravery on the battle-field; thus proving himself the worthy representative of a State which has just established impartial suffrage by the popular vote of its citizens.

In the Presidential campaign of 1868, Mr. Harlan took an active part in promoting the success of the Republican cause. To that end he addressed numerous and large audiences in the States of Pennsylvania, Iowa, Missouri, and Indiana. On the stump, Mr. Harlan is a popular and powerful speaker. Natural and graceful in his manner, candid in his presentation of facts, skillful in portraying whatever tends to arouse the human sensibilities, and logical in his mode of reasoning, he has few superiors as a popular orator.

Senator Harlan is in the prime of life, a Christian gentleman, a dignified Senator, of good habits, and in the enjoyment of vigorous health. He is an example to be admired and imitated by the young men of our country. As a youth he worked his way through college, acquiring an education in the face of trials and obstacles that would have deterred others from such an undertaking. As a man, by sterling integrity, a faithful discharge of his duties, and a close adherence to principle, he has earned the proud position he now occupies before the country, and in the affections of the people of his State. He is a bright exemplar of the benign influence of our free institutions, illustrating that, with energy and application, the poor and lowly may lift themselves up to the highest stations.

ALEXANDER G. CATTELL.

NOW that great financial problems, which concern the honor and even life of the nation, are to be solved, it is fortunate that there are men in the halls of National Legislation whose ability to grapple with such questions has been proven by their success in private business.

Such a man is Alexander G. Cattell, Senator from New Jersey. He was born at Salem, New Jersey, February 12, 1816. The town of Salem was the residence of his ancestors for more than a century. There lived his patriotic grandfather, who in the war of the Revolution was singled out as a special object of British vengeance on account of his conspicuous devotion to the American cause. One day as he was plowing in the field, the breeze of the morning wafted across the Delaware the thunder of the cannon of the battle of the Brandywine. Turning his horses loose, he went quickly to his house, took down his fowling piece, rowed across the river, and, like John Brown at Gettysburg, took post in the ranks and poured his fire into the enemy. His son, the father of Alexander G. Cattell, inherited the spirit and principles of his Revolutionary sire. He was for half a century a successful merchant, and recently died, greatly respected, at the age of nearly fourscore years.

Mr. Cattell being designed for mercantile business, received such an education as was deemed necessary for that pursuit forty years ago. At the age of thirteen he was placed behind the counter of his father's store, where he advanced, before he had attained his majority, to the head of a large and flourishing business of his own.

At the age of twenty-four, Mr. Cattell was elected to the Legislature of New Jersey, and in 1844 was a member of the Convention called to revise the State Constitution. Although the youngest member of that body, which embraced the leading men of the State, he was second to none in ability and influence. Distinguished for sound common sense, a choice command of language, and a graceful and forcible delivery, he never rose to speak without commanding the respectful attention, and generally securing the conviction of his auditors.

While success crowned his commercial operations in his native town, he possessed capabilities for a career of enterprise and competition in a more extensive field. Accordingly, in 1846, he removed to Philadelphia, where he entered into mercantile business, first with Mr. E. G. James, and afterwards with his brother, Mr. Elijah G. Cattell. He soon became extensively engaged in the shipment of grain and other produce to foreign markets. He soon became a prominent member, and afterwards President, of the Corn Exchange Association of Philadelphia, which won honorable eminence among the business boards of that city for its public spirit and patriotic devotion to the interests of the country. The Association is composed of many of the most liberal and wealthy merchants of Philadelphia. Through their enterprise, energy, and sagacious management, the grain trade of that city was developed, until it has become a commercial interest of the greatest magnitude.

The Corn Exchange became conspicuous, at the outbreak of the civil war, as a pre-eminently loyal body of citizens. When the news reached Philadelphia that the rebellion of the South had culminated in the attack on Fort Sumter, the Association then assembled for their daily business laid aside their "samples," and raising the flag of the country in front of their hall, pledged themselves to keep it floating till the rebellion should be subdued, and the honor of that flag vindicated. They contributed largely to aid in the enlistment of men, and the support of the families of such as went to fight the battles of the country. The Association recruited, organized, and equipped two and a half regiments for the field. Mr. Cattell was chairman of the special committee under whose supervision the patriotic service was performed.

As a testimonial of the esteem in which Mr. Cattell was held by his associates in this work, they voted that when the old flag-staff at the camp, around which their regiments had rallied, was taken down, it should be planted on the grounds of his country seat. When this was done, a magnificent flag was presented to him with interesting and appropriate ceremonies.

During the war for the suppression of the Rebellion, Mr. Cattell gave to Mr. Lincoln's administration the utmost support of his talents, money, and influence. Few enjoyed to a greater degree the respect and confidence of that great and good man.

During Mr. Cattell's residence in Philadelphia he was several times a member of both branches of the municipal government. As a legislator for the city he ever had a careful regard for the great public and private interests intrusted to his care.

No mercantile house in Philadelphia has stood higher than that of A. G. Cattell & Co. in a character for the enterprise and integrity that form the basis of commercial success. Mr. Cattell had other business connections, first as Director of the Mechanics' Bank, and then as President of the Corn Exchange Bank, proving himself to be an able financier, fully meeting the expectations which were formed of his character and talents from his previous career.

In 1855 Mr. Cattell resumed his residence in his native State, making his home in an elegant villa about three miles from the city of Camden, where he now resides.

In 1866 Mr. Cattell was elected a Senator in Congress, from New Jersey. "The esteem in which he is held by those who know him best," says Rev. Dr. Carrow, one of his biographers, "may be inferred from the fact that, at the last regular session of the Legislature, the Republican members refused to go into an election rather than fail to secure his triumph. In this case the members were influenced not so much by personal partialities as by their conviction of his pre-eminent fitness for the great post of a Senator in Congress in these critical times."

ALEXANDER G. CATTELL.

Senator Cattell, by his course in Congress, has shown that the confidence of his party was not misplaced. He has been firm, consistent, and able in his support of the principles he avows.

Since he took his seat in the Senate, December 3, 1866, the voice and vote of Mr. Cattell have been given in favor of all the great measures of public policy which have given to Congress so prominent a place in the history of the country. Mr. Cattell's speeches abound in facts and figures so combined as to be most effective in argument. At the same time his speeches are not devoid of rhetorical beauties calculated to charm the most indifferent hearer.

To illustrate this, and at the same time give a hint of Mr. Cattell's views concerning the results of the war, we quote the closing paragraphs of his speech, delivered in the Senate January 22, 1867, on a "Bill to Provide Increased Revenue from Imports:"

"The conflict is ended, and, God be praised, the right has triumphed; and having thus elevated four million human beings from chains and slavery to freedom and to manhood, let us address ourselves to the work of stimulating the industrial energies of the nation, so that free labor shall find its wonted employment, and receive its just reward.

"Perfect this bill, and then make it a law, and hope and courage will spring up throughout the nation. The fires of a thousand forges, and mills, and furnaces, will illumine the land, and the ceaseless hum of a million whirling spindles will chant the praises of the American Congress that had the wisdom to understand, and the fidelity to maintain the principles of the American system."

CHARLES R. BUCKALEW.

CHARLES R. BUCKALEW was born in Columbia County, Pennsylvania, December 28, 1821. He is of French descent, his ancestors having emigrated to this country on occasion of the Revocation of the Edict of Nantes. His father and grandfather were private citizens, undistinguished by wealth or position.

We have but scanty information concerning Mr. Buckalew in his boyhood, whether in respect to his youthful occupations, the extent of his educational advantages, or other circumstances of interest. He once narrowly escaped drowning, when he was the subject of those peculiar mental experiences which are thought to indicate for the soul a future existence independent of the body.

Mr. Buckalew adopted the profession of law, and was admitted to practice in 1843. From 1845 to 1847, he was Prosecuting Attorney for his native County, and from 1850 to 1856 was a Senator in the Pennsylvania Legislature. Meanwhile, he served also as a Commissioner to exchange the ratification of a treaty with the Government of Paraguay; and was, in 1856, a Senatorial Presidential Elector. In 1857, he was Chairman of the State Democratic Committee, was re-elected to the State Senate, and was appointed a Commissioner to revise the Penal Code of Pennsylvania. In 1858, he resigned the two latter positions, and was appointed by President Buchanan Resident Minister to Ecuador, whence he returned in 1861. In 1863 he was elected a Senator in Congress from Pennsylvania, by a majority of one vote, for the term ending in 1869.

Mr. Buckalew is not so frequent a speaker as many in the Senate, and yet he is not silent in that great national council. In the commencement of his speech on the "Basis of Representation," February 21, 1865, he remarked that he had previously refrained from speech-making, supposing that "while the passions of the country were influenced by the war, reason could not be heard." And he took occasion to express regret that "questions pertaining to the war still occupied the attention of Congress to the exclusion of those connected with economy, revenue, finance, ordinary legislation, and the administration of justice—questions which require intelligence, investigation, labor, and the habits of the student."

As an argument for changing the basis of representation as it existed, Mr. Buckalew gave statistical details showing the various ratios of representation in the Senate, as possessed respectively by the East, West, and South. He maintained that New England had too great a preponderance of power in the Senate, both as to membership and the chairmanship of committees. "While," said he, "the population of the East is less than one-seventh of the population of the States represented in the Senate, she has the chairmanship of one-third of the committees. The chairmanship of a committee is a position of much influence and power. The several distinguished gentlemen holding that position have virtual control over the transaction of business, both in Committee and in the Senate."

Mr. Buckalew thus presented the effect of restoration of representation to the Southern States upon the relative position of New England: "Twenty-two Senators from the Southern States, and two from Colorado—being double the number of those from the East— would reduce the importance of the latter in the Senate; and remit her back to the condition in which she stood in her relations to the Union before the war. True, she would even then possess much more than her proportion of weight in the Senate, regard being had to her population; but she would no longer dominate or control the Government of the United States."

Mr. Buckalew opposed also the proposition to grant negro suffrage in the District of Columbia. "The objection," said he, " which I have to a large extension of suffrage in this country, whether by Federal or State power, is this: That thereby you will corrupt and degrade elections, and probably lead to their complete abrogation hereafter. By pouring into the ballot-boxes of the country a large mass of ignorant votes, and votes subjected to pecuniary or social influence, you will corrupt and degrade your elections, and lay the foundation for their ultimate destruction."

Mr. Buckalew, by speech and vote, opposed the Civil Rights Bill, the Freedmen's Bureau Bill, and also the Military Reconstruction Bill.

In a speech on the last named measure, Mr. Buckalew thus presents his view of its character:

"Now, sir, what does this bill do? It provides, in a section of country thus subjected to military rule the most unlimited, for the organization of civil governments, State governments, and how? The military commander of the district is to appoint whomsoever he pleases, to act under whatever rules he may prescribe, according to his own pleasure, his own unregulated will, as agents and officers, to execute the plan of re-organization proposed, and these, his appointees, owing no obedience to any known law, and without rule or regulation for their conduct, other than that which he shall prescribe, are to proceed to enumerate the inhabitants, or rather, to register the electors among them, preliminary to what? Why, sir, to their exercise of the most valuable and fundamental privilege of freemen—the institution of government for themselves. And for any abuse of power, for any outrage, for any misconduct whatever, this bill and its predecessor are utterly destitute of any provision for punishment."

Mr. Buckalew is the ardent advocate of a "representative reform," by which minorities may have representation in the legislative bodies of the country, proportionate to their numbers. In advocacy of this scheme, he delivered an able and instructive address in Philadelphia, November 19, 1867. In illustrating what he termed the "cumulative vote," and its influence on elections, Mr. Buckalew said: "There are 60,000 voters in Vermont, of whom 40,000 are members of the Republican party, and 20,000 of the Democratic party. I speak in round numbers. By law that State is entitled to three Representatives in Congress, because her population, under the Constitution of the United States, authorizes the allotment of that number to her. Now, what ought to take place there? The majority should elect two Representatives, having 40,000 votes, and the minority should elect one, having 20,000 votes; but can that be so in point of fact at present? If the electors of that State vote for three Representatives by general ticket, the majority would elect the whole three. By cumulative voting, by authorizing the 20,000 minority electors of that State to give each three votes to one candidate, that candidate would receive 60,000 votes, and the majority cannot defeat him. The majority voting for two Representatives can elect them, but they cannot elect the third. Suppose they attempt to vote for three candidates, they can only give each of them 40,000 votes, and the minority candidate has 60,000. If they attempt to vote for two, as they ought to do, that being the number they are entitled to, they can give them 60,000 votes each, the same number that the minority candidate has. If they attempted to vote for one, they would give that one candidate 120,000; but of course they would not throw away their votes in that foolish manner. The practical result would be that the 40,000 majority electors in that State would vote for two candidates and elect them, and the 20,000 minority electors would vote for one and elect him, and results analogous to this would occur all over the United States if this system were applied."

JOHN CONNESS.

JOHN CONNESS is a native of Ireland, and was born in 1822. At thirteen years of age he came to this country, whither he had been preceded by some enterprising brothers. By their kindness he was favored with the advantages of academical education. Soon after arriving at manhood, he departed for California among the earliest emigrants to that country. There he devoted himself with success to mining and mercantile pursuits.

Turning his attention to politics, he was, in 1852, elected to the State Legislature, in which he held a seat during four successive terms. In 1859, he was a candidate for Lieutenant-Governor; and in 1861, he was the Union Democratic candidate for Governor. In 1863, he was elected a Senator in Congress from California for the term ending in 1869. He has served in the Senate on the Committees on Finance and the Pacific Railroad, Chairman of the Committee on Mines and Mining, and as a member also of the Committee on Post-Offices and Post Roads.

Mr. Conness ranks among the efficient and active members of the Senate. The record clearly shows him to be vigilant and awake to all the great questions naturally passing in review before the Senate. His speeches are generally brief and to the point, giving evidence of excellent sense, and a fearless aim to accomplish what appears to him to be his duty as a legislator, regardless of favor or reproach. As illustrative of all this, we may select almost at random various passages from his speeches on different occasions.

Pending the question of dropping from the roll of the army unemployed general officers, Mr. Conness, January 6, 1865, submitted the following remarks, which must impress the reader as both curious and interesting:

"Early in the conduct of this war, nominations for high ranks were easily obtained. The result was, that inefficient men—men unable and unfit to conduct our armies to victory and success—obtained the highest rank in the army; and the consequences were losses in every direction to the national cause. Why, sir, at a certain period, during the last session of Congress, we desired a new Department Commander for the Pacific Department, and, anxious to send an officer there of good ability, of high military skill, that that country might be organized and prepared for an emergency likely to arise—possible, at least, to arise—I had several conferences with the Secretary of War; I had an examination, with that officer, of the long list of unemployed major-generals and brigadier-generals then under the pay of the Government, and without public employment; and if I were at liberty here to repeat the comment that followed the name of each in those various conferences, it would demonstrate the necessity of action somewhere to rid the country of the unnecessary and profitless burden that those gentlemen in high rank, holding high commissions under the Government, imposed upon it. It was five months before an officer deemed competent to send to that department could be selected, by the exercise of the greatest wisdom, from the long list of the then unemployed generals in the United States army."

In the Fortieth Congress Mr. Conness has distinguished himself by the earnestness and ability with which he advocated measures designed to protect American citizens abroad. He successfully urged the passage of an "Eight-Hour Law." When this bill was pending in the Senate, he made a speech in which occurs the following passage:

"When I saw the column of Burnside, thirty thousand or forty thousand strong, marching through this city to the sanguinary fields between the Wilderness and Richmond and Cold Harbor, inclusive, and stood where I could see the eye of every man in the column,

I saw scarcely any but those who had the marks of toil and stalwart labor, black and white; and if I never before that time reverenced the men who labor, I should do it beginning at that period of my life; but it was not necessary for me to begin then.

"Now, Mr. President, there is considerable agitation in this country upon this question of whether a day's labor shall be constituted of eight or ten hours, and I have no doubt there are those who think if this bill be passed, and the example be set by the Government, the eight-hour rule will follow in other industries conducted in the country. Well, sir, I hope it will. A personal experience enables me to say that I could, myself, perform more labor in eight hours than in ten, taking any given week for the average; and then it gave more hours for study. Many and many a morning, at two o'clock, when I labored ten and eleven hours a day in my youth, found me yet endeavoring to enable myself to take my rank among my fellows in society; and I desire, by my vote and voice, if that can influence any one, to give an equal opportunity to the youths of the land connected with labor and toil. Let no man forget, because his task is made easy in this world, the thousands, the tens of thousands, and the hundreds of thousands who labor and toil for an ill-requited compensation, for a small compensation scarcely sufficient to furnish bread, much less to enable them to educate their children and bring them up fit to be citizens of this Republic. Make their path as easy as you can, by limiting their hours of labor. Give them time to think."

As a specimen of effective "stump oratory," we quote the following extract from a speech delivered by Mr. Conness in Cooper Institute, New York, September 30, 1868, before an immense audience composed largely of Irish-Americans: "I come before you to-night, fellow-citizens, as one of yourselves, as one of a class of Americans denominated Irish-Americans. [Applause.] I will not say, I know I could not say, that there can be any title higher than that of an American citizen. [Applause.] And while some of us may be denominated, and may be better known as Irish-Americans, it should be our boast peculiarly that we are Americans, and Americans alone—[Applause]—not forgetting our origin, not forgetting the trials of the land we came from, and the race from which we sprang, for that but sharpens the mental appetite for liberty, as we find it established here,—[Cheers]—but as American citizens simply, owning a part in the great cause of the Republic established by the fathers, and maintained by their sons, to go down, I trust, to all posterity for ever. [Applause.] We have a high title in having a part in that cause, and in being known as American citizens. [Cheers.] The American people, in a short time, are to determine who shall be the Executive, to give to the Republic a guardian of its interests; a safeguard, so far as an Executive can be such, to the principles upon which the Republic is founded, and we are to replace the man now filling that station by an accident—[Laughter and cheers]—with not only the greatest military leader of the world, but, greater than his military leadership, one of the simplest and the most virtuous citizens of America—a man who advanced, as he need not have done—and yet 'twas well done—that he is not to have a policy against at once the intelligence and the virtue of the American people—[Applause]—but whose policy, if he is elected President, will be to give reality and effect to that intelligence and virtue. [Cheers.] What is to be tried, and what is being tried, in the contest that is now going on for the Presidential office is, whether, after the nation, at the cost of hundreds of thousands of lives, and thousands of millions of treasure, maintained intact the national integrity—whether that integrity shall be continuously maintained, and, in addition, whether the great principles of liberty, law and humanity, vindicated and re-established by our grand successes against rebellion, shall also be maintained, and also whether, in addition still, the measures that the American people have found it necessary to enact to maintain the condition of things shall be carried out."

JAMES R. DOOLITTLE.

HE ancestry of the subject of this sketch is part English, part Irish, and part Scotch. The paternal line was entirely English, and in early times it was connected with the Puritans in England. On the mother's side the ancestors were Presbyterians from the north of Ireland. His parents were born in New England, but early in life they removed to the village of Hampton, Washington County, in the State of New York, where James R. Doolittle was born, January 3, 1815. Four years after his birth his parents removed to Wethersfield Springs, in Wyoming County. At that time this part of the country was a wilderness. But the father, man of great energy and prudence, was not long in acquiring property and influence in the community which grew up around him. Although without the advantage of a college education, he was always an earnest advocate of schools. He possessed a well balanced mind, firm religious principles and liberal views, and was the first to establish an Episcopal church at Wethersfield.

At the age of fifteen, young Doolittle entered college at Geneva, New York, and four years later graduated with the honors of his class. At school he was especially proficient in Mathematics and Greek. Even at that time he had developed unusual oratorical talent in the debating societies connected with the institution.

After leaving college, he read law with Isaac Hill of Rochester. During the three years of legal study then required before admission to the bar, he sometimes taught Mathematics, Greek, and Elocution. In 1836, he was admitted to practice law in the State of New York, and soon after was married to Miss Mary L. Cutting, of Warsaw. He established himself in Rochester, where he remained for two years.

The illness of a brother, which afterwards terminated in death, induced him to return to Wyoming County. There continuing in the practice of his profession, he was elected District-Attorney in 1845, in a county largely opposed to him in politics. He performed the duties of the office with ability, and to the satisfaction of his constituents.

In the year 1851, at the age of thirty-six, he removed with his family to Wisconsin, and took up his residence at Racine, which has since that time been his home. In a new State, surrounded by young and active men, he soon distinguished himself. He was employed by the Governor of Wisconsin to take charge of several cases for the State; on the ground, as the Governor said, that Mr. Doolittle was a man of ability, and could not be bought. He was successful in obtaining decisions in favor of the State. In 1853, he was chosen Judge of the First Judicial District of Wisconsin, but resigned in 1856, to resume the practice of the law.

At this time the country was agitated by the troubles in Kansas. The Democratic party, then in control of the Government, lent itself to the establishing of slavery in that Territory. When this course had been decided upon, he left the Democratic party, and assisted in the organization of the Republican party. The State of Wisconsin voted for Fremont, but Mr. Buchanan was elected President.

In 1857, the Legislature of Wisconsin elected Mr. Doolittle to the Senate of the United States, and in 1863 he was re-elected to the same position. In 1860, he sustained Mr. Lincoln; and in 1864 aided his re-election to the Presidency.

For many years he was chairman of the Committee on Indian Affairs of the Senate, and gave direction to the Indian policy of the Government. Always opposed to harsh measures, he sought to avert conflicts and to establish peaceful relations between the races on the frontier. In 1865, Congress appointed a joint committee to visit the Indian country, and ascertain the necessities of the situation. Mr. Doolittle was chosen chairman, and in this capacity, with Senator Foster and Hon. Lewis Ross of the House, as one portion of the Commission, visited the Indians of New Mexico, Colorado, and the

Plains. One result of this enterprise was the prevention of a war with the numerous nation of Camanches, by restraining one of our ambitious brigadier-generals from marching his troops across the Arkansas with the purpose of inaugurating hostilities. This one thing saved the Government at least thirty millions of dollars. An incident occurred at Denver in Colorado, which illustrates the character of the subject of this sketch. He was invited to address the people on Indian Affairs, for his views had much to do in determining the policy of the Government in that regard. It was only a few months after the Sand Creek massacre, where peaceable Cheyenne Indians of both sexes, old and young, had been slaughtered by wholesale at the instigation of Colonel Chivington. The meeting was held in the theater which only a short time before had been decorated with the scalps of more than a hundred Cheyennes, as trophies of the slaughter.

Mr. Doolittle commenced his speech, but had not proceeded far before announcing the opinion that the Indians should be treated with kindness and fairness, and allowed to pass away from the face of the earth in peace, and not exterminated by the whites. This opinion was no sooner stated than the whole audience raised a howl of rage, rose to their feet, some of them brandishing pistols, and tried to hiss the speaker from the stage. But they had mistaken the man. He folded his arms and gazed with cool defiance at the infuriated mass. They fired no shots, but in silence and awe soon resumed their seats, struck dumb by the courage and self-possession of the man. The speaker continued his remarks without further interruption, and did not spare the feelings or the prejudices of his audience. No man, unless possessed of physical and moral courage, could have braved such a storm of passion.

In dealing with the negro question, which for more than a quarter of a century has engrossed the attention of statesmen, and agitated and disturbed the country, he has maintained the theories of Jefferson, in which he was schooled in youth. He has always opposed slavery and its extension, and favored a gradual separation of the races by colonization or any other peaceful means. During a public life of twenty-five years, he has never swerved from those fundamental ideas. Always a Democrat, when his party did not attempt or connive at the extension of slavery, yet when any such attempt was made, he was always among the first to break from his party. In 1848, he was a Free-Soil Democrat. In 1856, when an attempt was made to force slavery into the Territory of Kansas, he abandoned the Democratic party in the pride of its power, and became a Republican. Before the Rebellion broke out, he often urged the Southern leaders to adopt a system of gradually colonizing the negroes of the South in Central America, and thus remove the only cause which was disturbing the peace of the country. But his admonitions were unheeded, as well by the extreme Republicans as by the men of the South. The same plan which Henry Clay had advocated, without material success, was again rejected, and the almost inevitable sequence, in the excited condition of the public mind, was civil war. The attempt to avert the impending conflict met with but little favor. And yet it is doubtful whether any other course could long have postponed the collision which followed.

During the war, Mr. Doolittle was a zealous supporter of the Union cause, and labored in the Senate, and before the people, to accomplish its triumph. After the overthrow of the Rebellion, he favored a policy of magnanimity towards the South, and sought to lessen the bitterness existing between the two sections, and allay the angry passions which the war had aroused. His voice has been heard pleading in eloquent tones for mercy to the vanquished, and pointing out the evils, present and future, of continuing the animosities of civil strife. Although much censured for this course, deserted by many of his best friends, and charged with ignoble motives, he has held his course without faltering, feeling that it was his duty, and trusting in the returning reason of his fellow-countrymen, at a future day, for his vindication. The advocates of leniency and magnanimity always are commended when the wild storm of passion has abated, and the clear light of reason breaks through the vanishing clouds.

As a member of the High Court of Impeachment, Mr. Doolittle

voted to acquit the President. During the consultation of the Senate, before the rendition of the verdict, he delivered an oral "opinion" on the case, of which the following is the closing paragraph:

"Sir, much may be forgiven, much must be forgiven in times of high party excitement, for the judicial blindness which it begets. But when this temporary and frenzied excitement shall have passed away, as pass it will, and when men shall carefully review this case and all the evidence given on this trial, their surprise will be, not that a few Republican Senators can rise above party prejudice and refuse to be driven from their clear convictions by party furor, but their utter astonishment will be, that any respectable Senator should ever for one moment have entertained the thought of convicting the President of the United States of a high crime or a misdemeanor upon the charges and evidence produced upon this trial."

As a public man, Mr. Doolittle is a statesman rather than a partisan. He has never felt himself bound to support party measures when he regarded them as prejudicial to the interests of the nation. Thoroughly a man of principle, in his daily life he conforms strictly to his convictions of duty. At times he seems to hesitate, but it is only for a moment. When convinced that a certain course is right, he assumes it without fear of consequences, and urges it with untiring zeal and unvarying consistency.

In a recent speech, delivered in the Senate, Mr. Howe, of Wisconsin, bore honorable testimony to Mr. Doolittle's integrity of character. "My colleague," said he, "has been a citizen of the State of Wisconsin since sometime about 1850 or 1851. He was for many years a leading lawyer in that State, very widely known to the profession, enjoying a very large practice. He was four or five years a Judge of the Circuit Court in that State, before he came to the Senate. I knew him for almost the whole time very well, personally and by reputation, and I have great personal satisfaction in saying here, and I think it is due to the State that I should say it, that in all that time I never heard the slightest imputation cast upon him, either for the conduct of business in the Courts over which he presided, or for the relations existing between him and his clients—never a whisper which could excite in the mind of any one a suspicion of his venality or corruption."

As an orator, Mr. Doolittle has a high reputation, which is well deserved. His speeches possess much argumentative force, graceful imagery, and frequent eloquence. His manner is earnest and dignified, his utterance is deliberate and distinct, without apparent effort.

Public men are praised more for their eloquence, wit, intellectual strength, and engaging manners, than for purity of character. But in forming a correct estimate of the character of a public man, private virtues, no less than public, should be taken into consideration. In this respect, the subject of this sketch will bear close scrutiny. In early manhood, he embraced the teachings of Christianity, and has lived a consistent, religious life. He is free from intemperance, and all its kindred vices.

AARON H. CRAGIN.

ARON H. CRAGIN was born in Weston, Vermont, February 3, 1821. He is of Scotch descent, one of his ancestors being John Cragin, who was among the prisoners taken by Cromwell at the great battle of Dunbar, September 3, 1650, and banished to America.

Aaron worked at farming and in a woolen mill until he became of age. His education was principally acquired at "Burr Seminary," Manchester, Vermont, and at the "Lebanon Liberal Institute," at Lebanon, N. H. Having finished his studies at the academy, he returned to his native town of Weston, and entered at once upon the study of law. He afterwards spent two years in law studies at Albany, New York, and was admitted to the bar in New York City, in the fall of 1847. The same year he moved to Lebanon, N. H., and commenced the practice of his profession.

In 1848, Mr. Cragin took an active part in the canvass for Gen. Taylor, and was an associate editor of the *Granite State Whig*, published at Lebanon. In 1852, he was on the electoral ticket for Scott and Graham, and made numerous speeches in behalf of those candidates. In the years of 1852, 1853, 1854, and 1859, he was a member of the New Hampshire legislature. He was elected to the Thirty-fourth Congress, a representative from the Third Congressional District of New Hampshire, by a majority of 3,000; although this District, before that time, had been strongly Democratic. He was re-elected in 1857, and served through the Thirty-fifth Congress.

Mr. Cragin was a delegate at large from New Hampshire to the Republican Convention at Chicago, in 1860, and voted first and last for Abraham Lincoln, and supported him upon the stump in every county in New Hampshire.

In June, 1864, he was elected to the United States Senate for the full term of six years, as the successor of John P. Hale.

Mr. Cragin is a staunch and able advocate of the measures enacted by Congress for the reconstruction of the Southern States.

On the 30th of January, 1868, he delivered an address in the Senate, in which he presented an able review of the Reconstruction acts, and the usurpation of Andrew Johnson. The speech closes with the following eloquent passage:

"The Republican party, sir, is the people's party. It is the hope of the country and the anchor of its freedom. It is the representative of the true democratic sentiment of the country. It bears aloft the banner of liberty, and pleads for those rights of human nature which God has given to man. It swears by the Declaration of Independence, and acknowledges the manhood of the whole human race. It teaches the great Christian democratic doctrine that 'all things whatsoever ye would that men should do unto you, do ye even so unto them.' It knows no baseness, cowers at no danger, oppresses no weakness. Generous and humane, it rebukes the arrogant, cherishes honor, and sympathizes with the humble. It asks nothing but what it concedes, and concedes nothing but what it demands. Destructive only to despotism and treason, it is the sole conservator of liberty, labor, and property. It cherishes the sentiment of universal freedom, of equal rights, and equal obligations. It sides with the weak and the down-trodden, and sympathizes with every effort to elevate the people and better their condition. A true Republican, while claiming an equality with the best, scorns any political immunities not accorded to the humblest of his fellows. The ark of our national salvation rests upon the shoulders of the men composing this party. I pray that they may be patient and strong, bold and prudent, patriotic and just, devout and self-sacrificing, and resolute and mighty, that we may transmit to uncounted millions and unborn generations the blessings of free, democratic government."

WAITMAN T. WILLEY.

AITMAN T. WILLEY was born in the county of Mongalia, Virginia, October 18, 1811. His birthplace was a "log cabin, just twenty feet square."

As soon as the little boy could well walk, he was put to work upon the farm until he was twelve years old—receiving, meanwhile, eight or ten months of schooling in a country school-house. From twelve to sixteen years of age—with the exception of tuition at a grammar school for two months—he continued at hard work upon his father's farm, at the end of which time he went to Madison College. He was distinguished in college by industry as a student, and success as a scholar, and at the end of his four years' course was graduated with the highest honors of his class, and was pronounced by the trustees of the institution as "well entitled to that honor."

In the following year, Mr. Willey—being yet under twenty-one years of age—commenced the study of law at Wellsbury, Virginia. He was admitted to the bar in 1833. As a lawyer he was successful, and soon secured a good and reputable practice. In 1840, he was a candidate for the State legislature. He was also on the Whig electoral ticket, and made forty speeches in behalf of his candidate. In 1841, in one and the same month, he was made Clerk of Mongalia County Court and of the Supreme Court. In 1850, he was elected a member of the Convention for re-forming the constitution of Virginia. In this Convention, Mr. Willey sustained a very prominent part. His speeches, which were somewhat numerous, were of decided ability, and were highly complimented, even by those whose views differed from his own. "He is," writes one of these, "a man of fine attainments, extensive reading, and high moral character; a bold thinker, an energetic and earnest speaker." His speech in this Convention, in favor of representation based upon suffrage, was deemed the best that was delivered on that side of this important question. In concluding this great speech, having alluded in glowing terms to the progress of popular liberty in the world, he adds this noble peroration:

"And yet, in the midst of all this, in the middle of the nineteenth century, beneath the noontide effulgence of this great principle of popular supremacy, a voice is heard in old Virginia, rising from almost the spot where the clarion voice of Henry awoke a nation to freedom, when he exclaimed, 'Give me liberty or give me death'— even here, where we should take off our shoes, for the earth on which we walk is holy—bearing in its consecrated bosom the remains of George Mason and Thomas Jefferson, the one the author of the Declaration of Independence, the other of the Virginia Bill of Rights— even here, a demand is made by honorable gentlemen to give superior political power to the property-holder, and virtually invest goods and chattels with the prerogative of legislating upon the rights and liberties of a vast majority of the people of this Commonwealth! I trust this can never take place."

In 1852, Mr. Willey was a Whig candidate for Congress, with no expectation of election, but to bring out a full Whig vote for General Scott.

At the State Convention of the Whig party, February 10, 1858, Mr. Willey was nominated as a candidate for Lieutenant-Governor. Alluding to this nomination, the Richmond *Whig* represented Mr. Willey as "one of the ablest and most eloquent men in Virginia," and "universally esteemed and popular." The Baltimore *Patriot* added: "A stronger name has never been presented to the freemen of Virginia. The name of Waitman T. Willey is a household word throughout the entire Northwest. A distinguished lawyer, with a reputation without a stain, his name upon the ticket secures at least five thousand votes that might have been considered doubtful."

In the canvass, Mr. Willey addressed the people daily until the election, and was everywhere acknowledged as a statesman, a patriot, an honest man, and an exemplary Christian. In the election he carried his own county, although his ticket ran behind.

In 1860, Mr. Willey, as might be expected, was exerting himself continually for the Union, and to strengthen the union sentiment of the State. In January, he published a long article for distribution on the general subject of disunion and secession. "Why, therefore," he writes, "should we madly rush into the perils of disunion? Our country was never more thrifty and prosperous, and what but the national Union secured to us all this happiness and prosperity? I shudder whenever I think of disunion. It does appear to me that some of our leaders, like the incendiary Erostratus, are aspiring after the infamous immortality which must eternally be attached to the names of the destroyers of the fairest fabric of national government ever devised by man, or bestowed on him by heaven."

In the winter of 1860-61, Mr. Willey was elected to a seat in the Richmond Convention, which resulted in the secession of Virginia. Referring to this Convention, he writes: "If the journal and proceedings of that body ever come to light, they will show how faithfully I resisted that terrible disaster."

In July, 1861, he was elected by the reorganized legislature of Virginia, sitting at Wheeling, to the United States Senate, and took his seat in that body during the special session of Congress then in progress. Also, in the fall of this year, he was a member of the Constitutional Convention assembled at Wheeling, to ordain a constitution for the proposed new State of West Virginia.

The attitude of Mr. Willey in the United States Senate, at this most trying crisis, was eminently just, enlightened, and patriotic, and worthy of Virginia in its wiser and better days.

"We may, with equal confidence," said he, "challenge a more minute examination of the policy and administration of the General Government affecting the States in rebellion. And here I do but allege what the records of the country will amply attest, when I say that in the bestowment of official patronage and emolument and position in every branch of the Government, the South has ever enjoyed an eminently liberal proportion of favor. The journals and acts of Congress will verify the assertion that every important measure of national policy has either originated with Southern statesmen, or has been made, sooner or later, essentially to conform to the demands of Southern sentiment. This is a broad assertion, but it is true. The South has always exercised a controlling influence in the councils of the Republic. She has had more than an equal share of Presidents; she has had more than a fair proportion of appointments in the Cabinet; the Supreme Court has been adorned with a full quota of her eminent jurists; the *corps diplomatique* has had no just cause of complaint for the want of representatives from south of Mason and Dixon's line; and the glorious annals of our army and navy attest on every page the valor and skill of Southern chieftains."

After unfolding the Southern conspiracy, he said: "Sir, truth will ere long strip these conspirators naked before the world, and the people whom they have so cruelly misled will rise up and curse them. History—impartial history—will arraign and condemn them to universal contempt. It will hold them responsible before man and God for the direful consequences already brought upon the country, and for the evils yet to come—for the desolations of war, its pillage and rapine, and blood, and carnage, and crime, and widowhood, and orphanage, and all its sorrows and disasters."

Mr. Willey, then and always, insisted upon the impossibility of dismemberment. "Sir," said he, "this Union cannot be dissolved. Nature and providence forbid it. Our rivers, and lakes, mountains, and the whole geographical conformation of the country rebuke the treason that would sever them. Our diversities of climate and soil and staple production do but make each section necessary to the other. Science and art have annihilated distance, and brought the whole family of States into close propinquity and constant and easy intercourse. We are one people in language, in law, in religion, and destiny. 'Whom God hath joined together, let no man put asunder.' The past is glorious; the future shall be sublime."

Mr. Willey, at the same session of the Senate, in an able and appropriate speech, gave a full and minute history of the new State matter, on the application of West Virginia for admission into the Union as a State. He met every objection, satisfied every reasonable doubt, and secured an early, favorable, and unanimous report from the committee, its triumphant and speedy passage through the Senate, and eventually through the House, until it received the sanction of the President.

The new State having been admitted, Mr. Willey in August, 1863, was elected one of the United States Senators from West Virginia. He drew the short term of two years, before the expiration of which he was re-elected for the term ending in 1871.

Thus far we have contemplated Mr. Willey in scarcely more than a single phase of his character, while to pause here would leave this sketch but half completed. Not only has he sustained an eminent reputation as a lawyer and statesman, but he has all along stood before the public as a Christian and a philanthropist. The very beginning of his professional life demonstrates the transparent integrity of his character. At thirty years of age, he writes:

"I was poor when I started; I am comparatively poor still. I was honest when I started, and, thank God, I am honest still. I would not give the consciousness of honesty and integrity for all the honors of ill-gotten gain." Elsewhere he adds, on occasion of somewhat straitened circumstances: "Poverty is far more desirable than ill-gotten wealth. I will live honest, if I die poor. I will live an honorable man, if I die in obscurity. I would not exchange the approbation of a good conscience for the hoards of Crœsus. I would not relinquish the pleasure and exalted happiness of conscious integrity for the crown of an emperor."

Mr. Willey is an active member of the Methodist Church, and his church connection seems early to have been with him a matter of gratulation and thanksgiving; while his religious experience, so far as it has been apparent to the eye of strangers, bears the marks of deep sincerity and genuineness. In 1853, we find him delivering a series of lectures on the "Spirit and Progress" of that branch of the church of which he is a member; wherein, among other things, he discusses the importance of an earnest faith in connection with the performance of Christian duty. Alluding to these lectures, the public prints alleged, and doubtless with much truth, that "he would fill a pulpit with no ordinary ability."

The cause of Temperance has ever held a warm place in the affections of Mr. Willey. He was early a member of various associations, here and there, for the promotion of this great enterprise. In 1853, he was, by the Grand Division of the Sons of Temperance of West Virginia, elected their lecturer on "Temperance and Legal Prohibition."

We find him also deeply interested in Sabbath-schools, and he is himself a Sabbath-school teacher. So likewise has the great missionary enterprise always enlisted his sympathies, commended itself to his judgment, and called forth his eloquence. Thus, he is not one of those lights that are hid under a bushel. At Washington, Mr. Willey has preserved his consistency. He has been here the friend of temperance, missions, the Sabbath-school, and every good work. The *National Intelligencer* says of him: "He devotes his hours of leisure from legislative duties in furtherance of good objects here. His late speech at the Foundry Church on Sunday afternoon on Sunday-schools, will not soon fade from the mind of any one present on the occasion."

More effective still seems to have been an address, delivered at Philadelphia, on a missionary occasion, when, in the course of his speech, he read various extracts from the highest authorities, illustrating the elevating power of the Gospel upon heathen nations. He further insisted that it was the best civilizing agency that was ever employed—that Magna Charta was not found at Runnymede, nor the Declaration of Independence at Philadelphia; but that both of these immortal documents were traceable to the Bible.

SAMUEL C. POMEROY.

SAMUEL C. POMEROY was born in South Hampton, Massachusetts, January 3, 1816, and his boyhood was spent upon his father's farm. In 1836, he entered Amherst College; but at the end of two years, leaving college, he went to reside in Monroe County, New York, where he continued about four years. He then returned to his native town of South Hampton.

In 1840, during the time of his residence in the State of New York, he heard that remarkable man, Alvan Stewart, on the subject of slavery, was deeply impressed with his eloquence, became a ready convert to anti-slavery principles, and began at once to labor zealously to promote them.

His first effort seemed rather discouraging. Proposing to organize a county liberty party, he issued a call for a meeting to be held at the county seat. On arriving at the place of meeting on the day appointed, after a ride of twenty miles in his own wagon, he found an audience of just two persons beside himself. After waiting an hour for other arrivals, and waiting in vain, nothing daunted, he called the meeting to order, one of the audience taking the chair, and the other acting as secretary. Mr. Pomeroy then delivered his speech, after which resolutions were presented and adopted, and a county ticket formed, which received at the election *eleven* votes in a population of twenty thousand. In six years afterwards, however, the liberty party ticket of this same county carried the election.

Returning to South Hampton, as we have seen, in 1842, Mr. Pomeroy, by his zealous efforts, had the satisfaction of seeing constantly increasing members added to the new party. He lectured in school-houses—preached from house to house—met objections—answered arguments—softened down prejudices, and made converts everywhere. Year by year the work prospered, and though slow, it was sure; for victory, at last, crowned his efforts. Annually, for eight years, he was on the anti-slavery ticket for the Massachusetts legislature, but was unsuccessful until 1852, when he was elected over both Whigs and Democrats. His characteristic anti-slavery zeal he boldly carried with him into the legislature. On the occasion of the rendition of the slave Burns to his assumed owner, he gave utterance to the following burst of eloquence:

"Sir," said he, addressing the Speaker, "when you have another man to enslave, do it as you did before, in the gray of the early morning. Don't let in the light of the brighter day upon the scene, for the sun would blush, if you did not, and turn his face away to weep. What! return a man to hopeless slavery! to a condition darker than death, and more damning than perdition! Death and the grave are not without their hope; light from the hill-tops of immortality cross the darkness and bid the sleepers awake, and live, and hope; and perdition with its unyielding grasp has no claims upon a man's posterity. But remorseless slavery swallows up not the man alone, but his hapless offspring through unending generations, for ever and for evermore!"

About the time of the passage of the Kansas-Nebraska Bill in 1854, Mr. Pomeroy was in Washington, and his call upon President Pierce happened to be at the very hour of his signing it. It is said, in fact, that the ink was not yet dry upon the parchment when Mr. Pomeroy addressed the President in these prophetic words:

"Sir, this measure which has passed is not the triumph you suppose. It does not end, but only commences hostilities. Slavery is victorious in Congress, but it has not yet triumphed among the people. Your victory is but an adjournment of the question from the halls of legislation at Washington to the open prairies of the freedom-loving West; and there, Sir, we shall beat you, depend upon it!"

The passage of the Kansas-Nebraska act at once "fired the heart" of the North. "Emigration to Kansas!" became a sort of watchword far and near. Freedom-loving men and women everywhere realized, for the first time, how much they were individually capable of doing. Organized emigration was at once initiated by the genius of Eli Thayer, who, under a charter obtained from the Massachusetts legislature, organized the "New England Emigrant Aid Company." In this enterprise, Mr. Thayer was ably seconded by Mr. Pomeroy, who discerned at a glance the value and practical nature of the idea. Of this company he immediately became the financial and general agent, taking an active part in procuring and distributing all necessary information relating to the history, soil, climate, distance, etc., of Kansas, together with rents, time of passage, and expense for reaching there. Moreover, he lectured extensively, and by word and deed stimulated all who could make the sacrifice to emigrate to Kansas, and offered himself to be their Moses to conduct them to the promised land.

It was on the 27th of August, 1854, that the first band of emigrants, under the leadership of Mr. Pomeroy, and numbering two hundred, started from Boston for the far West. At various points on their way, they received the greetings and sympathies of warmhearted and earnest men and women, like themselves, who bade them God-speed with many prayers, tears, and benedictions. On the 6th of September they came to Kansas City, Missouri, on the borders of the great land whither they were destined; and passing up the Kansas River, they pitched their tents at the end of three days' journey, and gave the name of *Lawrence* to the place of their sojourn. Another colony soon followed, whom Mr. Pomeroy met at St. Louis, and conducted them forward; and in November another still came on, and were likewise met and guided by him into the Territory. Meanwhile, Gov. Reed and other appointed officials came on to administer the government of the new Territory, and, in behalf of the emigrants, were welcomed by Mr. Pomeroy in such words as these:

"We welcome you to these rude homes of ours in the wilderness, which we have journeyed many weary miles to make, not because we look for better or for happier ones than we have left behind, but because we intend, in good faith, to meet the issues of the hour. In the spirit of the act which reclaims these territories from savage haunts, and organizes them into homes for civilized men, we came to do our share in the work necessary to accomplish it. In pursuance of this object, and in imitation of those who sought liberty with the *Mayflower*, we came bringing with us, as they did with them, the institutions of our faith and our freedom—our churches and our schools. With the Bible in one hand, and the school-book in the other, we propose to make this 'wilderness to bud and blossom as the rose.' This Bible we lay upon the altar of a free church—this primer upon the desk of a free school, and may the God of our Pilgrim Fathers aid us in the work!"

The limits of this sketch do not permit us to tell of the inroads of Southern banditti that followed this emigration—of their guns, bowie-knives, and whiskey—of how slavery sought eagerly to gain possession of the fair land of Kansas—how, for this purpose, and under the auspices of a weak and wicked administration of the General Government, it promptly introduced its hideous machinery of outrages, murders, house-breakings, and robberies.

Amid the disturbance and violence of this stormy year of 1856, Mr. Pomeroy was called upon to prove his fidelity to truth, and his courage in maintaining principle. Beaten, arrested, and twice imprisoned, threatened with death, and sentenced by a mob to be hung, he still escaped to complete the work yet remaining to be done. We find him in Washington conferring with the prospective Governor of Kansas—lecturing in various places in the East in its behalf—rallying and shipping Sharpe's rifles—forwarding ammunition, and thus variously preparing for the worst. But peace came soon, and 1857 opened auspiciously for the new Territory.

Thus far the career of Mr. Pomeroy had been that of a philanthropist. His political career now commences, and it commences with his righteous opposition to the infamous "Lecompton Constitution." Against this he fought day and night, and by addresses and public lectures, not only throughout Kansas, but the Northern States, until in 1858 Congress sent the swindle to the "tomb of the Capulets."

Along this period we have Mr. Pomeroy as Mayor of Atchison—as establishing the first free school of that town—building with his own private means a brick church, and presenting it to the Congregationalists—and entering heartily into plans for the relief of Kansas amid the terrible drought and famine of 1860.

It was in connection with this last-named effort that the noble disinterestedness of Mr. Pomeroy's character shone forth as conspicuously as in any other of his labors and sacrifices. Said he, at this time, to an intimate friend: "You know I intend to be a candidate for the United States Senate, and if I go into this relief business, it is certain to kill me; for every dollar that passes through my hands is sure to make an enemy of somebody. Some who don't need, will grumble because I refuse them; others who are helped, will be dissatisfied because I do not give them more; and my political enemies will make every mistake tell against me, whether it be mine or the fault of somebody else. They will lie about me in every way they can, and the result of the whole business will be, so far as the United States Senatorship is concerned, that I shall be killed as dead as Julius Cæsar. But still, if this people are in danger of suffering again, I mean to go in and help them anyhow, and let my political prospects go, and trust to God for the result;" and Mr. Pomeroy proved by the result of his confidence, that "Blessed are all they that put their trust in him." Accordingly, after aiding most efficiently in ministering the ample relief that flowed into Kansas from ten thousand benevolent hands, so well satisfied with him were the people, that they placed him, forthwith, in the United States Senate, where he took his seat at the extra session, which met July 4, 1861. In 1867 Mr. Pomeroy was re-elected for the Senatorial term ending 1873.

It seems quite unnecessary to write that Mr. Pomeroy's entire career in the Senate has been what might be expected from the antecedents of the man. The very first measure introduced by him was precisely characteristic, and was a "Bill to suppress the Slaveholders'

Rebellion." The very wording of the title evinces the intention of the author, which was to place the Rebellion directly at the door of the guilty party. His entire Congressional record, we believe, has been correspondent—all his speeches and votes have been eminently patriotic—and the true interests of the country have ever lain near his heart.

On the 5th of March, 1866, Mr. Pomeroy, advocating universal suffrage by Congressional enactment, which he maintained was "nothing less than throwing about all men the essential safeguards of the Constitution," used the following language: "Let us not take counsel of our fears, but of our hopes; not of our enemies, but of our friends. By all the memories which cluster about the pathway in which we have been led; by all the sacrifices, blood, and tears of the conflict; by all the hopes of a freed country and a disenthralled race; yea, as a legacy for mankind, let us now secure a free representative republic, based upon impartial suffrage and that human equality made clear in the Declaration of Independence. To this entertainment let us invite our countrymen and all nations, committing our work, when done, to the verdict of posterity and the blessing of Almighty God."

One of Mr. Pomeroy's friends has graphically said: "True to principle, true to his convictions, true to his country, and terribly true to his country's foes, he occupies to-day, as Senator of the United States, a proud position among his peers—a position that honors both representative and the represented. As a patriot, he is earnest; as a statesman, logical; as a politician, consistent; and as a man, genial generous, and just."

WILLIAM P. FESSENDEN.

WILLIAM PITT FESSENDEN, a son of the Hon. Samuel Fessenden, was born in Boscawen, N. H., October 16, 1806. Before he reached his twelfth year, he was fitted for college under the tutorship of a law student in his father's office, and at the age of seventeen was graduated at Bowdoin College, in the class of 1823. He immediately commenced the study of law, and in 1827, at the age of twenty-one, was admitted to the Portland bar. He immediately opened an office in Bridgeton, Me., and in 1829 removed to Portland.

In 1831, at twenty-five years of age, Mr. Fessenden was elected to the State legislature, of which he was the youngest member. He rose at once to distinction, both as a debater and a legislator. His insight into the details of political economy, for which, in later years, he became so distinguished, were thus early evinced in an important debate on the United States Bank, in which the youthful orator displayed remarkable spirit and ability.

From 1832 to 1839, Mr. Fessenden devoted himself exclusively to his profession, in which he very soon rose to the first rank, both as a counselor and an advocate. In 1838, he was solicited to become a candidate for Congress, but declined. In 1839, he was again chosen to the State legislature, a representative from the city of Portland. Although the House was largely Democratic, and Mr. Fessenden was a Whig always distinguished for an uncompromising assertion of his principles, nevertheless he was placed on the Judiciary Committee, and was made Chairman of the House Committee for revising the Statutes of the State.

Mr. Fessenden, in 1840, was nominated by acclamation as the Whig candidate for Congress, and was elected by a vote running considerably beyond the party limit. In Congress he participated in the current debates, and made speeches on the Loan Bill, Army Appropriation Bill, and against the repeal of the Bankrupt Law. In 1843, he was nominated for re-election, but declined, from a choice to remain in the practice of his profession; and, meantime, he received in the legislature of that year, the votes of the Whig party for a vacant seat in the United States Senate. In 1845, he was again elected to the State legislature, and was also chosen in the following year, but declined.

From 1845 to 1852, Mr. Fessenden was in private life, devoting himself to his profession with a constantly increasing practice and reputation. During this period he was associated with Daniel Webster in an important case before the Supreme Court at Washington, involving a legal question never before discussed in that court. The question was as to "how far the fraudulent acts of an auctioneer in selling property should affect the owner of the property sold—he being no party to the fraud?" In this case, Mr. Fessenden had to contend against the weight and influence of Judge Story's opinion and decision, which were against his client in the court below. But he was successful, and Judge Story's decision was reversed. His argument on that occasion was remarkable for its logical force and legal acuteness, and was said to have won the highest admiration from the most fastidious judges.

Once, during this period (1850) of Mr. Fessenden's career, he was elected to Congress, but his seat was given to his competitor through an error in the returns. Yet he declined to contest the case before Congress, from an unwillingness to serve in that body. This unwillingness he had decisively expressed in advance to the Conventions of the Whig and Free-Soil parties, which, against his wishes, had insisted upon nominating him.

Mr. Fessenden was a member of the National Convention which nominated Gen. Harrison for the Presidency in 1840; and of the

WILLIAM P. FESSENDEN.

National Convention which nominated Gen. Taylor in 1848; and also of that which nominated Gen. Scott in 1852. He was a member of the Maine legislature in 1853, the Senate of which gave him a majority vote for the position of Senator in Congress. But the House, being Democratic, failed by four votes to concur, and no election was effected at that session. The same House, however, though opposed to him in politics, associated him with the Hon. Reuel Williams in negotiating the purchase of the large body of wild lands of Massachusetts, lying in Maine, which was successfully accomplished.

In the following year, we find Mr. Fessenden in the State legislature, both branches of which were Democratic. But the Kansas-Nebraska question operating as a disturbing element, he was now elected United States Senator by both branches—a union being formed of the Whigs and Free-Soil Democrats. This event may be said to have been the preliminary step toward establishing the Republican party in Maine—the necessity of which, after the action of the Southern Whigs on the Nebraska Bill, Mr. Fessenden earnestly maintained. He was strongly opposed to this bill; and shortly after taking his seat in the Senate, and on the night when it was passed, he delivered one of the most electric and effective speeches that had been made against it. This great effort established his reputation in the Senate as one of its ablest members.. Among other important speeches of Mr. Fessenden subsequently made in the Senate, is his speech on our relations with England; also that on Kansas Affairs, and on the President's Message in 1856; on the Iowa Senatorial election in 1857, and on the Lecompton Constitution in 1858. In the general debates and business of the Senate, he has from the beginning taken a prominent part.

In 1859, by a unanimous vote of his party in the legislature, and without the formality of a previous nomination, Mr. Fessenden was re-elected to the United States Senate for the term of six years.

Toward the close of this term of service in the Senate, he was appointed, by President Lincoln, Secretary of the Treasury, in place of Salmon P. Chase, who had been elevated to the Supreme Bench. In the Thirty-seventh Congress, he was Chairman of the Senate Finance Committee, a position which he held until appointed to the Cabinet in 1864. In his capacity as Chairman of this important committee, Mr. Fessenden's labors were of a very arduous character. In the Thirty-seventh and Thirty-eighth Congresses there were all the vast appropriations of the Government to provide for, besides the labor of originating and putting in operation a financial system which would enable the Government to meet the demands of a civil war, waged on a scale of colossal proportions. In the accomplishment of all this, Mr. Fessenden bore a very prominent and conspicuous part. As Chairman of the Committee on Reconstruction, very much labor and care devolved upon him. He was authorized to write the Report of this Committee, which, in respect to ability, may be considered one of the capital achievements of his life.

As a laborer in the important work belonging to a legislator and statesman, probably few, if any, excel Mr. Fessenden. For clear, incisive common sense, the rarest and most excellent quality of a Senator, he is eminently distinguished. "There is no man in Congress," says one, "whose judgment is more true, whose discretion is more absolute, or whose conviction is more sincere." In great sagacity, catholic comprehension, and in that just estimate of what is practicable, he is probably unsurpassed.

Mr. Fessenden is equally eminent as a debater. He thinks closely, clearly, and accurately. He speaks readily—being prepared to discuss on the instant almost any subject that may be presented. His speeches are entirely extemporaneous, and are so accurately pronounced that they can be put in type without the change of a sentence or a word. And then there is scarcely a subject presented on which he does not have something to say—his remarks being brief and to the point. In opposition he is almost always reasonable, although, at times, the stern integrity of his character may render him somewhat impatient, particularly when in debate he is confronting mere rhetoric and sentimentality in place of argument and sound sense But he neither traduces nor defies his opponents; and his advocacy of measures is all the more effective that while firm, prudent, and pointed, he is, at the same time, usually genial and always respectful.

Mr. Fessenden's course and bearing in the progress of the reconstruction measures were invariably dignified and commendable. No one was more fully aware than he that the difficulties of the situation were to be surmounted, not by vituperation and crimination, nor by petty jealousies or lofty moral indignation; but rather by tranquil firmness and honest argument. Differing from the President, he forbore, however, to question his sincerity; and while convinced that certain conditions of reorganization were indispensable, he refrained from either exasperating the late rebel population, on the one hand, or flattering them, on the other.

Mr. Fessenden, as is well known, was one of those of the Republican party who, at the conclusion of President Johnson's Impeachment trial, voted for his acquittal.

In the "opinion" which he prepared on this occasion, he said: "It would be contrary to every principle of justice, to the clearest dictates of right, to try and condemn any man, however guilty he may be thought, for an offense not charged, of which no notice has been given to him, and against which he has had no opportunity to defend himself."

After proceeding at great length and with much learning to give reasons why he regarded the President not guilty on the several articles, he added: "In the case of an elective Chief Magistrate of a great and powerful people, living under a written Constitution, there is much more at stake in such a proceeding than the fate of the individual. The office of President is one of the great co-ordinate branches of the Government, having its defined powers, privileges, and duties; as essential to the very framework of the Government as any other, and to be touched with as careful a hand. Anything which conduces to weaken its hold upon the respect of the people, to break down the barriers which surround it, to make it the mere sport of temporary majorities, tends to the great injury of our Government, and inflicts a wound upon constitutional liberty. It is evident, then, as it seems to me, that the offense for which a Chief Magistrate is removed from office, and the power intrusted to him by the people transferred to other hands, and especially where the hands which receive it are to be the same which take it from him, should be of such a character as to commend itself at once to the minds of all right-thinking men as, beyond all question, an adequate cause. It should be free from the taint of party, leave no reasonable ground of suspicion upon the motives of those who inflict the penalty, and address itself to the country and the civilized world as a measure justly called for by the gravity of the crime and the necessity for its punishment. Anything less than this, especially where the offense is one not defined by any law, would, in my judgment, not be justified by a calm and considerate public opinion as a cause for removal of a President of the United States. And its inevitable tendency would be to shake the faith of the friends of constitutional liberty in the permanency of our free institutions and the capacity of man for self-government."

Mr. Fessenden's vote to acquit the President subjected him to considerable censure from a majority of the Republican press of the country. Subsequently, on declining an invitation to a public dinner tendered to him by some distinguished citizens of Boston, he took occasion to explain and defend his action in the case. Whatever may have been the surprise and regret of many of Mr. Fessenden's friends at his decision in this momentous trial, no one can reasonably call in question the integrity and purity of the motives by which in this, as in his other public acts, he seems to have been actuated.

ZACHARIAH CHANDLER.

ZACHARIAH CHANDLER is a native of Bedford, N. H., and was born Dec. 10, 1813. He received an academical education in addition to the usual school training given to New England boys.

As is common with such boys, he worked upon the farm until sixteen or seventeen years old. In the course of his youth he taught school two or three winters; and in 1833, when twenty-two years of age, he emigrated to Michigan, and engaged in mercantile business in Detroit. The country was then new, and Detroit was a town of but about 4,000 inhabitants.

Mr. Chandler is one of those fortunate men of the West who have grown up with the country. He commenced, at first, a small retail dry-goods store, but was soon enabled by a prosperous trade to enlarge his business to a wholesale trade, and extended, in course of time, his operations to all parts of the surrounding country, so that there were few of all the retail dealers in Northern and Western Michigan, Northern Ohio and Indiana, and in Western Canada, who were not numbered among his customers.

Mr. Chandler was a Whig in politics, but seems never to have sought for political honor, choosing, rather, to set the example of accepting office as an incident of the success of his party, than to strive for it as a primary object. His first official position was that of Mayor of Detroit, to which office he was elected in 1851. Here he served acceptably, and the following year was nominated for Governor of the State. His strong anti-slavery convictions, however, were brought into the canvass, and he preferred to be what he deemed right, than to be Governor. In denouncing the institution of slavery as the great curse of the nation, he lost the election. The progress of anti-slavery sentiment in Michigan was such that in 1856 he was elected to the Senate of the United States for six years, and took his seat on the 4th of March of that year.

During the important period of his first term in the United States Senate, Mr. Chandler was identified with all the leading measures of Congress for a general system of internal improvements—for preventing a further increase of slave territory, and for the overthrow of the powerful domination of the slave power, which had usurped the control of the nation. He was one of the few Northern men in the Senate at that time who foresaw the tendency of events, and that the country was drifting onward to a terrible war.

Mr. Chandler opposed all the so-called compromise measures of the South, as the virtual surrender of the liberties of the people. In all the Senatorial contests of that period, he stands on record as the unflinching defender of liberty, and the fearless advocate of the doctrines of the Declaration of Independence. These great doctrines he maintained by speech and vote in the Senate and before the people; and if an appeal to arms should be necessary, he welcomed the arbitration of war.

"The country," writes one of Mr. Chandler's admirers, "does not now appreciate how much it owes to his Roman firmness. The people have become too much accustomed to regard him as one of the great fortresses of their liberties, which no artillery could breach, and whose parapet no storming column could ever reach, that they have never given themselves a thought as to the disastrous consequences which might have followed on many occasions had he spoken or voted otherwise than he did. When did he ever pander to position or complain of being overslaughed by his party? Yet no man ever did braver work for a party, and got less consideration than he."

As the war came on, and seemed for a time to be prosecuted with indifferent success, particularly in the East, Mr. Chandler, with a multitude of other good men, chafed under what he considered the dilatory and unskillful management of army operations. He was prompt to discern and denounce the want of generalship in McClellan. His speech on this subject, made in the Senate, July 7, 1862—soon after the defeat of the army of the Potomac—was bold and incisive. "The country," he exclaimed, "is in peril; and from whom—by whom? And who is responsible? As I have said, there are two men to-day who are responsible for the present position of the army of the Potomac. The one is the President of the United States, Abraham Lincoln, whom I believe to be a patriot—whom I believe to be honest, and honestly earnest to crush out and put down this rebellion; the other is George B. McClellan, General of the Army of the Potomac, of whom I will not express a belief. * * Either denounce Abraham Lincoln, President of the United States, whom I believe to be a pure and honest man, or George B. McClellan, who has defeated your army. He took it to Fortress Monroe, used it guarding rebel property, sacrificed the half of it in the swamps and marshes before Yorktown and the Chickahominy, and finally brought up the right wing with only thirty thousand men, and held it there till it whipped the overwhelming forces of the enemy, repulsed them three times, and then it was ordered to retreat, and after that, the enemy fought like demons, as you and I knew they would, a retreating, defeated army. Tell me where were the left and center of our army? Tell me, where were the forces in front of our left and center? Sir, twenty thousand men from the left and the center to reinforce Porter on the morning after his savage and awful fight, would have sent the enemy in disgrace and disaster into Richmond."

Mr. Chandler, as we have seen, had no patience with any half-heartedness, or dilatory efforts in the prosecution of the war against the rebellion. He was for striking decided and heavy blows in order to crush the power of the enemy, and it was under the influence of such sentiments that he, in his place in the Senate, proposed a special "Committee on the Conduct of the War." This Committee was at once ordered. Mr. Chandler declined the chairmanship of the Committee, but was one of its most energetic members; and his zealous and faithful efforts, in connection with his associates, soon resulted in the removal of McClellan from his command. Equally active was he throughout the war in promoting its efficacy, looking after the interests of the soldiers, and encouraging all measures tending to a successful issue of the great struggle; a struggle he knew it would prove to be, in the very commencement of the revolt; and he then, in a letter addressed to the Governor of Michigan, intimated that blood must flow if the Government was to be preserved. Several years afterwards, when taunted in the Senate by a Democratic Senator in reference to this letter on "blood-letting," Mr. Chandler responded as follows: "It is not the first time that I have been arraigned on that indictment of 'blood-letting.' I was first arraigned for it upon this floor by the traitor John C. Breckenridge; and after I gave him his answer, he went out into the rebel ranks and fought against our flag. I was arraigned by another Senator from Kentucky, and by other traitors on this floor. I expect to be arraigned again. I wrote the letter, and I stand by the letter, and what was in it. What was the position of the country when that letter was written? The Democratic party, as an organization, had arrayed itself against this Government; a Democratic traitor in the Presidential chair, and a Democratic traitor in every department of this Government; Democratic traitors preaching treason upon this floor, and preaching treason in the hall of the other House; Democratic traitors in your army and navy; Democratic traitors controlling every branch of this Government; your flag was fired upon, and there was no response; the Democratic party had ordained that this Government should be overthrown; and I, a Senator from the State of Michigan, wrote to the Governor of that State, 'unless you are prepared to shed blood for the preservation of this great Government, the Government is overthrown.' That is all there was to that letter. That I said, and that I say again; and I tell that Senator, if he is prepared to go down in history with the Democratic traitors who then co-operated with him, I am prepared to go down on that 'blood-letting' letter, and I stand by the record as then made."

EDWIN D. MORGAN.

EDWIN DENNISON MORGAN is the seventh of her Governors whom New York has honored with a seat in the Senate of the United States. The others were DeWitt Clinton, Van Buren, Marcy, Wright, Seward, and Fish.

Mr. Morgan is a native of the town of Washington, Massachusetts, where he was born on the eighth of February, 1811. He here enjoyed the opportunities afforded by the public schools, until the age of twelve years, when his father removed to Windsor, Connecticut, where he attended the high school, and subsequently was a student in the Bacon Academy at Colchester. In the family exodus to Windsor, this youth of a dozen years drove an ox team loaded with household effects, performing a good share of the journey, some fifty miles, on foot. At the age of seventeen he entered the wholesale grocery and commission house of an uncle, in Hartford, as clerk. Anecdotes illustrative of his mature judgment and penetration are extant, qualities which early commanded his relative's attention, and, at the end of three years, procured for him admission to a partnership. He remained here engaged in mercantile pursuits until his removal to the city of New York, whither, in 1836, he went with a view to larger business opportunities. The period for such a change was perhaps fortunately chosen, for the financial crisis of 1837, which occurred a few months after his advent there, afforded, to a practical observer like himself, valuable lessons in the ethics of trade. At all events, his commercial house, since so successful, was established about this time on a sound and permanent basis. Enterprise, resolution, and honorable dealing, marked its course, and soon acquired for

Mr. Morgan a leading place among those engaged in pursuits like his own.

While vigilant in business, he was not unmindful of the claims implied in the right of citizenship, and from 1840 to the close of the canvass that resulted in the overwhelming defeat of General Scott, he labored assiduously in the Whig ranks, though realizing that the non-election of Mr. Clay, to whom he was devoted, destroyed the prestige of his party. He acted as Vice-President of the Republican National Convention held at Pittsburg, in 1856, and was there made Chairman of the National Committee. In that capacity he opened the Convention at Philadelphia, in 1856, that nominated Fremont, that at Chicago, in 1860, which nominated Lincoln, and also that of 1864, at Baltimore, which re-nominated Mr. Lincoln. In 1866, he was made Chairman of the Union Congressional Committee?

In 1849, he was elected to the Board of Assistant Aldermen in New York, of which he was chosen President. A few weeks after taking his seat in the latter body, the Asiatic Cholera broke out, and owing to the unfavorable sanitary condition of the city, it spread so rapidly as to create great alarm. Mr. Morgan was placed upon the Sanitary Committee, and so imminent appeared the danger from this pestilence that his whole time was devoted to the details of the position. Hospitals were to be improvised, the sale of food to be regulated, streets, yards, and places to be cleansed—indeed, many and pressing were the thankless duties incident to a critical moment like this, in a great city whose population is drawn from all quarters of the world. The efforts of the Board were attended with signal success, and in the fall of that year the Whig electors of the Sixth Senatorial District indicated their sense of his services by giving him a seat in the State Senate, and re-electing him two years afterward. In the Senate he was placed at the head of the Standing Committee on Finance, where he remained through his term. At the Session of 1851 he was made President *pro tempore* of that body, serving also in the same capacity at the extra meeting of that summer; and although the Democratic party had gained control of the Senate in 1852, he was unanimously chosen again as its temporary President, and also for the fourth time in 1853.

In 1855, he was appointed a Commissioner of Emigration, which place was held until 1858, when he was elected Governor. To the latter office, before the end of his term, two years afterward, he was re-elected by the largest majority ever given to a governor in the State of New York. Important duties lay in the four years he was destined to fill the gubernatorial chair; and as events proved, he possessed rare qualifications for their performance. A knowledge of men, a high standing in the commercial community, a thorough business training, and practical knowledge of the complex finances of the State, coupled with clear and enlightened views on questions falling within the scope of his functions, and freedom from petty prejudices, blended happily in the new Governor. He had need of all these advantages, as also of his tireless industry, equable temper, and robust physique. His first term, though marked with vigor and the initiation of important reforms, was preparatory to the second, whose duties in extent and importance no other Governor of the State has been called upon to perform.

On entering office, he found the State's high credit threatened, the public works still unfinished, though millions had been expended for their completion.

Popular expectation, disappointed often, and wearied at length by the languid progress of the enlargement, was giving way to a disposition, adroitly fostered, to sell the canals, thereby to create a great and controlling monopoly, most baneful in its character. The militia, as an organization, had by degrees, through years of peace, quite lost its efficiency, and the condition of the military property and arsenal supplies was sorry enough. His first message to the Legislature, like all his others, shows a clear and searching insight into the condition of the State in its varied interests. These papers are eminently clear and frank, and are wanting neither in force of diction nor soundness of doctrine. In his first communication to the Legislature occurs this sentence: "Upright intentions, a heart devoted to the interests of the commonwealth, and unceasing application, are all the pledges I can give for the faithful execution of the trusts delegated to me by the people of New York."

Pledge was never better kept, and he proceeded at once to make it good. The Canal finances received the first attention. The Canal revenues had fallen largely below the constitutional claims upon them, owing, in part, to an immense reduction in tolls, but most of all to a lax system of expenditure by the use of drafts upon the treasury, anticipatory of appropriations, to the extent of millions of dollars, in express defiance of the laws and the Constitution. This illegitimate paper was hawked in the markets, where it was known as "floating debt," a new form of obligation to New York's ledger of State indebtedness. It was daily growing in volume, and was prejudicing other forms of the State's credit. The proceeds were being used, it is true, though not with economy, in completing the Canals. He did not hesitate to present the whole subject to the Legislature, and to recommend early provision for its liquidation. "The people, thereby," said he, "are placed in the dilemma of paying an unauthorized debt, or seemingly incurring the stain of repudiation;" and while protesting against the whole system, adds, "but under no circumstances will the State of New York ever refuse to acknowledge and pay every and all just claims existing against her, or that have been contracted by any of her recognized agents." The question was submitted to a vote of the people, who legalized the debt, though by a majority so limited as to afford wholesome warning to any who might hereafter be tempted to repeat so evil a practice. As respected the current management of the Canals, he urged that the tolls be largely increased, and the cost of maintenance be essentially lessened. Both recommendations were adopted with most satisfactory results. He took decided ground against the sale of the Canals, and, with characteristic energy, urged their completion. Before retiring from the Executive office he had the satisfaction of announcing the Canal enlargement as fully effected.

The inadequate defenses of the harbor of New York were early adverted to by him with earnestness, and the series of labors performed by him in this connection, and also in conjunction with others, afford honorable example of public economy and practical wisdom. In response to an inquiry from the Inspector-General of the Army, he says, in December, 1867:

"You ask what steps were taken by me, as Governor of New York, in response to Mr. Seward's circular letter of October, 1861, upon the subject of perfecting harbor and coast defenses, and the amount of expense incurred by the State for that purpose. Immediately on the reception of Mr. Seward's letter, I proceeded to ascertain what mode of defense would be the most judicious to adopt, with a view to making temporary provision therefor. I had called the attention of the Legislature to the inadequate defenses of the harbor of New York in January, 1860, and, in view of dangers not necessary here to detail, the subject had not been lost sight of. Hence, I was the more ready to co-operate with the General Government in providing for the safety of the lake and sea-ports of the State, when the letter reached me to which you have called my attention.

"To the Legislature, on its assembling, I referred the whole subject, with the recommendation that, in default of prompt action on the part of the national authorities, it was the duty of the State to proceed without delay with such portions of the defense as prudence should dictate.

"Under apprehensions of hostilities growing out of the *Trent* affair, I had, in December, 1861, purchased a large quantity of timber for floating obstructions, at an aggregate cost of about $80,000, for use, if need be, in the form of cribs or rafts, connected by chain cables, to be anchored at the Narrows. The plan for its use, an eminently feasible one, had been carefully matured. When no longer necessary, the timber was sold, without loss to the State treasury.

"No expense was therefore incurred, either in 1861 or 1862, for the specific object of your inquiry. But early in 1863, the defenseless condition of the harbor of New York was again the occasion of disquietude, because of the unfavorable aspect of this country's relations with the two principal naval forces of Europe, and the liability to ravages of privateers. Accordingly, the Legislature appropriated $1,000,000 for the purchase of cannon, sub-marine batteries, and iron-clad steamers, and for providing such other means to protect the harbors and frontiers of the State as were deemed necessary by the commissioners named in the act, Governor Seymour, Lucius Robinson, comptroller, and myself.

"Popular apprehensions had, doubtless, magnified dangers sufficiently grave, and the commissioners lost no time in personally examining in detail all the fortifications in the harbor, and conferring with engineers thoroughly conversant with the subject. As Government was then rapidly placing the largest and most improved guns in the forts and progressing with the fortifications, there remained little to be done in that direction by the State authorities, whose duties could therefore be best performed by supplementing the labors of the Federal agents. And after due consultation with the Federal officers and other practical engineers, whose services, with the exception of the engineer in charge, it is but just to say, were gratuitously rendered, it was concluded to again resort to floating obstructions. Plans were at once advertised for, and, in due time, proposals for materials invited. As a precaution, my associates formally authorized me, in case of an unexpected attack upon the city of New York, to take such instant measures for defense as I might deem necessary, with liberty to use the whole appropriation, if required, for that purpose.

"When the bids were opened it was found that the enhanced price of timber and iron would so increase the cost of the proposed work as to render a further appropriation necessary, and, as meantime the relations of our country with certain foreign governments had become more pacific, it was decided to defer action until the regular meeting of the Legislature. Practically, however, the means for providing a defense were at all times within reach. Timber in sufficient quantities and suitable iron cables were at command in case of emergency, and as the plans for the use of these were well understood by a competent board of engineer officers who could be speedily convened, it was deemed unnecessary to urge further action. It only remains to be stated that of the appropriation but $5,000 were used; the balance of the million remains untouched in the State treasury."

The subject of executive pardons received more than ordinary consideration from him, and considered in proportion to the applications presented, he granted fewer pardons than any of his predecessors. The matter of special legislation and the want of specific accountability for appropriations to charitable objects engaged particular attention.

In common with close observers, he from the first held as serious the threats of secession that followed the election of Mr. Lincoln, but lent his influence to calm the popular mind, and to remove, so far as was consistent with principle, any pretext for the course finally pursued by the South. But the attack on Sumter ended all disposition on his part to placate that section. "This gratuitous violence, and this deliberate insult to the flag, conclusively proves to all," said he, "that it is the design of the leaders to break up the Government." Thenceforward, day by day, he bent every energy to the work of putting down the rebellion. No other State was looked to for so many men and so much money as New York. Her quota was about one-fifth part of all the troops called for. The Legislature was about to adjourn when the news from Charleston harbor reached Albany. A few earnest words served to present his views to the two Houses. In forty-eight hours they had appropriated three millions and a half in money for war purposes, and authorized the raising of 30,000 volunteers. With the aid of the State Military Board this number was soon enrolled and fully organized, and, by the third week in May, was hurried into the field, whither nine regiments of State militia, serving as minute men, had preceded them. So extensive had been the preparations of the rebels, as to leave it obvious that a single campaign would not end the struggle of the insurgents. Hence, Governor Morgan was averse to refusing volunteers after the State's quota was filled; and when the battle of Bull Run occurred, he was in Washington seeking authority to establish camps of instruction at two or three points in the State, with a view to greater efficiency of recruits, and to keep aglow the spirit of enlistment. Following the first great rebuff to Union arms, came the President's call upon New York for 25,000 men, and this demand was so far increased that on the first of January the State had raised 120,600 troops. On that day he was able to assert that "no requisition had been made by the Government that remained unhonored."

The city of New York was a common rendezvous for the several States; and many independent regiments were there forming, thereby impeding the State authorities. In view of these facts, and to secure other practical advantages, at the same time to express his sense of the important services rendered by Governor Morgan, the President, in September, 1861, appointed him a Major-General of Volunteers, and created the State into a military department under his command. It is proper to add that he declined any emolument for this duty of sixteen months.

Succeeding the ardent spirit of volunteering of the earlier months of the war, came a period when the disposition wholly ceased. The tardy movements of the eastern army and the unsuccessful series of battles of midsummer of that year had done the work. But the disaster that culminated at Malvern Hill, rendered a call indispensible, to be quickly followed by a second requisition of equal extent.

The quota of New York under the two was 120,000 men. Prompt action was vital, and a special incentive to secure the new levies became necessary. The public clamored for an extra session of the Legislature to authorize a bounty. But this involved the delay of days, possibly of weeks, when time was so precious. It was clear that the people of the commonwealth favored a bounty, and Governor Morgan did not hesitate to assume the responsibility of offering one. Accordingly he announced that the State would give $50 to each man enlisting for **three years**. The stimulus proved sufficient, and volunteering at once began again in earnest. A class of volunteers inferior to none who had ever taken up arms, were brought into the service. The aggregate sum expended for this object was about $3,500,000, which the Legislature at its next session, acting on the recommendation of Governor Seymour, lost no time in legalizing. The mode employed in this emergency, that of raising local regiments by committees of leading citizens for their respective Senate districts, proved to be wisely chosen. In a few days a regiment was ready for the field, and they followed each other with steady pace, at the rate of one a day until the great quotas were filled. Several of these regiments were equipped with arms purchased by the Governor, and most of them were uniformed and otherwise supplied from his purchases. They reached the field in time to take part in the battle of Antietam, inspiriting by their presence the hearts of the veterans whose rapid marches northward had prevented communication with friends, and who were needing such a stimulus. By the end of his term he had sent no less than 320,000 men into the field, being more than a fifth part of all that had yet entered the service. In addition to these, the State militia regiments were on three several occasions dispatched to Washington, to answer emergencies. The thanks of the President and the Secretary of War were frequently tendered Governor Morgan, for his promptness and efficiency in responding to their demands, and the extent of the aid that as executive of New York he was enabled to render. When he left the office, New York stood credited with an excess over all quotas.

Contracts for rations, clothing, arms and ordnance, to the extent of many million dollars, had been made by him in behalf of the General Government, in addition to what had been purchased for the State. All these business transactions have received the approval of the Federal authorities.

There were, during his latter term, causes of grave uneasiness to which the public gave no particular heed, but which occasioned him no little anxiety. The disorderly element in the city of New York, stimulated by persons not unfriendly to the South, and which a few months after his retirement originated the riot there, was watched by him with unceasing care. The rebel element in Canada, too, and the threatening aspect of the relations of this country with Great Britain in the earlier part of the war, made necessary, considering the proximity of the State to Canada and its extended and exposed frontier, a provision for prompt defense or retaliation; and in the winter of 1862, a plan was matured, the execution of which he would have intrusted to General Wadsworth, with the latter's approval, to secure the State from hostile dangers in that quarter. The subsequent raid at St. Albans and elsewhere along the northern borders, was but a feeble indication of what might have been in the earlier stages of the rebellion.

In February, 1862, he was elected to the Senate of the United States for the term of six years, to succeed Preston King. He took his seat at the called session of March of that year, and has served on the Committees on Commerce, Finance, the Pacific Railroad, as Chairman of the Joint Committee on the Library, on Manufactures, Military Affairs, Mines and Mining, and on Printing.

In February, 1865, on the retirement of Mr. Fessenden, he was asked by Mr. Lincoln to accept the position of Secretary of the Treasury. This he declined; but not disposed to forego the advantages which he believed Mr. Morgan's presence in the Cabinet at the head of the Finances would bring, the President, disregarding his expressed wishes, nominated him without his knowledge, and it was only after earnest objections on his part that Mr. Lincoln consented to withdraw his name and leave him in the Senate.

At its commencement, in July, 1867, Williams College, which is located in his native county of Berkshire, Massachusetts, conferred upon him the Degree of Doctor of Laws.

THOMAS A. HENDRICKS.

THOMAS A. HENDRICKS was born in Muskingum County, Ohio, September 7, 1819. He was educated at South Hanover College. He studied law at Chambersburg, Pennsylvania, where he completed his legal studies in 1843. He soon after settled in Indiana, of which State his uncle, Hon. William Hendricks, was an early Governor, and a United States Senator.

In the profession of law, Mr. Hendricks met with marked success, and attained great eminence. His professional business soon ceased to be of a mere local character, his practice extending largely into the highest courts of the State and the nation. In 1848, he was elected a member of the Indiana Legislature. In 1850, he was an active member of the Convention to amend the State Constitution. In 1851, he was elected a Representative in Congress from Indiana, and served two terms.

In 1855, Mr. Hendricks was appointed, by President Pierce, Commissioner of the General Land Office. During the four years of his service in this capacity, more business was transacted by the General Land Office than at any previous or subsequent period. Over four hundred thousand land patents were issued; and the land sold, located by warrants, and taken by grants, amounted to eighty millions of acres.

In 1860, Mr. Hendricks was the candidate of the Democratic party for Governor of Indiana, but was defeated. Two years later, his party having carried the State, he was elected a United States Senator for the term ending March 4, 1869.

In 1868, the name of Mr. Hendricks was prominently before the New York National Convention for the nomination as the Democratic candidate for the Presidency. It was deeply regretted by many of his party that he was not chosen as their leader in the great political struggle which ensued. He actively participated in the campaign, however, as the Democratic candidate for Governor of Indiana. After an exciting campaign and a close contest, he was defeated by a majority of about one thousand.

In the Senate of the United States, Mr. Hendricks was justly regarded as the ablest in the ranks of the minority. With great argumentative ability, and never-failing good humor, he advocated the policy of his party in opposition to the Reconstruction Acts of Congress. His great arguments on the Freedman's Bureau, the Civil Rights Bill, and on various questions of Reconstruction, were regarded by all as masterly presentations of Democratic principles and policy.

The career of Mr. Hendricks in the Senate has been marked by so much ability and courtesy as to win the respect and regard of his political opponents. In the course of a discussion in the Thirty-ninth Congress, a Republican Senator pronounced Mr. Hendricks "the best natured man in the Senate." On another occasion a Republican Senator remarked in debate, that if he had as much respect for the political opinions of Mr. Hendricks as for his abilities, they would seldom disagree.

As a speaker, Mr. Hendricks is graceful, deliberate, and impressive. He states legal and political propositions with clearness, and deduces conclusions with great logical skill, constantly giving evidence of careful investigation and thorough understanding of his subject. When feeling is to be aroused, or action to be urged, his earnestness of manner gives great weight to his appeals. He uses little ornament, relying for effect rather on plain statement than on rhetorical flourish.

On the 30th of January, 1868, Mr. Hendricks delivered in the Senate a speech on the Supplementary Reconstruction Bill then pending, from the concluding portion of which we make the following extracts:

"What objection have you to the constitutions of the Southern States as amended by the people? For two years you have made war against this policy; for two years you have kept these States out of the Union so far as representation was concerned; for two years you have kept this country disturbed and distracted; trade, commerce, and business have been uncertain and shivering; industry has been fearful to put forth its hand, or capital to trust to any enterprise; the spirit of harmony and of union has been passing away from both sections of the country, because of the strife that you have thus kept up. For what have you done it? What end have you attained? * * * You can lay your hand of logic upon but one thing. * * * You have taken the robes of political power off the shoulders of white men, and you have put them upon the shoulders of negroes. * * *

"A republican form of government is a form in which the people make their own laws through legislators selected by themselves, execute their laws through an executive department chosen by themselves, and administer their laws through their own courts. Is not that as near a republican form of government as you can have? That was the state of things when the Congressional policy sent five armies into the Southern States, when ten Governors were deposed by the paramount authority of the military power. * * * The property, the life, and the liberty of this people are placed at the control of the military authority; and this is a policy that is called a policy of reconstruction, of restoration, and this you claim to be done under the guarantee clause which directs this Government to guarantee to each State a republican form of government! You find no other point in the Constitution where you can stand. There is not a rock in the Constitution large enough for your feet to stand upon except this one, that it is your duty to guarantee a republican form of government to these States; and in the exercise of that power, in the discharge of that duty, you establish a military rule and despotism which is defined in the language of the Declaration of Independence, declaring the offenses of the British Crown toward the Colonies.

"This is all under the pretext of the guarantee clause. * * * I had some respect for it when it was claimed as under the military authority of the President, because when you say it is a military necessity I do not know any answer to that. Military necessity has no reply except obedience; but to say to an intelligent people that you are guaranteeing a republican form of government to States, when you are subjecting all the legitimate and rightful authority of their State governments to military rule, is, in my humble judgment, an insult to an intelligent people.

"I know the answer to this very well; that your establishment in the Southern States is only provisional; that it is only to last for a little time; and that out of its ruins there will 'spring up phœnix-like to Jove,' republican forms of government. You lay the foundations of free institutions on the solid rock of despotism, and expect it to grow up to a beautiful structure. I do not believe in the doctrine that you can do wrong and expect good to follow. I believe in the doctrine that good is the result of good, and that from a pure fountain. * * *

"Mr. President, my colleague has spoken of a column—the column of Congressional Reconstruction—and has said that 'it is not hewn of a single stone, but is composed of many blocks.' Sir, I think he is right. Its foundation is the hard flint-stone of military rule, brought from the quarries of Austria, and upon that foundation rests the block from Africa and it is thence carried to its topmost point with fragments of our broken institutions. That column will not stand. It will fall, and its architects will be crushed beneath its ruins. In its stead, the people will uphold thirty-seven stately and beautiful columns, pure and white as Parian marble, upon which shall rest for ever the grand structure of the American Union."

CORNELIUS COLE.

IN the year 1800 the grandparents of the subject of this sketch penetrated the wilderness of Western New York. David Cole, his father, was at that time twelve years old, and Rachel Townsend, his mother, was ten; the former having been born in New Jersey, and the latter in Dutchess County, New York.

Cornelius Cole was born in Seneca County, New York, September 17, 1822. He was afforded such educational facilities as the thrifty farmers of New York were accustomed to give their sons.

When he was about seventeen years old, a practical surveyor moved into the neighborhood and proposed to instruct some of the boys in his art. Flint's "Treatise on Surveying" was procured, and in eighteen days young Cole, without assistance, went through it; working out every problem, and making a copy of each in a book prepared for that purpose.

In the following spring, the instructor having died, young Cole entered into practice as his successor, executing surveys in the country about.

It was after this that he began in earnest preparation for college; first in the Ovid Academy, and afterwards at the Genesee Wesleyan Seminary.

He spent one year at Geneva College, but the balance of his collegiate course was passed at the Wesleyan University in Connecticut, where he was graduated in the full course in 1847. After a little respite he entered upon the study of law, in Auburn, N. Y., and was admitted to practice in the Supreme Court of that State at Oswego, on the 1st of May, 1848.

After so many years of close application, recreation was needed, and an opportunity for it was presented by the discovery of gold in California. On the 12th of February, 1849, he, in company with a few friends, left his native town for a journey across the continent. On the 24th of April, the party, consisting of seven, crossed the frontier of Missouri and entered upon the open plains.

At Fort Laramie the wagons of the company were abandoned, and the rest of the journey was made with pack and saddle animals alone; arriving at Sacramento City, then called the Embarcadero, on the 24th of July. After a few days of rest, he returned to the gold mines in El Dorado County, and worked with good success till winter, often washing out over a hundred dollars a day. When the rainy season set in, he first visited San Francisco, and in the following spring began the practice of law there. While absent in the Atlantic States in 1851, two most destructive fires visited that city, and he returned to find himself without so much as a law book or paper upon which to write a complaint. He visited some friends at Sacramento, and unexpectedly becoming engaged in law business, opened an office there.

Though he had been active in the political campaign of 1848, on the free-soil side, he took little or no part in politics in California beyond freely expressing his anti-slavery opinions, until his law business became entangled in it in this way: certain negroes had been brought out from Mississippi, and having earned much money for their master, were discharged with their freedom. Afterwards they were seized by some ruffians, with the purpose of taking them back to slavery. Cole unhesitatingly undertook their defense, and thus brought down upon himself at once the hostility not only of the claimants but of all their sympathizers, from the highest officers of the State down to the lowest dregs of society. California was at that time as fully subject to the slave power as any portion of the Union.

About this period he was united in marriage to a young lady of many accomplishments, Miss Olive Colegrove, who came from New York, and met him at San Francisco by appointment.

He contended vigorously with the elements of opposition in his profession until 1856, when, the presidential campaign opening, he was urged by the Fremont party to edit the *Sacramento Daily Times*, the organ of the Republicans for the State. The paper was conducted to the entire satisfaction of the party, and at the same time commanded the respect of the Democrats and Know-Nothings. After the election its publication was suspended, and Mr. Cole returned to his profession.

During the following four years he was the California member of the Republican National Committee and an active member of every convention of his party, always taking strong ground against both the Breckenridge and Douglas wings of the opposition, and never consenting to any party affiliation with either.

In 1859 he was elected District-Attorney for the city and county of Sacramento, being about the only Republican elected to any office in California that year.

His execution of that office during the two years for which he was elected was in the highest degree satisfactory to the people, and the subject of frequent favorable comment by both the courts and the profession.

In 1862 he visited the theater of the war. Before his return to the Pacific he had been named for Congress, and the following year was elected, receiving 64,985 votes.

In the Thirty-eighth Congress he was eminently successful in accomplishing results. He was a member of the Committee on the Pacific Railroad and of the Committee on Post-offices and Post Roads. As a member of the latter committee, he originated the project for mail steamship service between San Francisco and the East Indies, known as the "China Mail Line." The success of this great measure is universally conceded to be the result of his considerate management. His speech upon the subject was concise, and at the same time comprehensive and convincing.

He delivered a speech in favor of establishing a Mining Department at Washington, full of argument and statistics.

In February, 1864, when our arms were in their most depressed condition, he made a very effective speech in favor of arming the slaves.

Mr. Cole was among the most earnest advocates of the constitutional amendment abolishing slavery, and on the 28th January, 1865, made an effective speech in favor of the measure.

Mr. Cole's first term in Congress ended with the first term of Mr. Lincoln's administration. In him the war always found a warm supporter, and he enjoyed in an eminent degree the confidence of Mr. Lincoln. He was not elected to the Thirty-ninth Congress, but returned to California, to be very generally named for the United States Senate to succeed Mr. McDougall. In December, 1865, he was elected to that high office, receiving on the first balloting 92 votes out of 118, — having been nominated in the caucus of his party on the first ballot by a vote of 60 to 31.

Mr. Cole's career as a Senator, which has just begun, promises to be replete with useful service to the country, watchful regard for the interests of his State, and honor to himself. He is deliberate in forming his opinions, as he is firm in maintaining them when reached.

RICHARD YATES.

SOME who were not soldiers in the field, became conspicuous for their talents and patriotism amid the emergencies of the recent civil war. Prominent among these was Richard Yates of Illinois. He was born in Warsaw, Gallatin County, Kentucky, in 1818. In 1831 he removed with his father to Illinois, and settled in Springfield. He studied for one year in Miami University, Ohio, and subsequently entered Illinois College, where he graduated in 1838, the first graduate in any Western college. He subsequently studied law with Colonel John J. Hardin, who fell at the head of his regiment in the battle of Buena Vista. Having been admitted to the bar, Mr. Yates settled in the beautiful city of Jacksonville, Illinois, which has since been his home. In 1842 he was elected to the State Legislature, and served until 1850.

In 1850 he was nominated by a Whig Convention as a candidate for Congress, and was elected. In March, 1851, he took his seat in the House of Representatives, the youngest member of that body. A change was soon after made in his district, which, it was supposed, would secure a majority to the opposite party, yet he was re-elected over Mr. John Calhoun, a popular Democratic leader.

The district represented by Mr. Yates included the early home of Senator Douglas, where he had taught school, and commenced the practice of law. When Mr. Douglas became the author and champion of "Squatter Sovereignty" as applied to the territories of Kansas and Nebraska, his old friends warmly espoused the doctrine, partly through local pride and personal attachment to its author. The consequence was that, in 1854, Mr. Yates, who had opposed the "Nebraska Bill," was defeated as a candidate for re-election to Congress.

He subsequently devoted himself for several years to the practice of his profession and to the duties of president of a railroad. This interval of private life is looked back upon by himself and his friends as the happiest and most prosperous period of his career. Living in the midst of a community the most moral and intellectual of any in the West, surrounded by a young and interesting family to whose happiness he was devoted, and by whom he was ardently beloved, he passed a few years, which were the happiest of his life.

His family and near personal friends were reluctant to have Mr. Yates enter again upon political life, but his patriotic impulses and his ambition to mingle in more stirring scenes induced him to accept the nomination for Governor of Illinois in 1860. He had long been a devoted personal and political friend of Mr. Lincoln, and most gladly threw the power of his eloquence and the weight of his influence to promote his elevation to the presidential chair. As both the leading candidates for the presidency were citizens of Illinois, the contest in that State was especially interesting and exciting. The result, however, could not be doubtful, and Richard Yates was inaugurated as Governor of Illinois at Springfield a few weeks before Abraham Lincoln took the oath of office in Washington.

The inaugural address of Governor Yates was a most eloquent protest against the gigantic treason of South Carolina and other seceding States. Freshly crowned with the suffrages of a great State, his voice was heard throughout the Union as a truthful utterance of the people of the Northwest. "On the question of the Union of these States," said he, "all our people will be a unit. The foot of the traitor has never yet blasted the green sward of Illinois. All the running waters of the Northwest are waters of freedom and Union, and come what will, as they glide to the great Gulf, they will ever, by the ordinance of '87 and by the higher ordinance of Almighty God, bear only free men and free trade upon their bosoms, or their channels will be filled with the comingled blood of traitors, cowards, and slaves!"

The rebellion soon assumed proportions more immense, and the eloquent utterances of Governor Yates were put to a practical test. On the 15th of April, 1861, the Secretary of War issued an order requiring the Governor of Illinois to contribute six regiments to make up the force of 75,000 men called out by the President's first proclamation.

On the day the Governor received the call of the War Department, he issued a proclamation for a special session of the Legislature to provide the sinews of war.

Within ten days after the proclamation of Governor Yates was published, more than ten thousand men had offered their services. The work of enlistment still went on, and disappointment was everywhere expressed that the services of more men could not be accepted.

Cairo being a point of great strategic importance, situated at the confluence of the Ohio and Mississippi, and commanding both rivers, it was deemed important that it should at once be possessed and fortified by a Federal force. On the 19th of April Governor Yates ordered General Swift, of the State Militia, to take possession of Cairo. Forty-eight hours after the reception of this order, that officer left Chicago with four six-pounders and 495 men. On the morning of the 23d this force took possession of Cairo, which proved a most valuable military position during the war. It was fortunate for the country that this movement was made so promptly. A brief delay might have enabled the enemy to carry out their cherished purpose of waging the war upon Northern soil.

The Ohio and Mississippi Rivers were then thronged with steamboats engaged in the "Southern trade," and laden to the water's edge with Cincinnati dry goods, Northern produce, and Galena lead. The occupation of Cairo enabled Governor Yates to do a service to the Union by stopping this "aid and comfort" to the rebellion. The Governor having received information that the steamers *C. E. Hillman* and *John D. Perry* were about to leave St. Louis with military stores, he inaugurated the blockade of the Mississippi by telegraphing to Colonel Prentiss, commanding at Cairo, "Stop said boats, and seize all arms and munitions." The command was promptly and successfully obeyed, and all the strength which the commerce of the Mississippi and Ohio Rivers would have given to the rebel cause was at once cut off.

The War Department required but six regiments of soldiers from Illinois, and two hundred companies were ready and eager to be accepted. Governor Yates urged and finally secured the acceptance of four additional regiments. The disasters of the summer of 1861 aroused the General Government to a sense of the real danger of the country, and the necessity of a large army for putting down the rebellion.

Illinois had nobly responded to the enlarged demands. By the close of 1861 Governor Yates had sent to the field more than forty-three thousand men, and had in camps of instruction seventeen thousand more.

President Lincoln having on the 6th of July, 1862, called for three hundred thousand additional volunteers, Governor Yates replied: "Illinois, already alive with beat of drum and the tramp of new recruits, will respond to your call."

To the honor of Illinois it is to be recorded, that in the busiest season of the year, only eleven days were required to enlist more than fifty thousand men for the service of the country.

When the time arrived for the election of members for the General Assembly for 1863-4, there were at least one hundred thousand voters of Illinois absent from the State, in the service of the country. The consequence was the election of a Legislature with a majority opposed to the war for putting down the rebellion. It was in vain that the Governor recommended measures calculated to sustain and reinforce the soldiers of Illinois already in the field; in vain that he pleaded the necessity of providing and appropriating means for sustaining the financial and military credit of the State. The Legislature was not possessed of the patriotic impulses which moved the Governor and those who had responded to his call. Their time was wasted in unprofitable attention to other interests than those of the country in the great emergency which was upon her.

In June, 1863, a disagreement having occurred between the two houses as to the time of final adjournment, the Governor, in the exercise of a power placed in his hands by the constitution, prorogued the General Assembly to the 31st of December, 1864, the day when it's existence would terminate by law.

The people approved this brave and patriotic movement of their Governor, and in the following year elected a Legislature in sympathy with the country, and in harmony with the soldiers who were fighting her battles.

This Legislature elected Richard Yates to the Senate of the United States—a suitable reward to one whose ability and patriotism had contributed so largely to the honor of Illinois. During his administration a peaceful agricultural State, with scarcely a professional soldier within her limits, had grown to be one of the mightiest military commonwealths in history. Her army of two hundred and fifty thousand men, raised during the administration of Governor Yates, from the farms and shops of Illinois, was unsurpassed in effectiveness and valor. It was partly owing to the pride which the Governor took in the advancement of the soldiers of his State that so many of them had risen to high and distinguished rank as officers of the army. With honest pride the Governor said in his final message: "In response to calls for troops the State stands pre-eminently in the lead among her loyal sisters, and every click of the telegraph heralds the perseverance of Illinois generals and the indomitable courage and bravery of Illinois sons in every engagement of the war. The history of the war is brilliant with recitations of the skill and powers of our general, field, staff, and line officers. The list of promotions from the field and staff officers of our regiments to lieutenant and major-generals for gallant conduct and the pre-requisites for efficient and successful command, compare brilliantly with the names supplied by all other States; and the patient, vigilant, and tenacious record made by our veteran regiments in the camp, on the march, and in the field, is made a subject of praise by the whole country, and will be the theme for poets and historians of all lands for all time."

Mr. Yates took his seat in the Senate of the United States on the 4th of March, 1865, in time to aid in the complete restoration of the Union he had elsewhere assisted to save.

He immediately took rank among the foremost of those who have been denominated "Radicals." He announced himself as standing upon the broad principle "that all citizens, without distinction of race, color, or condition, should be protected in the enjoyment and exercise of all their civil and political rights." His faith in the final triumph of this principle was unwavering. On the 14th of February, 1866, Mr. Yates pronounced a speech of three hours' duration on a proposed Constitutional Amendment changing the basis of representation. "It is too late," he eloquently said on that occasion, "it is too late to change the tide of human progress."

Mr. Yates is one of the most popular orators of the country. Impelled by a warm humanitarianism and glowing imagination, he passes rapidly by dry technicalities and abstract theories to those grand and glowing deductions which the patriot delights to contemplate. He possesses a melodious voice, a graceful manner, with a ready and even rapid utterance. In person he is of medium hight, with a face which in his early years possessed a beauty quite uncommon among men of mark.

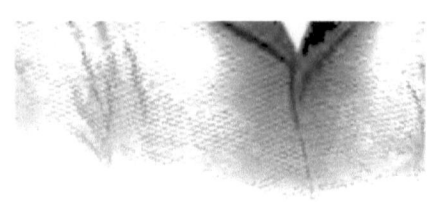

C. D. Drake

CHARLES D. DRAKE.

THE border States, upon the breaking out of the rebellion, were for a time the scene of severe conflicts between loyalty and treason; and during the whole progress of the war, only the presence of the military power of the Government secured the supremacy of the former. This condition of things brought out into prominence many men who had before taken little part in public affairs, and who did not enter the military service. Among these was Charles D. Drake, of Missouri. He was born in Cincinnati, Ohio, on the 11th of April, 1811, being the son of Daniel Drake, M.D., of that city, for many years eminent as a practitioner and teacher of medicine.

Mr. Drake's education was mainly received in the ordinary schools of the West. The only institutions of a higher grade which he attended were St. Joseph College, Bardstown, Kentucky, and Captain Partridge's Military Academy, Middletown, Connecticut. While at the latter, in April, 1827, he was appointed a Midshipman in the Navy, and in the following November entered upon active duty, and remained in the Navy until January, 1830, when he retired from the service and began the study of the law. He was admitted to the Cincinnati bar in 1833, and the next year removed to St. Louis, then a town of seven thousand five hundred inhabitants.

In 1838, he originated the St. Louis Law Library, now one of the most valuable in the country, and for more than twenty-one years was one of its Directors.

Mr. Drake's first appearance in public life was in 1859, when he was elected to the House of Representatives of Missouri, to fill a vacancy.

In 1860, he, for the first time since 1844, took part in politics, espousing the cause of Stephen A. Douglas for the Presidency, as a means of preventing the Electoral vote of Missouri from being cast for John C. Breckinridge. In August of that year, he delivered a speech at Victoria, in which the treasonable designs of the Southern States were exposed and denounced, and which, it was generally conceded, was the means of gaining the vote of Missouri for Mr. Douglas.

From the secession of South Carolina, Mr. Drake's course was open and pronounced against secession and rebellion. By speech and pen he labored for the Union cause, and it was in connection with those labors that he became prominent in Missouri and before the country.

In January, 1861, he delivered a speech in the Hall of Representatives of Missouri, in the presence of many members of the Legislature who were then plotting the secession of Missouri; in which he took the highest ground of unconditional loyalty to the Constitution and the Union.

On the following Fourth of July he delivered an elaborately prepared speech at Louisiana, Mo., upon all the issues of the hour; which was extensively published at the time, and was preserved in the "Rebellion Record." The concluding words of this speech were as follows:

"We are lost if our Constitution is overthrown. Thenceforward we may bid farewell to liberty. Never were truer or greater words uttered by an American statesman, than when Daniel Webster closed his great speech in defense of the Constitution, nearly thirty years ago, with that sublime exclamation: 'Liberty and Union, now and for ever, one and inseparable!' Union gave us liberty, disunion would take it away. He who strikes at the Union, strikes at the heart of the Nation. Shall not the Nation defend its life? And when the children of the Union come to its rescue, shall they be denounced? And if denounced, will they quail before the mere breath of the Union's foes? For one, I shrink not from any words of man, save those which would justly impute to me disloyalty to the Union and the Constitution. My country is all to me; but it is no country without the Constitution which has exalted and glorified it. For the preservation of that Constitution I shall not cease to struggle; and my life-long prayer will be, GOD SAVE THE AMERICAN UNION!"

On the 22d of February, 1862, he delivered, in St. Louis, an Address, in which he denounced Slavery as the cause of the rebellion, and used these words:

"Let it once be manifest that we are shut up to choose between our noble country, with its priceless Constitution, and Slavery, then, with every fiber of my heart and every energy of my nature, I will pass along the universal cry of all patriots—Down with Slavery for ever! I would then no more hesitate which to choose, than, in view of death, I would balance between eternal life and eternal perdition."

This Address was followed, at intervals, by others, during the progress of the rebellion, exposing its true character and aims, and denouncing Slavery as its sole cause. They were all gathered and published in a volume in 1864.

In 1863, Mr. Drake was elected a member, from St. Louis, of the Missouri State Convention, which was constituted in 1861, and which re-assembled in June, 1863, in pursuance of a proclamation of the Governor of the State, "to consult and act upon the subject of the emancipation of slaves." In that body he took ground in favor of immediate emancipation; but the Convention adopted a scheme so gradual as hardly to terminate Slavery before the year 1900. Mr. Drake, in a vigorous canvass, assailed it before the people; whence followed the rise of the "Radical" party in Missouri, of which he has for more than five years been the acknowledged leader.

In September, 1863, a delegation of seventy men from all parts of Missouri visited President Lincoln at Washington, to inform him of the actual condition of parties and affairs in Missouri. Mr. Drake was chairman of that body. Its address to the President attracted the attention of the people, and gave no inconsiderable impulse to Radicalism in all the loyal States.

In February, 1864, a Freedom Convention was held in Louisville, Ky., which Mr. Drake attended, and which he addressed on Washington's Birth-day, in a speech which attracted much notice and commendation from all parts of the country. The following are the concluding words of that address:

"The issue, upon one side or the other, of which every man in the nation must be ranged, is fully made up, between that Radicalism which will venture all, do all, and brave all for the Union and Freedom, and that Conservatism which, assuming loyalty, hangs back from the advanced positions of patriotism; professes enmity to Slavery, and yet cringes to it; avows hostility to treason, and yet counts traitors for partisan ends; ever finds something strong and resolute, which it were wise not to venture—something prompt and effective, that had better not be done—something daring and aggressive, which it is discretion not to be brave; and is content to stake less than all for country, that it may more cheaply win all for *itself*. When between two such forces the country's safety hangs, it is time that the banner of Radicalism were unfurled beyond the narrow limits of Missouri. The nation should behold it. Why not raise it here? And why not on this birth-day of Washington! Is there any better place or day? We have come to fling it to the breeze, and to plant it in the front rank, and we will do it. It is no paltry ensign of sectionalism, no drabbled banner of party, but the grand old standard of the Republic, with every broad stripe still firm and unstained; and look! with one more star in its azure field, than when treason struck at the beaming constellation; and that one riven, with her own blood-stained hand, from once brilliant, now poor, dismembered, fallen 'Old Virginia!' And see! its spreading folds reveal an inscription, inwoven in letters of gold, flashing in the orient sunlight! What are the words? Read them, ye downcast and oppressed, for they speak hope and cheer to you; read them, friends of Freedom, for they tell you of a brighter day; read them, champions of Slavery, for they proclaim your discomfiture; read them, traitors, for they thunder anathemas to you, as they say—' The Union without a slave; the Constitution amended to forbid Slavery for ever; and the arms of the Nation to uphold that Union and that Constitution to the latest generation!'"

In November, 1864, a new convention was elected in Missouri, to revise and amend the constitution of that State, and Mr. Drake was chosen one of its members from St. Louis County, and upon its assembling, in January, 1865, was made its vice president, and soon became its acknowledged leader. By that body slavery in Missouri was abolished on the 11th of that month. The convention was in session three months, and formed the present constitution of that State. In its formation so large a part was taken by Mr. Drake that he became more prominently identified with it than any other member of that body.

Mr. Drake was elected to the Senate of the United States in January, 1867, and took his seat in that body on the ensuing 4th of March.

In the subsequent consideration of the measures of reconstruction, he took a decidedly Radical stand; as, indeed, he had at all times taken on all questions relating to the suppression of the rebellion. His resolute adherence to Radical principles and policies was expressed in a published letter to Reverdy Johnson in November, 1867, in which he said:

"Here, Senator, at the close, as in the outset, we diverge. Cling, if you please, to purblind, droning, effete conservatism, and drift with it into the realms of the rejected and forgotten; but I will hold on to living, clear-sighted, resolute, and progressive Radicalism, be its fate what it may. If Americans, in this the meridian of their military renown, have not courage, persistence, and nerve to uphold such Radicalism as upheld and saved their country in the day of its deadliest peril, they will only exhibit a dishonoring example of a people unsurpassed in martial valor and achievement, but too timid for great civil conflicts, too feeble for sharp moral exigencies, too fickle for earnest struggles for the right, and too small for the mold of a grand and noble destiny."

Participating in the discussion of the Supplementary Reconstruction bill in the Senate, Mr. Drake earnestly advocated the substitution of voting by ballot for the method which had prevailed throughout the South of voting *viva voce*, and said:

"Once get the mode of voting by ballot fairly into the hands of a majority of the people down there, and they will be very likely to take care of it; but what I want is, that while this nation is undertaking to reconstruct these States upon the principle of loyalty to the Union, upon the principle of protecting the loyal people, the work shall be done thoroughly. Sir, I came from a State where we have dealt with this rebellion in some of its foulest aspects; and we have learned there, through a long and bitter experience, that the only way to deal with it is to apply the knife deep and strong down to the very fibers of the roots, leave not a single atom in which to germinate a future rebellion. I came here, Sir—I do not hesitate to avow in open Senate on the first occasion when I have undertaken to address this august body, that I came here as a representative, not of a conservative radicalism, but of a radical. radicalism, which believes in doing, and not in half doing."

HENRY W. CORBETT.

HENRY W. CORBETT was born at Westboro, Massachusetts, February 18, 1827. His father, Elijah Corbett, established one of the first ax manufactories in Massachusetts. In 1832, he removed to White Creek, New York, and subsequently settled in the town of Jackson, Washington County, New York. At the age of thirteen, Henry entered upon a clerkship in a store at Cambridge, New York, on a salary of fifty dollars a year. Here he remained two years, and about nine months of the time attended the Cambridge Academy. The following year he was a clerk in the establishment of Proudfit & Fitch, Salem, Washington County, New York.

In the spring of 1843, he went to New York City with letters of recommendation from his former employers, to enter upon a new life in the great metropolis. After much effort, he succeeded in obtaining a situation in a retail dry-goods store, his salary being $3 50 per week, out of which he paid his board, and slept on the counter. After remaining in this position for one year, he succeeded in obtaining a situation in a wholesale dry-goods store in Cedar Street, New York, where he continued as long as the firm remained in trade. In the fall of 1855, he was offered a situation in the dry-goods house of Williams, Bradford & Co. He remained with this firm until he conceived the idea of shipping a stock of goods to the Territory of Oregon. In the fall of 1850, he informed his employers that he desired to embark in this enterprise; and he proposed to them, if they would join him in the enterprise, he would divide the profits with them. They inquired of him what he knew of the country and its prospects.

They found him thoroughly informed on all points, and so implicitly did they believe in the success of any enterprise that his judgment approved, that they at once furnished him with a stock of goods, and cash to the amount of $24,000—a large amount of credit for a young man whose capital amounted to only $1,000, from his savings. After an absence of a year and a half, he returned to New York, repaid the $24,000—then divided his profits of $20,000 with those who assisted him. He was offered a co-partnership with his friends in New York, which he declined.

In February, 1853, he was married to Miss Cara E. Jagger, of Albany, New York; and in the following May he returned to Portland, Oregon, where he resumed his business, and was greatly prospered.

He now has an extensive wholesale hardware house in Portland, having two resident partners in that place, and one in New York. All his business enterprises have been attended with marked success, which his strict integrity and untiring energy have well deserved.

Mr. Corbett has been largely interested in many of the great enterprises for the development of Oregon, such as the establishment of manufactories of woolen goods, the erection of furnaces for the manufacture of iron, and the building of steamboats.

In 1866, he took the contract for carrying the daily mail from Lincoln, California, to Portland, Oregon, a distance of six hundred and twenty-four miles, stocked the road with four-horse teams and coaches, to the great satisfaction of the community.

In politics, Mr. Corbett was in early life a Whig. On the organization of the Republican party of Oregon in 1860, he was chosen chairman of the Republican State Central Committee. The energy with which this campaign was conducted, reduced the Democratic majority from about twenty-five hundred to thirteen. Hon. D. Logan, the Republican candidate for Congress, was defeated by only this small majority.

On the breaking out of the war, Mr. Corbett saw the importance of uniting all loyal men under the name of the Union party, for the purpose of crushing out the party of Secession in the State. By the prompt action of the Republican Central Committee in making a call, early in 1862, for all Union men to join them in a Convention, to be held at Eugene City, the peril of the State was averted. Mr. Corbett was an active member of that convention, and was instrumental in nominating a ticket that carried the State by about twenty-seven thousand majority. During the war he was active in raising money for the Sanitary and Christian Commissions, and contributed liberally for these as well as other worthy objects.

Mr. Corbett was chosen as one of the delegates to the Chicago Convention of 1860, that nominated Mr. Lincoln for the Presidency. He was a member of the Republican National Convention of 1868, which nominated Grant and Colfax.

Fully absorbed in his extensive business, and in his efforts to promote the success of the Union party in his State, Mr. Corbett has not been an ardent aspirant for political preferment. For some years he served the City of Portland as a member of its Council, and held the office of City Treasurer. On the 29th of September, 1866, he was elected a Senator of the United States.

In the Senate, Mr. Corbett has devoted himself with conscientious faithfulness to the discharge of his important duties. He has given much patient thought to the great financial questions which are now demanding attention. On these important topics he has delivered several speeches, which are marked by sound reasoning and wise deductions. On the 11th of March, 1868, he addressed the Senate on the Funding Bill, concluding his remarks as follows:

"When we look to the future of this great Republic, embracing twenty-three degrees in longitude by fifty-seven degrees of latitude, with all varieties of climate, producing the most delicate and delicious fruits of the South, with abundance of the more substantial productions of the temperate zone, and the hardy productions of the North— when we contemplate this vast and varied country, its climate, its production for the sustenance, comfort, and luxury of man, the vast resources of all its varied hidden riches of the earth, comprising metals for all the most substantial and useful arts of life, with all the most precious metals to tempt the cupidity of man; test the bowels of the earth, it sends forth its fatness in living streams of oil like the perennial fountain; add to these our beds of coal, our forests of timber, our mountains of iron, where is its equal? Have we the capacity to make them useful? —who doubts it? With all the thousands of inventors, combining the greatest inventive genius of the world, we can outstrip all other nations combined. A population from every land and nation under the sun, a land now happily free from the oppressor's rod, to be rebuilt upon a firm and enduring foundation, made sacred and cemented by the blood of a million of our noblest sons.

"Therefore, let us not crown this temple, hewn by the sweat of so many brows, reared by the blood of so many brave lads, with the cap-stone of repudiation. Let us do nothing, as a great and noble and suffering people, that shall detract from the honor of those that lie silent and cold in their blood-bought graves, with naught but their country's banner over them. To me, Mr. President, my duty is plain; my duty to the men that came forward to supply our suffering army, to succor our noble boys in the day of the national darkness and despair, and to the capitalists of Germany, of Frankfort, that took our securities, and spewed out the rebel bonds, and gave to us money, the sinew of war, to assist us in maintaining the life of the nation. I need not the example of other nations to tell me what is right between man and man or between nation and nation; it needs not the shrewd argument of a lawyer to tell me what is due to my creditor. If there is any one thing that I regard more sacred in life, after my duty to my God, it is to fulfill all my engagements, both written and implied, and nothing shall drive me from this position.

"If this be important and right in private affairs, how much more important in public affairs."

REVERDY JOHNSON.

ONE of the few remaining statesmen of the times who link the present with the past, is REVERDY JOHNSON, Senator from Maryland. JOHN JOHNSON, his father, was an eminent lawyer, who held the offices of Attorney General, Judge of the Court of Appeals, and Chancellor of Maryland. His mother was of French ancestry. The name of her family, REVARDI, is perpetuated, with a slight orthographic alteration in that of her distinguished son.

REVERDY JOHNSON was born in Annapolis, Maryland, May 21, 1796. He entered the Primary Department of St. John's College, in his native town, when six years old. Here he pursued his studies for ten years. At the age of sixteen he left the institution without graduating, yet having pursued a thorough course of classical and mathematical training.

On leaving college, he commenced the study of the law, under the direction of his father.

One day, as the young law-student was poring over his books, news came that the British were about to make an attack on Washington. The whole community was aroused, and a company of volunteers was hastily formed to aid in defending the Capital. Young Johnson joined them on such a sudden impulse that he did not stop to put off the slippers which he wore in the law-office; and the consequence was that, before he had marched half-way to Washington, he was completely barefoot. The company reached the neighborhood of Washington in time to participate in the battle of Bladensburg, on the 24th of August, 1814. Soon after this engagement young Johnson was attacked with a serious illness, which put a sudden termination to his military history.

Having resumed his law studies, Reverdy Johnson was admitted to the bar in 1815, and was soon after appointed Deputy Attorney General for Prince George's and St. Mary's counties.

In 1817 he removed to Baltimore, and while engaged in an extensive practice of the law, held the office of Chief Commissioner of Insolvent Debtors.

In addition to regular professional and official duties, he was, during a number of years, partially occupied in the literary labor of reporting judicial decisions, which were published in seven volumes, under the title of "Johnson's Maryland Reports."

In 1821 he was elected to the State Senate of Maryland for a term of five years, and was re-elected for a second term, but resigned after serving two years.

During twenty years which followed, he gave his undivided attention to professional business. In legal learning and skill he reached a rank and reputation unsurpassed in the American Bar. He was employed in arguing many important cases before the Supreme Court of the United States. His services were sought in distant portions of the United States and in Europe. He made journeys to New Orleans and California, to try important cases. On one occasion he went to England, as attorney in an important case which involved a heavy claim against the Government of the United States.

In 1833 Mr. JOHNSON met with an accident, which resulted in a partial loss of his eyesight. Mr. Stanley, a member of Congress from North Carolina, having been challenged to fight a duel by Henry A. Wise, of Virginia, went to Mr. Johnson's residence, near Baltimore, for the purpose of preparing for the conflict. He requested Mr. Johnson to assist him in some preparatory practice with his pistol. Mr. Stanley succeeding very badly in his practice, Mr. Johnson took the pistol, and fired at a small locust tree, about ten feet distant. He struck the target, but the ball rebounded and entered his left eye. A surgeon was summoned, and the bullet was extracted; but the sight of the eye was lost.

Mr. Johnson was a Whig in politics; yet, when the memorable Presidential contest of 1824 was narrowed down to a choice between Jackson and Adams, he favored the election of the former. He frankly told Mr. Clay, whose warm friend he was, that the great political error of his life was casting his influence for Adams instead of Jackson.

In 1845 Mr. Johnson was elected a United States Senator from Maryland, and, differing from a majority of his party, he favored the Mexican war. On the accession of General Taylor to the Presidency, in 1849, Mr. Johnson was appointed Attorney General of the United States, whereupon he resigned his seat in the Senate. On the death of President Taylor, he resigned his office, and resumed his private practice.

When the wicked policy of the Southern leaders had led the people to the verge of rebellion, Mr. Johnson, although in private life, did not fail to raise his voice and use his influence against the heresy of secession. In December, 1860, at the close of an argument before the Supreme Court, he pronounced one of the most eloquent eulogies on the Union, and presented one of the most thrilling delineations of the wickedness and folly involved in its overthrow, to be found in the annals of American oratory.

On the 10th of January, 1861, when Maryland was poised between loyalty and rebellion, Mr. Johnson addressed an assemblage of many thousands of the citizens of Baltimore, in an overwhelming argument against the crime of secession. He administered a withering rebuke to South Carolina, which he characterized as "that gallant State of vast pretensions, but little power." "If," said he, "the cannon maintains the honor of our standard, and blood is shed in its defence, it will be because the United States cannot permit its surrender without indelible disgrace and foul abandonment of duty."

This speech gave Mr. Johnson rank among the foremost defenders of the Union. In 1862 the Legislature of Maryland elected him as a Union man to the United States Senate, in which he took his seat in March, 1863.

Mr. Johnson has been one of the most faithful and laborious members of the Senate. He has generally acted with the minority, and yet has frequently shown that he is not bound by party trammels. In March, 1864, he gave his vote in favor of the constitutional amendment abolishing slavery.

As a member of the Joint Committee on Reconstruction, in the Thirty-Ninth Congress, he generally opposed the views of the majority and favored the immediate re-admission of the Southern States.

He opposed what was called the "Military Reconstruction Bill" when it was under discussion in the Senate, but when it was returned with the President's objections, he spoke and voted in favor of its final passage over the veto, as the mildest terms which the South were likely to obtain. He regarded it as the means through which the South might be "rescued and restored ere long to prosperity and a healthful condition, and the free institutions of our country preserved."

Mr. JOHNSON is of medium stature, with such a build of body as indicates great physical endurance. His countenance habitually wears a sober, serious expression, seldom relaxing into a smile. He possesses agreeable manners, combined with a dignity appropriate to his venerable age and high position. As a speaker, his manner attracts and retains the attention, which his matter abundantly repays. He enters with zeal into whatever subject of discussion deserves his attention and demands his utterance.

JOHN M. THAYER.

JOHN MILTON THAYER was born in Bellingham, Massachusetts, January 24, 1820. He graduated at Brown University, and studied law. In 1854, he emigrated to Nebraska, and settled there simultaneously with the organization of the Territory, selecting Omaha as the place of his residence.

Indian difficulties shortly after occurring, the Governor organized the militia, and appointed Mr. Thayer Brigadier-General, and gave him the command of the force. The Legislature, at its ensuing session, created the office of Major-General, and elected him as the incumbent. He was frequently selected to go as Commissioner to the Indians, for the purpose of stopping their hostilities, and, on several occasions, commanded expeditions against them.

From his youth, Mr. Thayer was imbued with the spirit of Anti-Slavery, and hence he early espoused the principles and course of the Republican party. In 1859, he was elected a member of the Convention for framing a State Constitution. Though an ardent Republican, he received this election from a county strongly Democratic—having the highest vote on the ticket.

In 1860, Mr. Thayer was elected to the higher branch of the Territorial Legislature. On the breaking out of the Rebellion, he applied immediately to the War Department for authority to raise a regiment of volunteers, and was instrumental in rallying the First Nebraska Infantry. Of this Regiment he was made Colonel, and served with it in Missouri during the first six months of the War. His regiment, with others, was selected by General Halleck to proceed to Fort Henry. On reaching that place, General Grant assigned to Colonel Thayer command of all the reinforcements which were arriving, and sent him down the Tennessee, and up the Cumberland, to Fort Donelson, while General Grant himself marched across by land. Colonel Thayer was then placed in command of the Second Brigade in General Lew Wallace's Division, and was engaged in the hardest of the fighting on the last day of the battle.

At the battle of Shiloh, Colonel Thayer had command of the extreme right, and for good conduct received the strong commendations of his commanders, and was made Brigadier-General.

A prominent share in the great struggles of the War seems to have fallen to General Thayer. He led one of the storming columns at Chickesau Bayou; his horse was shot under him at Arkansas Post; he was through all the seige of Vicksburg, and was at the first and second capture of Jackson, Mississippi. He was afterward placed in command of the "Army of the Frontier," and with it participated in the battles of Prairie de Ann, Jenkin's Ferry, and other engagements. He was made a Brevet Major-General for "distinguished services."

On returning to his State, after the close of the War, General Thayer was elected a United States Senator for the term expiring in 1871.

Mr. Thayer belongs to that class of legislators who, while not given to much speaking, are yet prompt and ready to speak whenever necessity or the public service requires it. From his long residence near the frontier, and the varied intercourse he has had with the Indian tribes, probably no member of the Senate possesses a more extensive knowledge of matters pertaining to these savage people than General Thayer. Hence his speeches bearing upon the Indian question have a special interest for those less familiar than himself with their sentiments and character. We are impressed, as we read and ponder these speeches, that though brief and unpretending, they are, however, the words of a man who knows whereof he affirms, and testifies of that which he has seen. "Mr. President," he says, in one of these addresses, "I rise simply to correct two misapprehensions of the Senator from Maine, [Mr. Morrill,] into which he has been led. He asks, where is there an Indian reservation which is not invaded today by the white people? Well, I respond to him by stating that there are five Indian reservations within the State of Nebraska, between which and the whites there has been the most perfect accord and friendship for the seven years past, not the slightest interference or collision between the Indians upon these reservations and the white settlers. That is my answer to his interrogatory. These troubles do not arise with the friendly Indians, but with the hostile Indians, who are away beyond Nebraska and Kansas, upon the plains, whose lands have not been invaded by the whites. Those who have committed these outrages and these murders are not the Indians whose lands have been interfered with by the whites. They are those who have come from their own section of the country down to the two Pacific Railroads, and there is where they are creating the difficulty. It is simply a question between civilization and barbarism. They are opposed to those two Pacific Railroads, and that is, after all, the real cause of the trouble."

In another speech, several days afterward, on the same general subject, Mr. Thayer remarked as follows:

"The Indians are opposed to the building of these two Roads (Pacific Railroads). There is no mistake about it. I have heard it from them myself. The reason they object is, that it cuts in two their buffalo range. The buffalo range, in certain seasons of the year, extends from away north of Nebraska down toward the Red River, and they think the Road will interfere with that. One Indian chief expressed his objection in this way: 'We do not object to the horse going through our country that goes so,' imitating in his manner the galloping of a horse; 'but,' he added, 'we do object to the horse that goes so,' imitating the noise of a steam-engine. That was his expressive way of giving utterance to his objection.

"The difficulty is, that the Indians do not like these Roads; and, hence, I have favored this bill, which proposes to open these two lines of road by taking the Indians away, and putting them on reservations to the north and to the south. * * *

When the Senate was preparing to proceed with the Impeachment Trial, Mr. Hendricks objected to Mr. Wade's being sworn, on the ground that being "interested, in view of his possible connection with the office, in the result of the proceedings, he was not competent to sit as a member of the court." Mr. Thayer spoke in answer to this objection, and from his remarks on the occasion, we make the following extract:

"I challenge the honorable Senator from Indiana to point me to one iota in the Constitution which recognizes the right of this body to deprive any individual Senator of his vote. No matter what opinions we may entertain as to the propriety of the honorable Senator from Ohio casting a vote on this question, he is here as a Senator, and you cannot take away his right to vote except by a gross usurpation of power. He is here as a Senator in the possession and exercise of every right of a Senator until you expel him by a vote of two-thirds of this body. Then he ceases to have those rights, and not till then. * * * In courts of law, if objections are made to any one sitting upon a jury, and he is excluded, an officer is sent out into the streets and the highways to pick up talesmen and bring them in to fill up the jury. Can you do that here? Suppose you exclude the honorable Senator from Ohio, can you send an officer of this Senate out into the lobbies or into the streets of Washington to bring in a man to take his place? By no means. I need not state that.

"Thus I come back to the proposition that we are a Senate, composed of constituent members, two from every State, sworn to do our duty as Senators of the United States; and when you attempt to exclude a Senator from the performance of that duty, you assume functions which are not known in the Constitution, and cannot for a moment be recognized. When you attempt to exercise the power, and do exercise it, are you any longer the Senate of the United States? The Senate, no other parties or bodies forming any part of it, is the only body known to the Constitution of the United States for this purpose, and the Senate is composed of two Senators from each State."

JAMES W. PATTERSON.

JAMES W. PATTERSON was born in Henniker, a small farming town in Merrimack County, New Hampshire, July 2, 1823. His father was a direct descendant of William Duncan and Naomi Bell, from whom originated some of the most superior men which New Hampshire has produced. The subject of this sketch was, however, born in poverty, and inured to toil and hardship.

When eight years of age he went with his family to Lowell, Mass., where he remained until he was thirteen. In 1836, he went back with the family to his native town, and subsequently for two years worked on a farm, in winter attending the academy in Henniker village, two miles and a half distant. In 1836, he returned to Lowell, and obtained employment in a cotton mill. The agent of the mill, John Aiken, Esq., a gentleman of penetration, practiced in reading character, soon took him from the mill into his counting room, where he continued two years. While in this position he was a leading member of a debating society, conducted at that period with great spirit by the young men of Lowell. It seems to have been largely due to the aspirations awakened by this society, that, with the approbation of his friend Mr. Aiken, he resigned his place in the counting room, for the purpose of seeking a liberal education. In the ensuing winter he taught a district school in his native place, and in the spring of 1842, went to the city of Manchester, where his parents then resided, and there entered with all his energies upon his preparation for college. The study of a single year, with little or no instruction, sufficed to fit him for college. In 1844, at the age of twenty-one, he entered Dartmouth College, and graduated with the first honors of his class in 1848. Subsequently for two years he was in charge of an academy in Woodstock, Conn., and at the same time he was pursuing a course of study with a view to the profession of the law. But becoming an intimate friend of Henry Ward Beecher, who at that period was accustomed to spend his vacations in Connecticut, he was induced through his influence to turn his attention to theology. In 1851, he entered the Theological Seminary at New Haven, of which the illustrious Dr. Taylor was then the leading spirit. In a single year he completed the prescribed studies of two, at the same time teaching in a ladies' seminary to pay his expenses.

From the Theological Seminary, Mr. Patterson was called back to Dartmouth College as tutor; and when the chair of Mathematics became vacant by the resignation of Prof. John S. Woodman, he was elected to that professorship. Subsequently, on the re-organization of the Departments, he was assigned to the chair of Astronomy and Meteorology, which he filled with conspicuous ability.

From 1858 to 1861, he was a member of the State Board of Education, and, as its Secretary, had the leading part of the work to do in preparing the Annual State Reports on Education. His duty as School Commissioner required him to address the people in various parts of the State, on the subject of Common School Education. The ability displayed by Mr. Patterson in these addresses, attracted the attention of the people, and caused them to demand his services in the wider fields of politics and statesmanship.

In 1862, he was sent to the State Legislature as a Representative of Hanover, the seat of Dartmouth College. His reputation and talents at once gave him a commanding position in that body.

In the spring of 1863, Mr. Patterson was elected a Representative from New Hampshire in the Thirty-eighth Congress. He was appointed on the Committee on Expenditures in the Treasury Department, and on that for the District of Columbia. In 1864, he was appointed a Regent of the Smithsonian Institution. In 1865, he was re-elected to Congress, serving on the Committee on Foreign Affairs, and on a Special Committee on a Department of Education. In June, 1866, he was elected United States Senator for the term ending in 1873, and is now serving on the Committee on Foreign Relations, and that on the District of Columbia.

In the popular branch of Congress, Mr. Patterson more than justified the high expectations which his entrance into that body awakened. His duties as a member of the Committee on the District of Columbia immediately made him acquainted with leading public interests and the prominent business men of Washington, and it is safe to say that from then till now there has been no member of either branch of Congress above him in the esteem and confidence of all classes in the District. His lively interest in free schools has especially won for him the regards of all connected with that cause in the District. To him belongs the honor of drafting and maturing the excellent existing School Law of the District, providing for the free education of all the children, without distinction of color, and placing the colored schools upon the same basis with the white schools. A crude bill looking to this result was presented at the time to the Senate Committee on the District of Columbia; but such was the deference to Mr. Patterson in such matters, that the bill was sent to the House Committee, of which he was then Chairman, with the understanding that he should draft a School Law covering that whole subject. From his first entrance into Congress, he has been recognized by the people of the District as the special champion of education, and has frequently been called upon to promote this cause by public addresses. At the inauguration of the Wallach School House, the first free school edifice worthy of the cause erected in the National capital, July 4, 1863, Mr. Patterson delivered an address, which is one of the best, as well as one of the earliest of his efforts in furtherance of education in the District.

Among the best specimens of Mr. Patterson's eloquence, is his eulogy upon the life and character of Abraham Lincoln, delivered at Concord, New Hampshire, June 3, 1865, at the request of the State authorities. This discourse delineates the wonderful character of the illustrious martyr with remarkable discrimination and comprehensiveness, while it often rises to the highest style of this species of commemorative eloquence. The following paragraph doubtless owes something of its terse and truthful brevity to the fact that the orator was enunciating the results of stern personal experience. He says of President Lincoln:

"Poverty brought labor and habits of industry; privations gave a broad experience and sympathy with those who eat bread in the sweat of their brows; the irrepressible impulses of a mind conscious of strength, induced study and thought. These were the sources of that intelligence, that tender sensibility to the misfortunes and sorrows of the humblest citizen, and that large executive ability which characterized his subsequent career."

Perhaps the ablest, most finished, and most eloquent of all his published discourses is that which he pronounced on the "Responsibilities of Republics," August 29, 1865, at Fort Popham, Me., on the 258th Anniversary of the planting of the Popham Colony. A single passage taken almost at random is here introduced. After a compact and philosophical statement of the fundamental ideas comprised in the American system, and of the process by which those ideas were developed into a Government, the orator adds:

"But the end is not yet. We, too, have work to do; for the foundations of the republic are not yet completed. We cannot escape the responsibility of those who build for posterity. The great architects of our system reared the framework, and other generations have labored faithfully and successfully upon it. The star-lit flag which symbolizes its existence, more beautiful than the pearly gates of morning closed with bars of crimson, has been unfurled over fleet, and camp, and court, but the broad substructure of this great nation cannot be settled firmly and compactly in its bed in a hundred years.

"'I am a long time painting,' says an old Greek artist; 'for I paint for a long time.' This is the laconic language of a universal truth. Whatever is destined long to survive, comes slowly to maturity. The primeval forests of cedar and oak, whose giant strength has resisted the forces of decay through half the life-time of man, slowly lifted their gnarled and massive forms through centuries of growth. The earth's deep plating was laid, stratum above stratum, through the lapse of the silent, unchronicled ages; for it was to be the theater of man's historic career. While the old cathedrals of Europe have risen slowly to their grand and solemn beauty, kings, their founders, have moldered back to dust within their vaults, and the names of their architects have perished from memory. Succeeding generations have added a tower, a stained window, or a jeweled altar, and lain down to rest beneath their shadow, and the work still lingers; but there they stand, firm as the hills, perpetuating in histories of stone the moral life and intellectual growth of the world, through many of its most eventful centuries. These are but types of national life.

"From the foundations of Rome, eight centuries, crowded with the reverses and triumphs of a heroic people, had passed into history, ere she became the mistress of the world.

"The republic of Venice, too, which at first fled from Rome's insatiable lust of power, and hid herself in the islands of the sea, dropping her bridal ring into the Adriatic, while the white-haired Doge pronounced the '*Desponsamus te, mare, in signum veri perpetuique dominii,*' wedded the waves to her sweep of power through thirteen hundred years of freedom."

One of his ablest speeches in the House was that which he delivered in 1864, on the Consular Bill, and which was recognized in Congress, at the State Department, and elsewhere, as an eminently able and exhaustive presentation upon that important subject. His speech on the Constitutional Amendment may also be mentioned as one of the best of the many able arguments made in the House at the time of the passage of that great measure. His services in the last two Presidential Campaigns have made his finished and popular eloquence familiar to every section of the country. On the stump he is perhaps surpassed by no orator in the country in the popularity and effectiveness of his eloquence. In all these efforts he deals almost exclusively with the great philosophical principles of Government and of parties, appealing to the understanding, and not to the passions of his audiences.

In the Senate, Mr. Patterson has already reached a high position. His broad, liberal culture, the deliberative character of his eloquence, and his habit of grappling with subjects in their foundation principles, all combine to give him great influence in the Senate. He fills the seat vacated by Judge Daniel Clark, and it is a just and ample tribute to say of him that he adorns the place that for ten years was occupied by that able and eminent Senator.

Mr. Patterson seems to have been exceedingly fortunate in his career, but his success has been the natural result of the fact that every public duty to which he has successively been called, has been executed wisely and well. From his first entrance into public life he has been a favorite with all classes in his State, and in Congress as well as at home at the present time he has the respect of all as an honest, able, and enlightened Statesman.

HENRY WILSON.

HENRY WILSON was born at Farmington, N. H., February 16, 1812, of poor parentage. He was early apprenticed to a farmer in his native town, with whom he continued eleven years, during which period his school privileges, at different intervals, amounted to about one year. He early formed a taste for reading, which he eagerly indulged on Sundays and evenings by fire-light and moon-light. Thus, in the course of his eleven years' apprenticeship, he read about 1,000 volumes—mainly of history and biography.

On coming of age, young Wilson left Farmington, and with all his possessions packed upon his back, walked to Natick, Mass., and hired himself to a shoemaker. Having learned the trade, and labored nearly three years, he returned to New Hampshire for the purpose of securing an education. His educational career, however, was suddenly arrested by the insolvency of the man to whom he had entrusted his money, and in 1838 he returned to Natick to resume his trade of shoemaking.

Wilson was now twenty-six years of age, and up to this period his life had been mainly devoted to labor. It was in allusion to this that when, in 1858, he replied on the floor of Congress to the famous "mudsill" speech of Gov. Hammond of South Carolina, he gave utterance to these eloquent words:

"Sir, I am the son of a hireling manual laborer, who, with the frosts of seventy winters on his brow, 'lives by daily labor.' I, too, have 'lived by daily labor.' I, too, have been a 'hireling manual laborer.' Poverty cast its dark and chilling shadow over the home of my childhood; and want was sometimes there—an unbidden guest. At the age of ten years—to aid him who gave me being in keeping the gaunt specter from the hearth of the mother who bore me—I left the home of my boyhood, and went forth to earn my bread by 'daily labor.'"

From his youth, Mr. Wilson seems to have been deeply and permanently imbued with the spirit of hostility to Slavery, and few men have dealt more numerous or heavy blows against the institution. His political career commenced in 1840. During this year he made upwards of sixty speeches in behalf of the election of Gen. Harrison. In the succeeding five years, he was three times elected a Representative, and twice a Senator, to the Massachusetts legislature. Here his stern opposition to Slavery was at once apparent, and in 1845 he was selected, with the poet Whittier, to bear to Washington the great anti-slavery petition of Massachusetts against the annexation of Texas. In the same year he introduced in the legislature a resolution declaring the unalterable hostility of Massachusetts to the further extension and longer continuance of Slavery in America, and her fixed determination to use all constitutional and lawful means for its extinction. His speech on this occasion was pronounced by the leading anti-slavery journals to be the fullest and most comprehensive on the Slavery question that had yet been made in any legislative body in the country. The resolution was adopted by a large majority.

Mr. Wilson was a delegate to the Whig National Convention of 1848, and on the rejection of the anti-slavery resolutions presented to that body, he withdrew from it, and was prominent in the organization of the Free Soil party. In the following year he was chosen chairman of the Free Soil State Committee of Massachusetts—a post which he filled during four years. In 1850 he was again a member of the State legislature; and in 1851 and 1852 was a member of the Senate, and president of that body. He was also president of the Free Soil National Convention at Pittsburg in 1852, and chairman of the National Committee. He was the Free Soil candidate for Congress in 1852. In 1853 and 1854 he was an unsuccessful candidate for Governor of Massachusetts. In 1853 he was an active and influential member of the Massachusetts Constitutional Convention. In 1855, was elected to the United States Senate to fill the vacancy occasioned by the resignation of Mr. Everett.

Mr. Wilson took his seat in the Senate in February, 1855, and, by a vote nearly unanimous, has been twice re-elected to that office. As a Senator, he has been uniformly active, earnest, faithful, prominent, and influential,—invariably evincing an inflexible and fearless opposition to Slavery and the slave-power. In his very first speech, made a few days after entering the Senate, he announced for himself and his anti-slavery friends their uncompromising position. "We mean, sir," said he, "to place in the councils of the Nation men who, in the words of Jefferson, have sworn on the altar of God eternal hostility to every kind of oppression over the mind and body of men." This was the key-note of Mr. Wilson's career in the Senate from that day to this.

In the spring of 1856 occurred the assault upon Mr. Sumner by Preston S. Brooks of South Carolina. Mr. Wilson—whose fearlessness is equal to his firmness and consistency—denounced this act as "brutal, murderous, and cowardly." These words, uttered on the floor of the Senate, drew forth a challenge from Mr. Brooks, which was declined by Wilson in terms so just, dignified, and manly, as to secure the warm approval of all good and right-minded people.

At the commencement of the rebellion, the Senate assigned to Mr. Wilson the Chairmanship of the Military Committee. In view of his protracted experience as a member of this committee, joined with his great energy and industry, probably no man in the Senate was more completely qualified for this most important post. In this committee originated most of the legislation for raising, organizing, and governing the armies, while thousands of nominations of officers of all grades were referred to it. The labors of Mr. Wilson, as chairman of the committee, were immense. Important legislation affecting the armies, and the thousands of nominations, could not but excite the liveliest interest of officers and their friends; and they ever freely visited him, consulted with, and wrote to him. Private soldiers, too, ever felt at liberty to visit him, or write to him concerning their affairs. Thousands did so, and so promptly did he attend to their needs that they called him the "Soldier's Friend."

As clearly as any man in the country, Mr. Wilson, at the commencement of the rebellion, discerned the reality and magnitude of the impending conflict. Hence, at the fall of Fort Sumter, when President Lincoln issued a call for 75,000 men, the clear-sighted Senator advised that the call should be for 300,000; and immediately induced the Secretary of War to double the number of regiments assigned to Massachusetts. In the prompt forwarding of these troops Mr. Wilson was specially active. Throughout that spring, and until the meeting of Congress, July 4th, he was constantly occupying himself at Washington, aiding the soldiers, working in the hospitals, and preparing the necessary military measures to be presented to the national legislature.

Congress assembled; and, on the second day of the session, Mr. Wilson introduced several important bills relating to the military wants of the country, one of which was a bill authorizing the employment of 500,000 volunteers for three years. Subsequently Mr. Wilson introduced another bill authorizing the President to accept 500,000 volunteers additional to those already ordered to be employed. During this extra session, Mr. Wilson, as Chairman of the Military Committee, introduced other measures of great importance relating to the appointment of army officers, the purchase of arms and munitions of war, and increasing the pay of private soldiers,—all of which measures were enacted. In fact, such was his activity and efficiency in presenting and urging forward plans for increasing and organizing the armies necessary to put down the rebellion, that General Scott declared of Mr. Wilson that he "had done more work in that short session than all the chairmen of the military committees had done for the last twenty years."

After the defeat at Bull Run, Mr. Wilson was earnestly solicited by Mr. Cameron, Mr. Seward, and Mr. Chase, to raise a regiment of infantry, a company of sharp-shooters, and a battery of artillery. Accordingly, returning to Massachusetts, he issued a stirring appeal to the young men of the State, addressed several public meetings, and in forty days he succeeded in rallying 2,300 men. He was commissioned colonel of the Twenty-second Regiment, and with his regiment, a company of sharp-shooters, and the third battery of artillery, he returned to Washington as colonel; and afterwards, as aid on the staff of General McClellan, Mr. Wilson served until the beginning of the following year, when pressing duties in Congress forced him to resign his military commission.

Returning to his seat in the Senate, Mr. Wilson originated and carried through several measures of great importance to the interests of the army and the country. Among these was the passage of bills relating to courts-martial, allotment certificates, army-signal department, sutlers and their duties, the army medical department, encouragement of enlistments, making free the wives and children of colored soldiers, a uniform system of army ambulances, increasing still further the pay of soldiers, establishing a national military and naval asylum for totally disabled officers and men of the volunteer forces, encouraging the employment of disabled and discharged soldiers, securing to colored soldiers equality of pay, and otherwise and judicious provisions.

Invariably true and constant in his sympathies for the downtrodden and oppressed, Mr. Wilson never once forgot the slave, for whose freedom and elevation he had consecrated his time and energies for more than a quarter of a century. He actively participated in the measures culminating in the anti-slavery amendment to the Constitution. He introduced the bill abolishing Slavery in the District of Columbia, by which more than three thousand slaves were made free, and Slavery made for ever impossible in the capital of the Nation. He introduced a provision, which became a law, May 21, 1862, "providing that persons of color in the District of Columbia should be subject to the same laws to which white persons were subject; that they should be tried for offenses against the laws in the same manner as white persons were tried; and, if convicted, be liable to the same penalty, and no other, as would be inflicted upon white persons for the same crime." He introduced the amendment to the Militia Bill of 1795, which made negroes a part of the militia, and providing for the freedom of all such men of color as should be called into the service of the United States, as well as the freedom of their mothers, wives, and children. This, with one or two other measures of a kindred character, introduced by Mr. Wilson, and urged forward through much and persistent opposition, resulted in the freedom of nearly 100,000 slaves in Kentucky alone.

After the close of the war, Mr. Wilson was no less active and influential in procuring legislation for the suitable reduction of the army than he had been in originating measures for its creation. Making an extended tour through the Southern States, he delivered numerous able and instructive addresses on political and national topics.

He was among the first to declare himself in favor of General Grant as the Republican candidate for the Presidency. After the nomination, Mr. Wilson entered with great zeal into the canvass, and made some of the ablest speeches of the campaign.

Amid the pressure of public duties, Mr. Wilson has found time for literary pursuits. He is the author of a "History of the Anti-Slavery Measures of the Thirty-seventh and Thirty-eighth Congresses," and "History of the Reconstruction Measures of the Thirty-ninth Congress."

In his personal character Mr. Wilson is without reproach. He possesses purity as stainless as when he entered politics, and integrity as unimpeachable as when first elected to office. He is one of the most practical of statesmen, and one of the most skillful of legislative tacticians. His *forte* as a Senator is hard work—the simple and efficient means by which he has arisen from humble origin to his present high position.

JACOB M. HOWARD.

JACOB M. HOWARD was born in Shaftsbury, Vermont, July 10th, 1805. His father was a substantial farmer of Bennington County, and the sixth in descent from William Howard, who settled in Braintree, Massachusetts, in 1635, five years after the town was established.

The subject of this sketch, although frequently in requisition to assist in farm labors, early evinced a taste for study, which he was permitted at intervals to gratify by attendance at the district school. Subsequently pursuing preparatory studies in the academies of Bennington and Brattleboro, he entered Williams College in 1826. His studies were much interrupted, in consequence of his want of means and the necessity of teaching to pay expenses, yet, with characteristic perseverance, he made his way through college, and graduated in 1830. He immediately commenced the study of law in Ware, Massachusetts, and in July, 1832, he removed to Detroit, then the capital of Michigan Territory, where he was admitted to the bar in the following year. In 1835 he was married to Catharine A. Shaw, a young lady whose acquaintance he had formed at Ware.

In his professional career, Mr. Howard was ever faithful to the interests of his clients, bringing to their service great industry, a mind well stored with legal learning, much native sagacity and force of logic.

In 1835 he was a Whig candidate for a seat in the Convention to form a State Constitution, but was not elected.

In the controversy of 1834 and 1835 between the Territory and Ohio, respecting a tier of townships which had ever belonged to Michigan, on her southern border, embracing the present city of Toledo, Mr. Howard took strong ground against the claim of Ohio;

and, having employed his pen in repelling it, finally, when Mr. Mason, the territorial governor, thought it necessary to employ military force against a similar force from Ohio, Mr. Howard volunteered, and proceeded with arms to make good the arguments he had advanced. The expedition was, however, productive only of wasteful expenditure to the Territory, and a large slaughter of pigs and poultry.

In 1838, Mr. Howard was a member of the State Legislature, and took an active part in the enactment of the code known as the Revised Laws of that year; in the railroad legislation of the State; and in examining into the condition of the brood of "free banks," known as "wildcat banks," that had come into pernicious existence under the free-banking system enacted the year before. This examination developed such a scene of fraud and corruption in the local currency of the State, that the paper of those banks soon lost all credit; and the State Supreme Court, as soon as the question was fairly brought before it, adjudged them to be all unconstitutional and void; a decision in which the community most heartily acquiesced.

In the presidential canvass of 1840, which resulted in the election of General Harrison, Mr. Howard was a candidate for Congress, and was elected by 1,500 majority. During the three sessions of the Twenty-seventh Congress he engaged but seldom in debate, but was an attentive observer of the scenes which passed before him. His feelings and opinions had ever been against slavery, its influences, its crimes, its power. John Quincy Adams and Joshua R. Giddings, both members of the House, championed the anti-slavery cause. Henry A. Wise, Mr. Gilmer, and Mr. Mallory, of Virginia, and Thomas F. Marshall, of Kentucky, were the leading combatants on the other side. The conflict, which occupied a large portion of that Congress, was fierce and fiery.

With what interest did Mr. Howard, then a new member and a young man, drink in the words of the "old man eloquent," as he unfolded his mighty argument against the "sum of all villainies," and the dangers it menaced to the liberties of our country!

He left that Congress with the full conviction that the final solution of the great question would be in a civil war, though hoping that some measure might be devised less radical and terrible, that should calm the deeply-stirred passions of the people. He remained steadfastly attached to the Whig party, and in the presidential canvasses of 1844, 1848, and 1852, exerted himself to promote the election of Mr. Clay, General Taylor, and General Scott.

In the trial of a slave case, under the fugitive slave act of 1850, in the United States Circuit Court, before Judge McLean, he denounced that act as a defiance, a challenge to the conflict of arms, by the South to the North, and predicted that sooner or later it would be accepted; and characterized its author (Mr. Mason, of Virginia,) as an enemy of his country and a traitor to the Union.

On the defeat of General Scott he resolved to withdraw entirely from politics; but on the passage of the act of 1854, repealing the Missouri compromise, he again entered the political arena in resistance to that flagrant encroachment of the slave power. He was among those who took the earliest steps to effect an organization for the overthrow of the Democratic party of the North, which had become the willing ally of the pro-slavery or secession party of the South. He saw that such a party must embrace all the elements of popular opposition to the principles and aims of the slaveholders. The old Whig party, never as a party having made its influence felt in opposition to those principles and aims, had become powerless as an agency whereby to combat them—or even to move the hearts of the people. Yet by far the greater portion of its members in the free states were in sentiment opposed to the schemes of the slave power, now too manifest to be misapprehended or viewed with indifference. To count upon this portion of the Whig party was obvious. The great end to be obtained was a firm and cordial union of this with two other elements, the old Abolition party proper, and the "Free Soil Democracy." In Michigan, these last two had already coalesced and had put in nomination a State ticket, at the head of which was the name of Hon. Kinsley S. Bingham as their candidate for Governor. A call, numerously signed, was issued, inviting all freemen of the

State, opposed to the recent measures of Congress on the subject of slavery, to assemble at Jackson on the 6th of July. The assemblage was numerous, and the utmost harmony and good feeling prevailed. "Whigs," "Abolitionists," "Free Soilers," and "Liberty Men," met and shook hands like a band of brothers. A deep seriousness pervaded the whole, and a prescience of the events soon to develop themselves, seemed to teach them that this was the "beginning of the end" of slavery. Mr. Howard was the sole author of the series of resolutions that were adopted. They strongly denounced slavery as a moral, social and political evil, as a source of national weakness and endless internal strife; they condemned the repeal of the Missouri compromise and the consequent opening of all the new territories to slavery; they encouraged in no equivocal terms the free settlers of Kansas to resist the tyranny and outrages with which the slave power was seeking to crush them. They went further—they demanded, not the restoration of that compromise, but, as an indemnity for the future, as just and necessary safeguards against the grasping ambition of slaveholders, the banishment of slavery, by law, from all the territories of the United States, from the District of Columbia, and all other places owned by the Government. They invoked the cordial co-operation of all persons and parties for the attainment of these great ends; and gave to the new party there consolidated the name of "REPUBLICANS,"* by which it has since been known.

Mr. Bingham was here again nominated for Governor, and Mr. Howard, against his own earnest remonstrances, put in nomination for Attorney-General of the State. At the ensuing November election, the whole ticket was elected by a large majority, notwithstanding the earnest appeals of General Cass and other speakers from the stump, struggling against the popular current.

Mr. Howard was a member of the committee on the address at the first national Republican convention held at Pittsburgh, February 22d, 1856. He held the office of Attorney-General of Michigan for ix years, and left it January 1st, 1861. While holding that impor-

---

* Mr. Greeley suggested the name of " Democratic Republican party," but as the Democratic party had been the authors and abettors of the measures complained of, the new party rejected even any *nominal* connection with them.

tant office, his incessant labors attested his fidelity to his trust; and the published reports of the Supreme Court evince his thoroughness and talents as a lawyer. To him the State is indebted for its excellent law, known as the registration act, by which all voters are required to enter their names on the proper books of townships and wards.

Mr. Bingham was elected to the United States Senate in January, 1859, and died in October, 1861. On the assembling of the Legislature in January following, Mr. Howard was chosen to fill the vacancy. He was an active member of the Senate Committee on the Judiciary and that on Military Affairs. He gave an earnest support to all the measures for the prosecution of the war to subdue the rebellion, and was among the first to recommend the passage of the Conscription Act of 1863, being convinced that the volunteer system could not safely be relied upon as a means of recruiting and increasing the army. Every measure for supplying men and means found in him a warm supporter. He favored the principle of confiscation of the property of the rebels, and one of his most elaborate and eloquent speeches was made on that subject in April, 1862. A careful observer of the movements of parties, he early came to the conclusion that General McClellan was acting in the interest of the anti-war portion of the Democratic party, and consequently lost all confidence in his efficiency as a commander. Influenced by this feeling, he called on President Lincoln, in company with Senator Lane of Indiana, in March, 1862, and earnestly urged the dismissal of that General from the command of the Army of the Potomac. But Mr. Lincoln thought it best, as he said, "to try Mac a little longer." He added: "Mac is slow, but I still have confidence in him." And thus McClellan was retained in command.

Mr. Howard was among the first to favor an amendment of the Constitution, abolishing slavery throughout the United States, in the Judiciary Committee of the Senate, who reported the amendment as it was finally passed by both houses and ratified by the State Legislatures. He drafted the first and principal clause in the exact words in which it now appears. Some members of the Committee remarked despairingly: "it is undertaking too much; we cannot get it through the Legislatures, or even the houses of Congress." Mr. Howard replied with animation: "We can! Now is the time. None can be more propitious. The people are with us, and if we give them a chance they will demolish slavery at a blow. Let us try!" In January, 1865, Mr. Howard was re-elected to the Senate for the full term commencing on the 4th of March of that year. The successes of our arms in the southwest, and the hope of converting rebels into union men there, had induced President Lincoln to send General Banks with a large force to New Orleans, and by formal instructions to invest him with authority to hold, under his own military orders, elections of members of new State conventions, to result finally in the reconstruction of the State governments. This strange plan of reconstruction required the assent of only one-tenth part of the white voters. The crudest and most unsatisfactory of all plans of reconstruction, it went into operation in Louisiana, and was in truth the suggestion of that stupendous plan of usurpation of the powers of Congress under the pretense of reconstructing the rebel States afterwards, in the summer of 1865, attempted to be carried out by Andrew Johnson, when he became President by the assassination of Mr. Lincoln. A joint resolution for the recognition of Louisiana, organized under the military orders of General Banks, came before the Senate from the Judiciary Committee, and was the subject of animated and elaborate discussion. Mr. Howard opposed it, and on the 25th of February, 1865, delivered a speech in which he fully and clearly demonstrated, that in the reconstruction of the seceded States the authority of Congress was supreme and exclusive, and that the executive as such was invested with no authority whatever. He insisted that by seceding from the Union, and in making war upon the Government, the rebel States became *enemies* in the sense of the laws of nations, and thus forfeited their rights and privileges as States; that consequently, when subdued by the arms of the Government, they were "conquered" and lay at the mercy of their conquerors, for exactly the same reason as prevails in cases of international wars; that it pertained to the law-making power of the United States, not to the President, to deal with the subjugated communities, and that Congress in its own discretion was to judge of the time and mode of re-admitting them as States of the Union. And this is the doctrine that has practically and finally prevailed, after a most gigantic struggle between the two branches of the Government.

In the reconstruction legislation of 1867 and 1868, the principles of constitutional law, thus affirmed by Mr. Howard, were fully recognized and put into practice; for that legislation rests exclusively upon the ground that Congress, and not the President, is vested with the power of reorganizing the rebel States.

During the session of 1865-6, he served on the joint committee on Reconstruction, one of whose duties was to inquire and report upon the condition of the rebel States. For convenience the committee divided them into several districts, and to Mr. Howard was assigned Virginia, North Carolina and South Carolina. The voluminous report of this committee, containing the testimony of the numerous witnesses examined, shows the extent of their labors and the perplexing nature of the subjects committed to them. As the principal result of their labors, they submitted to Congress a proposition to amend the Constitution, now known as the Fourteenth Article: a most important amendment, which, after thorough discussion, in which Mr. Howard took a leading part, passed both houses of Congress and was submitted to the State legislatures for ratification. Had it been ratified by the State governments of the rebel States, inaugurated by the executive proclamations of Mr. Johnson, all the troubles that followed would have been avoided. But that singular man and a majority of his cabinet strenuously opposed and defeated it in those bodies. The result is known. Forced to vindicate their own authority, and to prevent anarchy in those States, Congress, in March, 1867, enacted the first of that series of statutes known as the reconstruction acts, by which they declared those States without legal governments, and subjected them to a *quasi* military rule until proper State constitutions could be formed on the principle of impartial suffrage of whites and blacks, and until Congress should formally re-admit them. In the earnest struggle to uphold this legislation, Mr. Howard was ever at his post of duty. He drew the report of the Committee on Military Affairs, on the removal of Hon. E. M. Stanton, Secretary of War, by President Johnson, strongly condemning that act, and exposing Mr. Johnson's complicity in the " New Orleans Riots."

When the contest between the two branches of the government resulted in the impeachment of Mr. Johnson by the House of Representatives, Mr. Howard voted the accused guilty of the high crimes and misdemeanors charged in the articles of impeachment. He is a man of medium stature, compact frame, and much power of endurance. He is an eloquent speaker and a formidable antagonist in debate. He is as exemplary in his private life as honorable in his public career.

TIMOTHY O. HOWE.

TIMOTHY O. HOWE is a native of Livermore, Maine, and was born on the 24th of February, 1816. Many generations since, his ancestors settled in Massachusetts. His father was a physician, living in a strictly rural district, having a wide practice among the farming community of fifty years ago.

After receiving a good common school education, Mr. Howe studied law, first with Hon. Samuel P. Benson, of Winthrop, and subsequently with Judge Robinson, of Ellsworth. In 1839 he was admitted to the bar, and immediately commenced the practice of his profession, at Readfield. In 1841 he married Miss L. A. Haynes.

In politics, he was an ardent Whig, and a devoted admirer of Henry Clay. Taking a warm interest in political questions, he was elected by the Whigs of his district as a member of the popular branch of the Maine Legislature of 1845. The Hon. William Pitt Fessenden was a member of the same body. In the Legislature he took an active part in discussions, and was recognized as a young man of unusual promise.

In the latter part of that year he removed from Maine to the Territory of Wisconsin, and opened a law office at Green Bay, which, at that time, was a small village, separated from the more thickly settled parts of the Territory by a wide belt of forest, extending for forty or fifty miles to the southward. He soon became known, however, to the people of the Territory, and upon its admission into the Union, in 1848, was nominated by the Whigs for Congress. The district being largely Democratic, he was defeated. In 1850 he was elected Judge of the Circuit Court. At that time the Circuit Judges of the State were also Judges of the Supreme Court, and Judge Howe was, during a part of his term, Chief Justice of the State. In

TIMOTHY O. HOWE.

1854, immediately after the passage of the Nebraska bill, the Whigs, Free Soilers, and Anti-Nebraska Democrats, of Wisconsin, met in mass convention at Madison, the capital, and organized the Republican party in that State. This occurred two years before the national organization of the party. Judge Howe was then on the bench, and took no active part in politics, but published a letter expressing his hearty approbation of the movement. The following year he resigned his office as Judge and resumed the practice of the law. He bore a leading part in the State canvass of that and the following year, as a speaker, in the advocacy of Republican principles and the election of the nominees of the Republican party.

The year 1856 was signalized by one of the most remarkable judicial trials in the history of jurisprudence. At the general election in November, 1855, Hon. Wm. A. Barstow, then the Governor of Wisconsin, was the Democratic candidate for re-election. The candidate of the Republican or opposition party was Hon. Coles Bashford, recently a delegate from the Territory of Arizona in the Fortieth Congress.

The canvassers determined that Mr. Barstow had received the greatest number of votes. In pursuance of that determination a certificate of election was issued to him, signed by the Secretary of State, and authenticated by the great seal of the State, and on the opening of the next political year Mr. Barstow took the oath of office, and was re-inaugurated with imposing ceremonies and much display of military force. Mr. Bashford averred that, in fact, the greater number of legal votes were cast for him, and not for Mr. Barstow. He contended that the canvass was fraudulent and false, and he resolved to try the validity of Mr. Barstow's title by a suit at law. Accordingly he also took the oath of office. On the 15th of January the Attorney-General filed, in the Supreme Court of the State, an information in the nature of *quo warranto* against the acting Governor. That is supposed to be the only instance in the history of Government, when the people of a State have appealed to the judicial authority to dispossess an incumbent of the executive office.

Some of the best professional talent in the State was employed in the conduct of the cause, and in its progress party feeling was stirred to its lowest depths. An attempt was made to deter the prosecution by threats that the litigation would be protracted so that no judgment could be obtained during the Gubernatorial term. It was broadly hinted on the argument, and freely asserted by a portion of the press, that, if the court should give judgment for the relator, the respondent, having already the command of the militia of the State, would not submit to the judgment. For the relator appeared, besides Mr. Howe, Mr. E. G. Ryan, Mr. J. H. Knowlton, and the late Postmaster-General, Hon. A. W. Randall, while the defence was managed by Mr. J. E. Arnold, Judge Orton and the present Senator Carpenter.

It was expected that Mr. Ryan would lead the prosecution. He was a Democrat in politics, and so was politically opposed to his client; and, moreover, was a lawyer unsurpassed for ripe learning and forensic ability by any member of the profession in the United States. But an unfortunate disagreement between him and the court, in the commencement of the contest, induced his temporary withdrawal from the case, and thereupon the lead was assigned to Mr. Howe.

A sketch of the progress of the case would hardly fail to interest both the professional and the general reader; but space forbids. The prosecution, however, was completely triumphant. In spite of threatened delays, the court unanimously gave judgment for the relator, on the 24th day of March, 1856 — but little more than two months from the commencement of proceedings — and in spite of threatened resistance, the relator was, on the next day, quietly and peaceably installed in the office.

The reputation won by Judge Howe, in the management of that great State trial, gave to his name marked prominence as a candidate for the U. S. Senate in the place of Hon. Henry Dodge, whose term expired on the 4th of March, 1857.

When the Legislature assembled, his election was regarded as almost certain. But no sooner had the canvass for Senator fairly opened, than a novel question was raised in the party, for an explanation of which it is necessary to refer to events that had transpired some years before. In 1854 a fugitive slave from Missouri was arrested at Racine, Wisconsin, taken to Milwaukee, and there thrown into jail for security, while the master was engaged in complying with the legal forms necessary to enable him to reclaim his human property. The fugitive had been treated with great barbarity at the time of his arrest, and popular feeling, inflamed by this circumstance, and by detestation of Slavery and the Fugitive Slave act, became so turbulent that it resulted in the organization of a mob which broke open the jail, released the fugitive, and sent him to Canada. Some of the prominent actors in this proceeding were arrested for violating the provisions of the Fugitive Slave law, but were released upon a writ of habeas corpus, partly upon technical grounds, and partly on the ground that the Fugitive Slave act was unconstitutional. Subsequently the case came before the Supreme Court of the State, and one of the Judges delivered a very elaborate opinion, pronouncing the Fugitive act unconstitutional, and affirming the most ultra doctrines of the State Rights school of Southern politicians, but applying them to the detriment instead of the support of slavery. The decision became at once immensely popular with a great number of radical anti-slavery men in the State, and was thought by them to be an admirable example of capturing the guns of an enemy and turning them against him. This class of Republicans regarded what they termed an anti-State Rights Republican as a little worse than an out and out pro-slavery Democrat. Accordingly, when the senatorial election approached, in the winter of 1857, the friends of other candidates raised the cry of State Rights, and averred that Judge Howe was unsound on that issue. In a caucus of the Republican members of the Legislature a resolution was adopted in substance identical with the first of the celebrated Kentucky resolutions of 1798, declaring the right of each State to be the final judge of the constitutionality of laws of the United States, and in case of infractions upon what it held to be its rights, that it should determine for itself as to the mode and measure of redress. Each of the candidates was requested to declare whether or not he approved of the doctrines of the resolution. Judge Howe alone refused to endorse them. He preferred to remain a private citizen rather than secure a seat in the Senate by endorsing doctrines which he regarded as unsupported by the Constitution, and in practice fatal to the perpetuity of the Union. The result was that he was defeated, and the Hon. James R. Doolittle elected. But his defeat on such grounds attached to him, by the strongest ties of personal esteem and devotion, a large body of influential members of the party who were in harmony with him on the question of State Sovereignty. They agreed with their opponents that the Fugitive Slave law was an infamous statute, and they thought it unconstitutional; but they denied that a State court possessed the right of passing final judgment upon a law of the United States. Upon this question a dangerous division continued among the Republicans of Wisconsin, until the breaking out of the rebellion. Judge Howe was the leader of the Republicans who repudiated the State Sovereignty theory. At every Republican State Convention the question arose, and the opponents of State Sovereignty, only by dint of the most strenuous efforts, succeeded in fighting off an endorsement of the principle in the Republican platform of the State. On two occasions, once before a Republican State Convention, and again in the Assembly Chamber during the session of the Legislature, Judge Howe met in debate the ablest and most brilliant champions of the State Sovereignty theory, the Hon. Carl Schurz, then a resident of Wisconsin, and Judge A. D. Smith, the author of the opinion pronouncing the Fugitive law null and void, and achieved a signal victory over them in the argument of the question. The next senatorial election in Wisconsin occurred in the winter of 1861. In the pretended secession of the Southern States, justified upon the ground of the sovereignty of each State, the people had a practical illustration of the ultimate consequence of the doctrine. It was the vindication of Judge Howe. The quality of his Republicanism was no longer questioned, and a Republican Legislature elected him to the Senate. From that time to the present he has borne himself in all the new and perplexing crises, that have occurred in our political history in such a manner as to secure the approbation of his constituents, and the esteem and confidence of his associates. During the war he served on the Senate Committee on Finance, and several minor committees, and in the Fortieth Congress was Chairman of the Committee on Claims, and a member of the Committee on Appropriations, and on the Public Library. He was among the earliest advocates of Emancipation, of Universal Suffrage, and of the right and expediency of establishing Territorial Governments over those districts of country in which Civil Government was overthrown by Rebellion. As a consequence he was among the foremost of those who took issue with the policy of President Johnson—and some of his ablest speeches in the Senate were delivered in the winter of 1865-1866, at the time when the division between the Radical and the Johnson Republicans began to assume the form of an open rupture.

Upon the expiration of his term, in 1867, Senator Howe was re-elected. Few representatives have ever received so signal evidence of the esteem and confidence of their constituency as was awarded him on that occasion. Every Republican member of the Legislature favored his re-election. No other candidate was spoken of. He was the unanimous choice of his party. In his senatorial career, he had displayed so much of ability, so much of consistency and steadfast adherence to principle, that the people of his State demanded his re-election with unexampled unanimity. As a consequence, no legislative caucus was held to nominate a candidate for Senator, and Mr. Howe received the unanimous vote of the Republican members when the election occurred.

In politics, as may be gathered from the above, Senator Howe is a Radical. He would abridge no man's rights on account of creed, or race, or complexion. As a speaker, he is deliberate and impressive, with a ready command of language and all the resources of extemporaneous oratory. He appears, indeed, to the best advantage in the sudden exigencies of debate, the excitement of the occasion stimulating his faculties, and rousing them to the fullest action. In private life, he is social and genial, attaching men to him by his cordiality and frankness, and winning their enduring respect by his purity of character and genuine worth.

JOHN SHERMAN.

IN 1634, three Shermans—two brothers and a cousin—emigrated from Essex, England, to the infant colony of Massachusetts Bay. One of them settled in Connecticut, where his family remained and prospered for many years. A great-grandson of the emigrant, who had become a Judge of one of the Connecticut Courts, dying in 1815, his son, Charles Robert Sherman, himself a thoroughly educated lawyer, removed to Ohio, where he soon acquired an extensive practice, and in 1823 became one of the Judges of the Supreme Court. He married young, and had a family of eleven children. In 1829, he died suddenly of cholera, leaving his family in destitute circumstances. One of his sons was William Tecumseh Sherman, now General of the Army. The eighth child of the family was John Sherman, who was born in Lancaster, Ohio, May 10, 1823. He went steadily to school at Mount Vernon, Ohio, until he was fourteen years old. He was then sent to the Muskingum Improvement, to earn his own support, and to learn the business of a civil engineer, and was placed under the care of Colonel Samuel R. Curtis, the resident engineer of the work. He was thus employed for two years, in which he acquired the best part of his early education, in learning the methods and forms of business, and acquiring habits of industry and self-reliance. The election of 1838, which brought the Democratic party into power, was followed by the removal of Colonel Curtis from his position, and the consequent loss of employment by John Sherman.

His engineering apprenticeship closing thus abruptly, he commenced the study of law with his brother, Charles T. Sherman, now United States District Judge in Ohio, who was then engaged as a lawyer, in Mansfield, Ohio. The day after he was twenty-one years old, he obtained a license to practice law, and immediately entered into a partnership with his brother, which lasted for eleven years. Entering at once upon an extensive practice, he soon obtained a wide reputation as a laborious, honest, and successful lawyer.

In politics, John Sherman took a profound interest, although, as an ardent Whig, in a strongly Democratic district, he had no hope of obtaining office. He was sent as a delegate to the Whig National Conventions of 1848 and 1852, and in the latter year was chosen a Presidential Elector.

When the Nebraska issue arose in 1854, he felt the necessity of combining all the elements of opposition against the further extension of Slavery, and earnestly labored to build up the political organization which soon developed into the Republican party. He accepted a nomination for Representative in Congress, from the Thirteenth Ohio District, and, to his surprise, was elected. He entered the House of Representatives of the Thirty-fourth Congress, fully equipped for useful and successful public service. Fluent in debate, patient of details, laborious in investigation, conciliatory in temper, and persistent in purpose, he entered at once upon a successful congressional career.

In the first session of the Thirty-fourth Congress, he served upon the Kansas Investigating Committee, and prepared the famous report which the Committee presented to the House of Representatives and to the country. This brought him at once into honorable prominence before the people. At the close of the session the Republican members of the House, through the influence of Mr. Sherman, adopted the amendment to the Army Bill, denying the validity of the slavery-extending laws of Congress. Had the Republican party stood upon that declaration as a platform, they would probably have carried the presidential election of 1856. Mr. Sherman wrote an address to the people of the United States, elaborating the principle contained in that declaration. Although it was agreed upon by the Republican members of the House, Mr. Seward and other Senators dissented, and the doctrine was not promulgated.

In the Thirty-fifth Congress, Mr. Sherman took an active part in the heated contest over the Lecompton Constitution and the English Bill, and made many powerful speeches. He served as Chairman of the Naval Investigating Committee which made a most damaging exposure of the complicity of Buchanan and Toucey with the crimes of the slavery propagandists. He made an important speech upon the public expenditure, which was widely circulated as a campaign document.

At the opening of the Thirty-sixth Congress occurred the memorable contest for the Speakership, in which Mr. Sherman was the candidate of the Republicans. He had signed a recommendation of Helper's "Impending Crisis," and this was made the pretext by the Southern members for a violent opposition to his election. Through a long series of ballotings he lacked but one or two votes of an election. In order to secure an organization, his name was finally withdrawn, and Mr. Pennington was elected. Mr. Sherman was at once honored with the Chairmanship of the Committee of Ways and Means, by virtue of which he became leader of the House of Representatives. He distinguished himself as chairman of this committee by putting through the House the Morrill Tariff, a measure greatly promotive of material prosperity to the country.

In an important speech, delivered in reply to Pendleton, February, 1861, he displayed a statesmanlike perception of the result of the conflict to which the South was rushing with such arrogant confidence, predicting that slavery would be destroyed, and that the North would triumph.

Mr. Sherman was elected as a Representative to the Thirty-seventh Congress, but on the resignation of Mr. Chase, as a United States Senator, he was elected by the Legislature to a seat in the Senate. He was placed upon the most important committee of the Senate, that of Finance. He introduced the National Bank Bill, and had charge of that important measure, as well as of the Legal Tender Acts, on the floor and in the debates.

His labors were chiefly confined to finance and taxation—to providing money and maintaining credit to carry on the war. In January, 1863, he delivered a speech against the continuance of the

State Banking system, and one in favor of the National Banks, both of which were of decisive influence.

In the Thirty-ninth Congress he introduced a bill to fund the public indebtedness, which if passed, would have resulted in the saving of $20,000,000 of interest per annum, the wider dissemination of the loan among the masses, and the removal of the debt from its present injurious competition with railroad, mercantile, manufacturing, and all the other vital interests of the country. Unfortunately for the public interests, the bill was mutilated in the Senate and defeated in the House.

In the second session of the Thirty-ninth Congress, Mr. Sherman proposed the substitute for the Reconstruction bill which finally became a law.

In the Fortieth Congress, Mr. Sherman was Chairman of the Senate Finance Committee, and in this important position exerted a marked effect upon Congressional legislation. In the second session he reported a new bill for funding the National Debt, and converting the notes of the United States. He advocated this bill as a measure of just and wise public policy, in a speech of remarkable ability.

In person, Senator Sherman is tall and spare, with a large head, and countenance expressive of decision, firmness and self-control. He speaks smoothly and rapidly, making no effort at display, aiming only to produce conviction by clear statement of facts and arguments.

SIMON CAMERON.

SIMON CAMERON was born in Lancaster County, Pennsylvania, March 8th, 1799, and was left an orphan at nine years of age. He educated himself while pursuing his employment as a printer in Harrisburg and in Washington City. He edited and published a paper, called the "Pennsylvania Intelligencer," at Doylestown, and subsequently, before he reached the age of twenty-two, he was editor of a newspaper published at Harrisburg. In 1832 he established the Middletown Bank. He devoted much attention to the railroad interests of Pennsylvania, and became president of two railroad companies.

Before reaching the age of thirty he was appointed by Governor Shultze, Adjutant-General of Pennsylvania. In 1845 he was elected United States Senator for four years.

Retiring from office in 1849, he resumed active business, and devoted himself to internal improvements and financial affairs. In 1857 he was again elected to the United States Senate for six years, but resigned in 1861 to become Secretary of War under President Lincoln. In this position he favored the most vigorous measures for prosecuting the war, and insisted on arming the negroes. These views being at variance with those of the Administration, he retired from the Cabinet, and accepted the appointment of Minister Plenipotentiary to Russia. On his arrival at St. Petersburg, he found the Czar engaged in the noble work of emancipating the serfs, and his first act was to congratulate him for doing that justice which our country could not then be induced to do, predicting at the same time that events would force this nation to follow his great example. During his stay at St. Petersburg, the unbroken and continuous news of Federal disasters strengthened his fear that the policy of the Government foreboded ruin, and deeming it yet possible to impress his views on the Administration, and believing that the salvation of the country depended on a change of policy, he resigned his office and hastened home to take an active part in the mighty struggle. The Government would not yet yield to the growing pressure for vigorous measures, and he threw himself into the work of recruiting the Federal army, and supporting the Union cause in Pennsylvania and the loyal States. At last, the negroes were accepted for soldiers, and, finding that the work of their enlistment was unpopular, he offered his services to Mr. Lincoln to recruit a brigade of negro soldiers for the war, and lead them. His offer being declined, he continued to devote himself to the Union cause, to the utmost of his ability, until the end of the war. In 1867 he was elected for the third time to the Senate of the United States, for the term ending in 1873, and taking his seat in that body he was placed on the Committees on Foreign Relations, Military Affairs, and Ordnance, and was made Chairman of the Committee on Agriculture. He was steadfast in his opposition to the policy of the late Executive, and voted for conviction in the great Impeachment Trial.

He was one of the founders of the Republican party, and, in 1860, was prominent as a candidate for nomination to the Presidency. Whether in the cabinet, on diplomatic duty, or in senatorial service, he has been unswerving in his adherence to Republican principles. If not unanimously allowed the highest rank in statesmanship, he is acknowledged to be unsurpassed in shrewdness as a politician. Eminently successful as a financier, he uses his wealth with great public spirit and liberality in promoting worthy ends.

WILLIAM M. STEWART.

WILLIAM M. STEWART was born in Wayne County, New York, August 9th, 1827. When eight years old he removed with his father to Trumbull County, Ohio. He worked on a farm in summer, and attended school in winter, until thirteen years old, when he left home with the consent of his parents and worked at farming for various persons, at six, eight, and twelve dollars a month, until 1844. In the Spring of that year he drove a herd of cattle to Pennsylvania, and visited Philadelphia, the first large city he had seen. He thought of going to sea, and went on board the receiving ship with a view to getting into the Navy. While on board he saw a boy badly treated, and thinking the situation not congenial to him, he started back to Ohio.

In the summer of 1845, he taught school in Hampden, Ohio, and subsequently attended an academy at Farmington. He then returned to his native county in New York, where he taught school, and prosecuted his studies, making especial proficiency in Mathematics. He entered Yale College in 1848, remaining there until the winter of 1850, when he started for California, and arrived there by way of the Isthmus in the following April. He worked two years at mining with varied success. He ran for Sheriff of Nevada County in the Spring of 1851, but there being several opposing candidates, who made a combination, he was defeated by a few votes. Soon after he commenced the study of law, and in the fall of 1852 was admitted to the bar, and appointed District-Attorney on the same day. The next year he was elected to the same office by the Democratic party. In 1854, the Attorney-General of California left the State on leave of absence for six months, and Mr. Stewart was appointed in his place. He subsequently went to San Francisco and formed a law partnership with Ex-Governor Henry S. Foote of Mississippi, and Judge Aldrich, which continued about two years. In the fall of 1855 he married a daughter of Governor Foote, and went back to Nevada, where he remained practicing law until 1857. He then went to Downieville, where there was a great deal of litigation growing out of mining disputes. He got the lead of the practice, and received very heavy fees. In the spring of 1860 he went to the Territory of Utah — now Nevada—where he was employed by the first locators of the Comstock Lode to manage their heavy litigations.

When the Legislature was organized, he was in the Territorial Council. He took an active part in organizing the Union party, and in 1863 he was a member of the Constitutional Convention. On the admission of Nevada into the Union, he was elected to the United States Senate, and was admitted to his seat February 1st, 1865. His term closing in 1869, he was re-elected for the term ending in 1875.

Upon his entrance into the Senate, he was appointed to the important Committees on the Judiciary, Public Lands, Pacific Railroad, and Mines and Mining. Of the last-named committee he was in the Forty-first Congress appointed chairman.

He took a prominent part in the important discussions of the Thirty-ninth and Fortieth Congresses. In February, 1866, he made a speech, occupying parts of two days in its delivery, in which he maintained the right of the loyal people in the recent rebel States to be represented in Congress. On the 24th of May, 1866, he made a speech, of three hours' duration, on a pending Constitutional Amendment, in which he advocated "pardon for the rebels, and the ballot for the blacks." He stood in the Fortieth Congress among the firm opponents of President Johnson's policy. He is a ready and effective off-hand debater, never thrown off his guard, and never losing his good humor.

WILLIAM SPRAGUE.

WILLIAM SPRAGUE was born in Cranston, Rhode Island, September 11, 1830. He is a nephew of William Sprague, who was Governor of Rhode Island in 1838, and United States Senator in 1842. He received an academical education at Tarrytown, New York, and subsequently engaged in the calico print works founded by his father and uncle, in which he is now a partner. He engaged also in other branches of manufactures, became president of several banks, and a director of various insurance companies. In his eighteenth year he joined an artillery company in Providence, and became a colonel.

In 1860, he was nominated for Governor of Rhode Island by a portion of the Republican party, and elected, in consequence of a coalition between them and the Democrats. In February, 1861, foreseeing the outbreak of the civil war, he offered to the President and General Scott 1,000 men and a battery of artillery, and as soon as the call for troops was made, hastened to raise regiments, and went with them to the field. The commission of Brigadier-General of Volunteers was offered to him in May, but he refused it. He fought with the Rhode Island troops at Bull Run, and in several engagements of the Chickahominy campaign. He was chosen United States Senator for six years from March 4, 1863, and was re-elected for the term ending in 1875. A few years ago he married a daughter of Chief-Justice Chase.

In the Senate he served as Chairman of the Committee on Manufactures, a position for which he was fitted by his business-like habits and thorough understanding of commercial law.

In the Impeachment trial he voted the President guilty of high crimes and misdemeanors, as charged in the indictment. During his first term in the Senate, he seldom spoke, but in March and April, 1869, he startled the Senate and the country by a series of remarkable speeches on national affairs. The first was on "The Financial Condition," and depicted ruin in store for the country unless it should pause in the "forced policy pursued since the close of the war." Two speeches on the Civil Tenure Act drew glowing pictures of the future of the country under "a government of lawyers and judges, educated in one line, practiced in one pursuit; educated upon the quarrels and the exhibitions of the worst passions of human nature; practiced in the dissensions, influenced by the vices of the people." Speeches on "The National Currency" and "The Tax Bill" presented the injurious effects upon the country of large accumulation of capital, illustrated by reference to prominent citizens of Rhode Island.

Mr. Sprague is somewhat slight in person—with a grave expression, and thoughtful attitude. Retiring and reticent, he has none of the qualities of the noisy demagogue. Although the richest man in Congress, he makes no personal ostentation of wealth. As a speaker he is slow and deliberate, uttering his convictions rather with the earnestness of the conversationalist rather than the art of an orator.

JAMES W. NYE.

THE son of one of the substantial farmers who have given to the Empire State its rapid development and great prosperity, James W. Nye was born in De Ruyter, Madison County, New York, June 10, 1815. The labors of the farm, to which he was inured in boyhood, developed great physical strength and power of endurance. As a youth he enjoyed the advantages of superior schools, in which he laid the foundation of a good education and manifested remarkable ability as a speaker. He studied law and practiced in his native county, and afterward in New York City. He entered actively into political life, and soon became conspicuous for his eloquence, fearlessness, and thorough mastery of all political subjects. He was identified with the Free-Soil movement from the beginning, and on the organization of the Republican party he became one of its members, and eloquently advocated the election of Fremont in 1856. In 1860 he was a Police Commissioner for the city of New York, under the Metropolitan Police Act. In the campaign which ended in the election of Mr. Lincoln, in 1860, Mr. Nye was one of the most efficient workers, by his convincing logic and moving eloquence winning multitudes to the support of the Republican candidates.

Though never actively engaged as a soldier, Mr. Nye has frequently shown his interest in the military movements of the country. He was a General of the New York State Militia, and raised a regiment for service in the war with Mexico. He would have devoted himself to military service in the war for the suppression of the Rebellion, but the President believed that he could better promote the interests of the nation as Governor of the new Territory of Nevada, which needed the moulding and guiding influences of such a man, and he was accordingly appointed to that position in 1861. When Nevada was admitted into the Union as a State he was elected United States Senator, and took his seat in 1865. Two years later he was re-elected for the term ending in 1873.

In the Senate he immediately took rank among the most fearless and able of the Radical Republicans. Entering Congress just at the close of the war, he aided in carrying all the great measures of re-construction. He opposed the policy of President Johnson, and voted for his conviction. Serving at first as Chairman of the Committee on Revolutionary Claims, he was afterward advanced to the more important position of Chairman of the Committee on Territories.

As a speaker, Mr. Nye is graceful, fluent, and sometimes eloquent. His trenchant logic and luminous facts command the respectful attention of the Senate, while his pungent satire, ready repartee and keen wit delight the popular audience in the galleries.

L. Trumbull

LYMAN TRUMBULL.

LYMAN TRUMBULL was born in Colchester, Connecticut, October 12th, 1813. He was educated at Bacon Academy, in his native town, which in those times was one of the best institutions of learning in New England. In his sixteenth year he became a teacher in a district school; and at twenty years of age went to Georgia, taking charge of an Academy at Greenville in that State. While engaged in teaching, he employed his leisure time in studying law with a view to preparing himself for the legal profession.

Having been admitted to practice at the bar in Georgia, in 1837 he removed to Illinois and settled in Belleville, St. Clair County. In 1840, he was elected a Representative in the State Legislature from that county; and before he had served out his term, he was, in 1841, appointed Secretary of State of Illinois. After serving in this office for two years, he returned to his profession, and gained an eminence therein second to no other lawyer in the State. In 1848, he was nominated and elected one of the Justices of the State Supreme Court, and, in 1852, was re-elected for nine years. As a Judge on the bench he distinguished himself by great acuteness of discrimination, accuracy of judgment, and familiarity with organic and statute laws. He resigned his place on the bench in 1853, and in the succeeding year was elected to represent the Belleville District, then embracing a wide extent of territory, in Congress; but before taking his seat in the House, the Legislature elected him to the Senate of the United States for the term of six years from March 4, 1855.

During the great political contests which attended the passage of the Fugitive Slave Law and the organization of the Territories of Kansas and Nebraska, Mr. Trumbull, both at home and in the halls of Congress, took a bold stand against the policy and doctrines of the old Democratic party, with which he had been actively identified, and espoused the cause of freedom, of which he became one of the strongest of champions. He opposed his colleague, Mr. Douglas, in all questions having reference to slavery, and especially in his celebrated "popular sovereignty" plan of settling that question in the Territories and future States. With such distinguished ability did he contest this question with Mr. Douglas and his friends, that he at once gained a national reputation.

In 1860, he earnestly and ably advocated the election of Abraham Lincoln, his fellow-citizen and friend, to the Presidency. During the early part of the next year, just previous to Mr. Lincoln's inauguration, and when the war of the rebellion had already virtually commenced, Mr. Trumbull was one of the leaders of the Union party in the Senate, and favored prompt and decided measures for the maintenance of the Union. In 1861, Mr. Trumbull was re-elected for a second term, and in 1867 for a third term in the Senate of the United States.

As Chairman of the Judiciary Committee of the Senate, a position which he has held uninterruptedly since 1861, he framed and advocated some of the most important acts which were passed by Congress during and since the war. He was one of the first to propose the amendment of the Constitution abolishing Slavery in the United States, which proposition passed Congress, and was ratified by the requisite votes of two-thirds of the States.

He ably advocated the acts establishing and enlarging the Freedman's Bureau, and eloquently championed the Civil Rights Bill. He voted for the acquittal of President Johnson on the Articles of Impeachment.

Senator Trumbull continued his residence at Belleville until 1849, when he removed to Alton, and subsequently, in 1863, to Chicago, where he now resides. He is of medium stature, with a cast of countenance which marks the man of thought. Lacking the warmth of temperament calculated to win personal friendship, he possesses talents which command universal respect.

OLIVER P. MORTON.

OLIVER P. MORTON was born in Wayne County, Indiana, August 4, 1823. His parents dying when he was quite young, he was placed under the care of a grandmother and two aunts, in the State of Ohio. He served for a while with his brother at the hatter's trade; but this not being a congenial employment, at the age of fourteen he entered the Wayne County Seminary. He is described by his preceptor as "a timid and rather verdant-looking youth, too shy to bear, with head erect, a master's look." After completing his preparatory studies, he entered Miami University, at Oxford, Ohio. He displayed much talent as a student, and made great proficiency in his studies, and especially in forensic exercises. Leaving college without graduating, he returned to Indiana, and entered upon the study of law with Hon. John S. Newman. He was admitted to the bar in 1846, and, as a jurist and an advocate, soon took rank among the first lawyers of the State.

In 1852, he was elected Judge of the Circuit Court. Two years later, the Democratic party, of which he was a member, repealed the Missouri Compromise, and passed the Kansas-Nebraska bill. Mr. Morton, with many others who had been known as free-soil Democrats, abandoned his old party relations, and aided in forming the Republican party.

In 1856, he was nominated by the Republicans as their candidate for Governor of Indiana. He made a thorough and vigorous canvass of the State, in company with his Democratic competitor, Ashbel P. Willard. A party so powerful, championed by a leader so eloquent and popular, could not be overcome in a single campaign. Mr. Morton lost the election by about five thousand votes; but his speeches, delivered throughout the State, did much to build up and consolidate the Republican party in Indiana.

Anticipating the importance of the great political struggle of 1860, the Republicans of Indiana made an exceedingly strong ticket, with Henry S. Lane for Governor, and Oliver P. Morton for Lieutenant-Governor—both unsurpassed for eloquence and effectiveness in political debate. The Republican State ticket was triumphantly elected in October, and, in November, Indiana stood in the unbroken column of Northern States that elected Abraham Lincoln to the Presidency.

On the 14th of January, 1861, Mr. Morton, entering upon the office of Lieutenant-Governor, took his seat as President of the State Senate. He occupied this position but two days, when, in consequence of the election of Henry S. Lane to the Senate of the United States, he became Governor of Indiana.

Never before had a Governor of the State been inaugurated amid circumstances so difficult and trying. The election of Mr. Lincoln to the presidency was used as a pretext for rebellion, which was already showing its formidable front in various portions of the South. The State of Indiana was divided on the question of the right of secession. Men were heard to say in the State Legislature, that they would rather take their muskets and assist the Southern people to obtain their independence, than to support the Government. The Southern traitors believed that should the Administration pursue a coercive policy, Indiana would secede and join the Southern Confederacy. To repress treason, to foster loyalty, and hold the entire State true to the Union, and to hurl its concentrated moral and physical force against the rising rebellion, constituted the extraordinary work before the newly-inaugurated Governor.

Convinced of the importance of prompt action in defence of the Government, he visited the President in person, and assured him that if he would adopt a vigorous policy, Indiana would support him. Soon after his visit to Washington, the bombardment of Fort Sumter inaugurated actual hostilities and produced the great uprising of the North.

Upon receiving the President's proclamation, Governor Morton issued calls to every part of the State for men. Forty thousand men, more than six times the number required, volunteered for the defence of the Union. In three days, six regiments, the quota of the State, were in readiness for service, fully armed and equipped. Twenty regiments were tendered in addition, and when they were not accepted by the Government, most of them were mustered into the State service, put in camp and drilled until the time came when the Government was glad to take them.

No sooner were their first troops in the field than the Governor sent agents to look after their interests, to see that their necessities were supplied while in health, and that they were properly cared for when sick.

To meet the extraordinary emergencies of the occasion, Governor Morton called an extra session of the Legislature. His message to this body, delivered April 25th, 1861, was a patriotic and eloquent presentation of the true relations of the States to the Federal Government, and the duty of Indiana to aid in crushing the rebellion.

During the extra session of the General Assembly the labors of the Executive Department were augmented to an extent never before equalled in the history of the State. Great discernment and discretion were exercised by the Governor in the selection of men to aid in recruiting, organizing and equipping the regiments. He laid aside party prejudices, and, in dispensing favors, rather showed partiality to his former political foes than to his friends. Loyalty and capacity were the only qualifications for position which he demanded, and during the early stages of the war he appeared to look for these in the Democratic party.

The doubtful attitude of the State of Kentucky gave additional anxiety and labor to the Governor of Indiana. Governor Magoffin, at heart a secessionist, had refused most positively to respond to the President's call for volunteers. While making professions of a desire to hold Kentucky in a neutral position, he was really rendering the rebels all the aid in his power. He artfully laid his plans to induce Indiana, Ohio, and other Northern border States, to assume the character of sovereign mediators between the Government and the seceded States. To his overtures Governor Morton promptly responded, "There is no ground in the Constitution, midway between the Government and a rebellious State, upon which another State can stand, holding both in check. A State must take her stand upon one side or the other; and I invoke the State of Kentucky, by all the sacred ties that bind us together, to take her stand with Indiana, promptly and efficiently, on the side of the Union."

From this time until the close of Magoffin's administration, Governor Morton was practically the governor of Kentucky. He dispatched numerous secret agents to watch the movements of Kentucky secessionists. Thus he was constantly advised in reference to the traitorous designs of Kentucky rebels and their Confederate allies. In view of the defenceless condition of the Indiana and Ohio border, he urged upon the President and the War Department the importance of gunboats and fortifications along the Ohio river.

From the beginning of the difficulties in Kentucky he unremittingly pressed upon the attention of the Government the necessity of taking decided steps toward the occupation of the State by the United States forces.

On the 16th of September, 1861, Governor Morton learned, through one of his secret agents, that the rebel General Zollicoffer had marched his brigade through Cumberland Gap, into Kentucky. On the same day General Buckner, who had for some time been stationed at Bowling Green in command of a body of "neutral State Guards," set out with his men for Louisville. General Rousseau had organized a brigade at Jeffersonville, Indiana, but out of respect for Kentucky's neutrality was ordered to St. Louis. Governor Morton, having been apprised of the movements of Zollicoffer and Buckner, had General Rousseau's marching orders countermanded. He was ordered to cross the Ohio into Kentucky; thus Louisville was saved from falling into the hands of the rebels, and the fatal charm of neutrality was broken.

Governor Morton withdrew his secret agents and appealed to the people of Indiana to render all possible aid in rescuing Kentucky from the hands of the secessionists. Many regiments responded to the call, and ere the lapse of many months Bowling

Green, a strongly fortified position, was occupied by a Federal force Zollicoffer was defeated and slain at Mill-spring, and the soil of Kentucky cleared of rebel troops.

The important agency of Governor Morton in bringing about these results was universally acknowledged. The "Louisville Journal" said of him, "He has been, emphatically, Kentucky's guardian spirit from the very commencement of the dangers that now darkly threaten her very existence. Kentucky and the whole country owe him a large debt of gratitude. Oh, that all the public functionaries of the country were as vigilant, as clear-sighted, as energetic, as fearless, as chivalric, as he."

The wants of Indiana troops in Missouri, West Virginia, and the Department of the Potomac, received his constant attention, and his numerous efficient agents were actively employed in every camp where Indiana regiments were stationed.

The reverses of the national arms had such a discouraging effect upon the country, that in most of the States the work of recruiting progressed slowly. Not so in Indiana. The faithfulness of Governor Morton in looking after his soldiers, and providing for their families at home, inspired the people of Indiana with such a degree of confidence that the volunteering spirit among them did not abate because of national disasters, and by the 11th of December, 1861, an aggregate of forty-four volunteer regiments from Indiana were in the service of the United States.

The approach of the first winter of the war seemed likely to find large numbers of our troops almost destitute of comfortable clothing, owing to the misappropriation of supplies, by incompetent and unprincipled quartermasters. Governor Morton sought to remedy this deficiency, so far as the Indiana troops were concerned, by taking the matter of supplying them with clothing into his own hands. Notwithstanding the obstructions thrown in his way, and the insults offered him by thieving officials, by indefatigable energy, he carried his points, and had the satisfaction of being assured by his messengers that his soldiers would not suffer from lack of clothing amid the rigors of winter in the mountains of Western Virginia.

Governor Morton's popularity among the soldiers, and his reputation in other States, having excited the jealousy of certain ambitious politicians, they gave currency to vague charges of mismanagement in State military matters, of corruption in the appointment of officers, and the awarding of contracts. In compliance with Governor Morton's urgent request, a Congressional Investigating Committee visited Indianapolis, and made rigid inquiry into the management of military matters in Indiana. The published report of the proceedings of this committee not only exonerates him from all blame, but shows the greatest care on his part to prevent fraud and peculation. It was stated by this committee that, notwithstanding the Indiana troops had been better armed and equipped than those of any other western State, the expense attending their outfit was less, in proportion to the number of men furnished, than that of any other State in the Union.

Governor Morton steadily rose in the estimation of the President and the Cabinet, until his influence became greater in Washington than that of any other man in the country outside the Executive Departments. Many times was his presence requested in Washington, and his counsel solicited in matters of the greatest moment to the Government.

Before the close of the year 1862, more than one hundred thousand men had enlisted from Indiana in the service of the United States. Most of these being Republicans, their absence greatly depleted the strength of the party at home. Mismanagement of officers and reverses in the field had cooled the ardor of many who had been supporters of the war. These causes operated to produce a defeat of the Republican party in Indiana in the autumn of 1862, and the election of Democratic State officers, and a majority of the Legislature. Fortunately for the State, Governor Morton held over, having been elected for a term of four years. He stood as the sole obstacle in the path of reckless men who desired to drag the State into alliance with the rebels.

The Governor transmitted to the Legislature a message in which he accurately set forth the condition of the State, and with calmness and dignity made such suggestions as were appropriate to the emergencies of the State and Nation. The Legislature insultingly refused to accept this message, and by a joint resolution complimented, and virtually adopted, the message of Governor Seymour of New York.

The Democratic majority in caucus drew up a bill designed to take all the military power of the State away from the Governor, and place it in the hands of four Democratic State officers. This bill was engrossed and only prevented from becoming a law by the withdrawal of the Republican members, leaving the Legislature without a quorum. When the Legislature was thus broken up, no appropriations had been made to defray the expenses of the State government for the next two years, and Governor Morton must either call the Legislature back at the risk of having the State involved in civil war, or borrow the money to carry on the State government. He determined to take the latter course, and succeeded in raising nearly two million dollars, with which he paid the expenses of the State government and the interest on the State debt. The money was borrowed from loyal counties in the State, from railroad companies, banks, private persons, and from the house of Winslow, Lanier & Co., in New York. During these two years he acted as Auditor and Treasurer of State, kept the accounts in his own office, and disbursed the money upon his own checks. The next Legislature examined his accounts, and adopted them without the slightest exception, paid up all his borrowed money, and thus relieved him of the great responsibilities he had incurred.

The most persistent and dangerous opposition to Governor Morton's administration was a secret association, popularly known as "Knights of the Golden Circle." It had a lodgement in every section of the State, but became most numerous in those places where the people, not having frequent access to the mediums of public intelligence, became readily the dupes of designing men. The ultimate exposure of this organization showed that it numbered over 80,000 men, bound together by the most solemn oaths, thoroughly drilled and ready to obey the call of their masters at any time.

It was the plan and purpose of the conspirators to rise and seize the government arsenals, release rebel prisoners at various points in the North, furnish them with arms, and after assassinating State and United States officers, to take forcible possession of the government.

To ferret out and defeat the schemes of these conspirators was a work of no ordinary magnitude, but it was fully accomplished. The Governor employed secret detectives, through whose activity and tact he obtained an inside view of almost every lodge within the State. He was fully informed of all their plans, their financial resources, and their strength. Large quantities of arms, consigned to the conspirators, were seized and confiscated. Several of the chiefs of the conspiracy were arraigned, tried, convicted of treason and punished. The opportune discovery and exposure of this plot prevented a terrible outbreak and massacre on the soil of Indiana, and rescued the State from infamy and ruin.

In the fall of 1864, Governor Morton was re-elected by a majority of 22,000 votes. He continued with energy and ardor to prosecute the work which for four years had occupied his time and attention. He continued to raise soldiers, by volunteering and by draft, until the last call was more than met.

He passed the last year of the war in unceasing activity. At Washington, in council with the President; at the front, beholding the brave achievements of his soldiers, moving in person through the hospitals to ascertain the wants of the sick and wounded, and directing the operations of his numerous agents; at home, superintending sanitary movements, appointing extra surgeons and sending them to the field, projecting additional measures for the relief of dependent women and children, and attending personally to all the details of the business of his office—his labors were unsurpassed by those of any man in the civil or military service of the country.

The sudden collapse of the rebellion, and the return of the surviving heroes of the war, varied, but did not diminish, the labors of the Governor of Indiana. He made the amplest arrangements for the reception and entertainment of the Indiana volunteers at the State capital. Every regiment was received and welcomed by him in person. He gave special attention to the pay department, and saw that no unnecessary delay detained the veterans from their homes and families.

Finally, the war being ended, and the soldiers dismissed to their homes, the long excitement ended, and the day of relaxation came. For five years his powers of mind and body were taxed to the utmost. The immense weight of his official responsibilities, the embarrassments which beset him, the gigantic difficulties he had overcome, had, apparently, made no inroads upon his frame. The cessation of labor and excitement developed the evil results of over-work. In the summer of 1865 he was attacked with partial paralysis. The efforts of physicians to afford relief were fruitless, and a change of scene and climate was advised as the only means of obtaining relief. Accordingly, he devolved his official duties upon the Lieutenant Governor, and sailed for Europe. After an absence of several months he returned, partially relieved, and resumed his official duties.

In January, 1867, he was elected to the United States Senate, and resigning the Governorship, he took his seat on the 4th of March, for the term ending in 1873.

In the Senate he has not failed fully to meet the high expectations of the country. Though somewhat disabled by disease, he has performed all the work of a Statesman and a Senator. His speeches, heard by crowded galleries and an attentive Senate, have fallen with marked effect upon the country. Though often necessitated to speak in a sitting posture, he retains the commanding presence and the impressive delivery essential to the highest success in oratory. Unsurpassed in executive ability, as proved by a splendid career in another field, he has shown himself the peer of the greatest statesmen in legislative talent.

DAVIS.—FRELINGHUYSEN.

GARRETT DAVIS was born at Mount Sterling, Kentucky, September 10, 1801. After receiving an English education, and spending some time in classical study, he obtained employment as a writer in the County and Circuit Courts of his district. He was thus familiarized with legal forms, and was naturally led into the profession of law, to the practice of which he was admitted in 1832. Ten years later, he made his first appearance in the State Legislature, to which he was twice re-elected. He was a member of the State Constitutional Convention in 1839. In the same year he was elected a Representative in Congress, of which he continued a member until 1847, when he declined a re-election. In 1861 he was elected a United States Senator, and, on the expiration of his term, in 1867, was re-elected for the term ending in 1873. Though much immersed in the labors of his profession and the cares of politics, he has for many years given attention to agricultural pursuits. In the early part of his political career he was a Whig, and an intimate personal friend of Henry Clay. In his later life he has been an ultra pro-slavery Democrat.

FREDERICK T. FRELINGHUYSEN was born in Millstown, Somerset County, New Jersey, August 4, 1817. Being left an orphan, he was reared in the family of his uncle, Hon. Theodore Frelinghuysen. He graduated at Rutgers College in 1836, and, having studied law, was admitted to the bar in 1839. He was appointed Attorney-General of New Jersey in 1861, and was reappointed in 1866. He was appointed, and subsequently elected, a Senator in Congress, to fill the vacancy occasioned by the death of William Wright, and took his seat January 24, 1867. He served on the committees on Naval Affairs, the Judiciary, and Claims. His term of service expired with the close of the Fortieth Congress, March 4, 1869. During his brief term in the Senate he won golden opinions for sound statesmanship, legal learning, and forensic ability.

LOT M. MORRILL.

LOT M. MORRILL was born in Belgrade, Maine, May 3, 1813. In 1834, at the age of twenty-one, he entered Waterville College, but soon after left the institution to commence the study of law. Five years later he was admitted to the bar, and entered upon a lucrative practice. Taking an active part in politics, he soon rose to prominence as a leader in the Democratic party. In 1854 he was elected a Representative in the State Legislature, and in 1856 he was elected to the State Senate, of which he was chosen President.

He had never been an apologist for slavery, though acting with the Democrats, and when they attempted to force slavery by fraud and violence upon the people of Kansas, he denounced the scheme and severed his connection with the party. In 1857 he was nominated by the Republican party for Governor of the State, and was elected by a majority of fifteen thousand votes. He administered the State Government to the satisfaction of the people, and was by them twice re-elected. In 1861 he was elected to the United States Senate to fill the vacancy created by the resignation of Hannibal Hamlin. He took his seat on the 17th of January of that year, and in 1863 he was re-elected for the term ending March 4, 1869. In the senatorial election, for the ensuing term, the contest was very warm between the friends of Mr. Morrill and Mr. Hamlin. In the Republican caucus the latter was nominated by a majority of one vote, and was accordingly elected by the Legislature.

In the Senate his record is that of a consistent Republican. A promoter of the Congressional plan of reconstruction, he opposed the "policy" of President Johnson, and voted for his conviction.

DAVID T. PATTERSON was born in Greene County, Tennessee, February 28, 1819. He commenced life as a papermaker, and subsequently worked as a miller. He afterwards adopted the profession of law, and settled in Greenville, where he married a daughter of Andrew Johnson, and was elected Judge of the Circuit Court. He was a member of the Convention that re-organized the State of Tennessee in 1864. He was chosen a delegate to the Republican National Convention of 1864, and was a member of the Board of Trustees of the West-Point Military Academy. He was elected to the United States Senate, and was admitted to his seat July 26, 1866, for the term ending in 1869.

JOHN B. HENDERSON was born near Danville, Virginia, November 16, 1826. He removed to Missouri with his parents when a child, and spent his boyhood on a farm. He obtained an academical education, and for several years engaged in school-teaching. He studied law, and was admitted to the bar in 1848. In the same year he was a member of the State Legislature, and was re-elected in 1856. He was a presidential elector on the Buchanan ticket, and in 1858 was a candidate for Congress, but was defeated by a large majority. In 1860 he was an elector on the Douglas ticket, pledging himself to vote for either Douglas or Bell, to carry the State against Breckenridge, the Secession candidate. He was again defeated as a candidate for Congress in 1860. In the following year he took a prominent part as a Union member of the State Convention, called to determine whether Missouri should secede. In June, 1861, he procured arms and equipped a regiment of loyal State militia, and went into service with them. On the expulsion of Trusten Polk from the United States Senate, in January, 1862, he was appointed to fill the vacancy, and in 1863 was elected for the term ending in 1869, when he was succeeded by Carl Schurz.

EDMUNDS.—ABBOTT.

GEORGE F. EDMUNDS was born in Richmond, Vermont, February 1st, 1828. After obtaining such education as the common schools afforded, he received the instruction of a private teacher. He studied law, and was admitted to the bar in 1849. For several years he devoted himself unremittingly, and with much success, to his profession. In 1854 he entered the Vermont Legislature, and was several times re-elected, serving three years as Speaker. On the breaking out of the rebellion he aided in forming a coalition between the Republicans and War Democrats, and drew up the resolutions which formed the basis of union for the country. He was appointed to the United States Senate to fill the vacancy occasioned by the death of Solomon Foot, and took his seat April 5th, 1866, and was subsequently confirmed in his position by a vote of the Legislature. On the expiration of this term, March 4th, 1869, he took his seat by re-election for the full term of six years.

JOSEPH C. ABBOTT was born at Concord, New Hampshire, July 15th, 1825. Having received an academic education, he studied law and was admitted to the bar in March, 1852. He was editor and proprietor of the "Manchester American" for five years, and subsequently was editor of the "Boston Atlas." In July, 1855, he was appointed Adjutant-General of New Hampshire, and held the office until July, 1861, when he resigned. In September, 1861, he received authority from the War Department to raise a regiment of infantry, of which he was commissioned Lieutenant-Colonel. In November, 1863, he was promoted to be Colonel, and in January, 1865, was brevetted Brigadier-General for "gallant services in the capture of Fort Fisher." At the close of the war he settled in North Carolina, and entered into business. In September, 1867, he was elected to the State Constitutional Convention, and to the State Legislature in the following April. In July, 1868, he was elected to the United States Senate for the term ending March 4, 1871.

ORRIS S. FERRY was born in Bethel, Connecticut, August 15th, 1823. He graduated at Yale College in 1844, studied law, and was admitted to the bar in 1846. In 1847 he received the commission of Lieutenant-Colonel in the First Division, Connecticut Militia. In 1849 he was appointed Judge of Probate for the District of Norwalk. He was elected to the State Senate in 1855 and in 1856, and was subsequently appointed State's Attorney for the county of Fairfield. He continued to hold this office until his election, in 1859, as a Representative to the Thirty-sixth Congress. He served as a member of the special committee of thirty-three on the rebellious States. In the civil war he served the country with distinction, as Colonel and Brigadier-General. He was elected to succeed Hon. Lafayette S. Foster as a Senator in Congress, and March 4th, 1867, took his seat for the term ending in 1873.

JOSEPH S. FOWLER was born near Steubenville, Ohio, August 31, 1822. When quite young he was left dependent on his own resources, but by industry and perseverence succeeded in obtaining a collegiate education, graduating at Franklin College in 1843. In that institution he was Professor of Mathematics for four years; and, subsequently, was Principal of a seminary near Nashville, Tennessee. On the breaking out of the Rebellion he warmly espoused the Union cause. In September, 1861, he left the State under the forty days' proclamation of Jefferson Davis, and went to Springfield, Illinois, where he resided until April, 1862. Returning to Tennessee, he was appointed Comptroller under Governor Johnson, and took a prominent part in re-organizing the State Government. In 1865 he was elected a Senator in Congress from Tennessee, but was not admitted to his seat until July, 1866. He was elected as a Republican, but sided with President Johnson near the close of his administration, and acted with the Democrats.

JAMES DIXON.

JAMES DIXON was born at Enfield, Connecticut, August 5, 1814. He pursued his preparatory studies at the High School of Ellington, and at sixteen years of age entered Williams College, where he graduated in 1834. After leaving college he studied law in the office of his father, William Dixon, Esq.; and after being admitted to the bar, commenced the practice of his profession in his native town, which for two years he represented in the State Legislature. Subsequently he removed to Hartford. In October, 1840, he was married to Miss Elizabeth L. Cogswell, daughter of Rev. Dr. Cogswell, Professor in the Theological Institute of East Windsor, and soon after went upon a European tour, which occupied him until the following summer.

Mr. Dixon devoted much attention to literature. He contributed poems of much merit to the "New England Magazine," and the "Connecticut Courant." Mr. Everest, in his "Poets of Connecticut," says, "Mr. Dixon's articles display truly poetical powers, and his sonnets in particular are characterized by a chasteness of thought and style which entitle them to a high place amongst the poems of their order."

He was re-elected to the lower branch of the Connecticut Legislature in 1844, and was a member of the State Senate in 1849 and 1854. He served as a Representative in Congress from Connecticut, from 1845 to 1849. He was elected a United States Senator from Connecticut, and entered upon the duties of this office in 1857, and was subsequently re-elected for the term which ended March 4th, 1869. He was elected as a Republican, but joined President Johnson in his defection from that party. In the spring of 1869, he was a candidate of the Democratic party for Representative in Congress, and was defeated.

ROSCOE CONKLING was born in Albany, in 1828. His father, Hon. Alfred Conkling, was a member of the Seventeenth Congress, United States District Judge for the Northern District of New York, and Minister to Mexico. The present Senator was educated for the bar, and pursued that profession with success. In 1849 he was appointed District-Attorney for Oneida County, and in 1858 was Mayor of Utica. He was elected a Representative from New York to the Thirty-sixth Congress by a large majority, and was re-elected to the three Congresses succeeding, by increased votes. He was also elected a Representative to the Fortieth Congress; but in January, 1867, he was chosen a Senator of the United States, for the term ending in 1873. He took his seat in the Senate on the 4th of March, 1867, and was appointed Chairman of the Committee on the Revision of the Laws of the United States. He is a popular orator, an effective debater, and an earnest Republican.

THOMAS W. TIPTON was born at Cadiz, Ohio, August 8, 1817, and spent his early life on a farm. He graduated at Madison College, Pennsylvania, in 1840. Having studied law and divinity, he was admitted to the bar and the ministry. In 1845 he was a member of the Ohio Legislature, and subsequently for three years was at the head of a division of the General Land Office. He then removed to Nebraska, where, in 1860, he was a member of the Territorial Council, and was chosen a delegate to the Convention to frame a State Constitution. On the breaking out of the Rebellion he was chosen Chaplain of the First Regiment of Nebraska Infantry, and served in that capacity during the war. On the admission of Nebraska into the Union he was elected a Senator in Congress from the new State, and drew the short term, commencing in 1867 and ending in 1869. He was subsequently re-elected for the term ending in 1875.

GEORGE VICKERS was born in Chestertown, Maryland, November 19, 1801. Having received an academical education, he studied law, and was admitted to the bar in 1832. In 1836 he was a candidate for the Maryland Senate. He declined appointments as judge, tendered him by the Governors of Maryland, but accepted that of Major-General of Militia, in 1861. He was a delegate to the Baltimore Convention of 1852, and was a presidential elector in 1864. He was a member of the State Senate in 1866 and 1867, and on the rejection of P. F. Thomas, he was, in 1868, elected to the United States Senate for the term ending in 1873.

ADONIJAH S. WELCH was born in the State of Connecticut, in 1821. He graduated at the University of Michigan, and afterwards became one of its professors. He was for fifteen years at the head of the Normal School of Michigan. On the breaking out of the Rebellion he entered the Union Army, and served until the close of the war. Having settled in Florida, he was elected by its Legislature a Senator in Congress, and on the reconstruction of that State he was admitted to his seat, which he held but a few months, his term closing in March, 1869.

W. P. WHYTE was born in Baltimore, Maryland, August 9, 1824. He was educated by a private tutor, and was for nine months in the counting-room of George Peabody. He graduated at the Harvard Law School in 1845, and afterwards practiced law. In 1851, and in 1857, he was a Democratic candidate for Congress, but in both instances was defeated by small majorities. In 1853 he was elected Comptroller of the State of Maryland. He was appointed to the United States Senate to fill the vacancy occasioned by the resignation of Reverdy Johnson, serving until March 4, 1869.

DANIEL S. NORTON was born in Mount Vernon, Ohio, April 12th, 1829. He was educated at Kenyon College, and served in the war with Mexico. He subsequently went to California, and thence to Nicaraugua, where he spent a year. Returning to Ohio, he studied law, and was admitted to the bar in 1852. He emigrated to Minnesota in 1855, and was two years after elected to the Senate of that State, to which he was three times reelected. In 1865 he was elected a United States Senator for the term ending in 1871.

WILLARD WARNER was born in Granville, Ohio, September 4, 1826, and graduated at Marietta College, Ohio, in 1845. He entered the Union army, as Major of the 76th Ohio Volunteer Infantry, in 1861. During the Atlanta campaign he served on General Sherman's staff as Assistant Inspector-General. In October, 1864, he was appointed Colonel of the 180th Ohio Volunteer Infantry, was brevetted Brigadier and Major-General for meritorious services. He was subsequently elected to the Ohio Senate, in which he served two years. Having removed to Alabama, he was in July, 1868, elected as a Senator in Congress from that State for the remainder of a term ending in 1871.

ALEXANDER McDONALD was born in Clinton County, Pennsylvania, April 10th, 1832. In 1857 he removed to Kansas, and subsequently to Arkansas, engaging in mercantile pursuits. He took an active part in raising and equipping Union troops during the civil war. He was the founder and first President of the National Bank at Fort Smith, and afterward of the Merchant's National Bank at Little Rock. He was the first signer of the call for a State Convention under the Reconstruction Acts, and was elected a member of the convention. He was elected to the United States Senate, as a Republican, and took his seat on the reconstruction of Arkansas, for the term ending in 1871.

HENRY B. ANTHONY.

HENRY B. ANTHONY was born of Quaker ancestors, in Coventry, Rhode Island, April 1, 1815. He graduated at Brown University, in 1833, and adopted the profession of journalism, in which he was successful. In 1838, he assumed the editorial charge of the "Providence Journal," which he retained for many years. During the period of his editorial supervision, that newspaper had much influence in moulding the politics and the public opinion of the State of Rhode Island. It was an emphatic testimony to his editorial success and his general ability, that he was in 1849 elected Governor of Rhode Island. He served with success, and was re-elected, but declined re-election for a third term. Retiring from official life, he devoted himself with renewed ardor and enlarging influence to his profession.

In 1858 he was elected a Senator in Congress from Rhode Island, and took his seat on the fourth of March ensuing, for the term ending in 1865. He served with efficiency on the floor of the Senate, and as Chairman of the Committee on Printing. He was re-elected to the Senate for the term ending in 1871, again serving as Chairman of the Committee on Printing, and as a member of the Committees on Claims, Naval Affairs, Mines and Mining, and Post Offices. At the opening of the Forty-first Congress he was elected President of the Senate *pro tempore*.

Mr. Anthony is recognized among the most radical of the Republican members of the Senate. He has stood almost alone in the Senate as an advocate of woman suffrage.

As a Senator he has much influence, consequent upon his ability in debate, and large experience in public affairs. He has dignified bearing and commanding presence, with regular features, florid complexion, and a profusion of iron-gray hair.

USTIN S. MORRILL was born in Strafford, Vermont, April 14, 1810. Having received an academic education, he engaged in mercantile pursuits until 1848, when he turned his attention to agriculture. He was elected a Representative from Vermont to the Thirty-fourth Congress, and was five times re-elected. In the Thirty-ninth Congress he was Chairman of the Committee of Ways and Means. In October, 1866, he was elected a Senator in Congress for Vermont, for the term ending in 1873. He is a careful thinker and a sound reasoner, especially upon financial and economical subjects, to which he has given much attention. His name is connected with the tariff, which is a source of immense revenue and protection to the industry of the country.

ETER G. VANWINKLE was born in New York City, September 7, 1808. Having received an academic education, and studied law, he went to what is now West Virginia in 1835.. He practiced his profession until 1852, when he became treasurer, and subsequently president of a railroad company. He was a member of the Virginia State Constitutional Convention in 1850. In 1861 he was a member of the Convention assembled at Wheeling to frame a Constitution for the proposed new State of West Virginia. He was a member of the Legislature of that State from its organization to June, 1863. In November of that year he was elected to the United States Senate, for the term which ended March 4th, 1869.

OHN S. HARRIS was born at Truxton, Cortland County, New York, December 18, 1825. Having received an academical education, in 1846 he removed to Milwaukee, Wisconsin, where he embarked in commercial and financial pursuits. In 1863 he removed to Concordia Parish, Louisiana, and engaged in the cultivation of cotton. He was elected to the Constitutional Convention of that State in 1867, and to the State Senate in April, 1868. He was elected to the United States Senate in July, 1868, and the same month took his seat for the term ending in 1871.

THOMAS W. OSBORN was born at Scotch Plains, New Jersey, March 9, 1836. He graduated at Madison University in 1860, and studied law at Watertown, New York. In 1861 he entered the Union army as captain in the 1st New York Artillery. He afterwards served successfully as Chief of Artillery of the Army of Tennessee. He was Assistant-Commissioner of the Bureau of Refugees and Freedmen for Florida from January, 1865, to August, 1866. He practiced law in Tallahasse, and held the office of Register in Bankruptcy. He was a member of the Constitutional Convention of Florida under the Reconstruction Act, and was elected to the United States Senate for the term ending in 1873.

GEORGE E. SPENCER was born in Jefferson County, New York, November 1, 1836. He removed to Iowa, and served as Secretary of the Senate of that State in 1856, and was admitted to the bar. He entered the army in 1862 as Captain and Assistant Adjutant-General of Volunteers. He commanded a brigade of cavalry in Sherman's grand march, and was brevetted Brigadier-General for gallantry in the field. At the close of the war he settled in Alabama, and in May, 1867, was appointed Register in Bankruptcy for the Fourth District of that State. In July, 1868, he was elected to the United States Senate for the term ending in 1873.

JOHN POOL was born in Pasquodunk County, North Carolina, June 16, 1826. He graduated at the University of North Carolina in 1847, and adopted the profession of law. He was elected to the State Senate in 1856, and was re-elected in 1858. He was the Whig candidate for Governor in 1860. He was a member of the State Constitutional Convention in 1865. In the same year he was elected to the United States Senate from North Carolina, but was not admitted to a seat. In 1868 he was again elected to the United States Senate, and in July of that year he was admitted to his seat for the term ending in 1873.

JAMES A. BAYARD is a native of Delaware, and son of a distinguished Senator of the United States, who was American Minister to France, and aided in negotiating the celebrated treaty of Ghent. The younger Bayard graduated at Princeton College, and adopted the profession of law. He was elected to the United States Senate in 1851, was re-elected in 1857, and was again re-elected in 1863, but resigned, January 29, 1864. He was appointed to fill the vacancy occasioned by the death of George Read Riddle, and took his seat April 1, 1867. His term of service expired March 4, 1869, when he was succeeded by his son.

WILLIAM PITT KELLOGG was born in Vermont, December 8, 1830, and was educated at Norwich University. He removed to Illinois in 1848, studied law in Peoria, and was admitted to the bar in 1853. In 1860 he was appointed Chief-Justice of Nebraska, by President Lincoln, but resigned the same year, and was commissioned as Colonel of the Seventh Illinois Cavalry. He served under General Pope in Missouri, and commanded a cavalry brigade, until the evacuation of Corinth. In April, 1865, he was appointed Collector of the port of New Orleans, his commission being signed by Mr. Lincoln on the day of his assassination. In July, 1868, he was elected by the Legislature of Louisiana a Senator in Congress, for the term ending in 1873.

THOMAS J. ROBERTSON was born in Fairfield County, South Carolina, August 3d, 1823. He graduated at South Carolina College in 1843, and subsequently turned his attention to agricultural pursuits and railroad interests. During the Rebellion he was an avowed Union man. He was a member of the South Carolina Constitutional Convention, under the reconstruction acts, and at the first meeting of the General Assembly under the new Constitutional Convention he was elected to the Senate of the United States, and took his seat July 22, 1868, for the term ending in 1871.

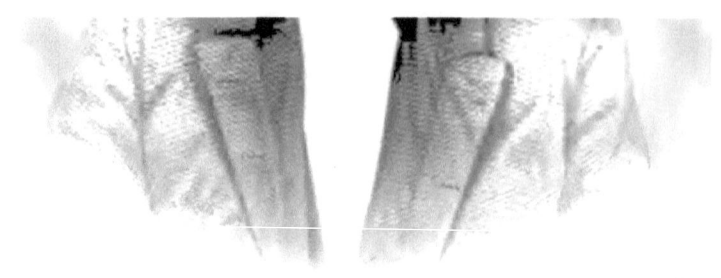

Geo H Williams

GEORGE H. WILLIAMS.

GEORGE H. WILLIAMS was born in Columbia County, New York, March 23, 1823. He received an academical education in Onondaga County, and studied law. He was admitted to the bar in 1844, and immediately emigrated to Iowa. In 1847 he was elected Judge of the First Judicial District of Iowa, and in 1852 he was a presidential elector. In 1852 he received from President Pierce the appointment of Chief-Justice of the Territory of Oregon, and was re-appointed by President Buchanan in 1857, but resigned. He was a member of the Convention which formed a Constitution for the State of Oregon.

When Oregon was under the absolute control of the Democratic party, Judge Williams declared himself a Republican, and did much to promote the ultimate triumph of that party in his State. In 1864 he was elected a United States Senator from Oregon for the term ending in 1871. He at once took an active part in the important legislation of the Thirty-ninth Congress. On the first day of the second session of this Congress he brought before the Senate a bill to "regulate the tenure of offices," which was referred to a committee, and subsequently, with modifications, passed over the President's veto. On the 4th of February, 1867, Mr. Williams introduced " A bill to provide for the more efficient government of the insurrectionary States," which was referred to the Committee on Reconstruction. It was subsequently reported and passed as the "Military Reconstruction Act." He has served with much ability on the Committee on the Judiciary, and as Chairman of the Committee on Private Land Claims.

As a Speaker Mr. Williams is deliberate, logical, and impressive. He is a wise, comprehensive, and practical statesman, having a large and increasing influence in the Senate.

JAMES W. GRIMES was born in Deering, Hillsboro County, New Hampshire, October 16, 1816. He graduated at Dartmouth College in 1836, and soon after removed to Iowa, where he was, in 1838, elected to the first Territorial Legislature. From 1854 to 1858 he was Governor of the State of Iowa. In 1859 he was elected a Senator in Congress, and in 1865 was elected for a second term, which will end in 1871. He received the degree of LL.D. from Iowa College in 1865. During the greater part of his term in the Senate he has served as Chairman of the Committee of Naval Affairs, and in this position rendered important service to the country during the war. His vote to acquit the President in the Impeachment Trial elicited much criticism from his political friends.

EDMUND G. ROSS was born in Ashland, Ohio, December 7th, 1826. He went to Wisconsin, and worked as a printer in the office of the "Milwaukee Sentinel." Emigrating to Kansas at the beginning of the troubles there, he became editor of the "Kansas Tribune." He was a member of the Constitutional Convention of 1859, which framed the present Constitution of the State. At the breaking out of the rebellion he entered the Union army as a private, and was promoted to the rank of major. He was appointed to the United States Senate, to fill the vacancy occasioned by the suicide of James H. Lane, and took his seat July 25th, 1866. He was regularly elected by the Legislature, in the following January, for the term ending in 1871.

WILLARD SAULSBURY was born in Kent County, Delaware, June 2, 1820. He was educated at Delaware College and at Dickinson College, Pennsylvania. He studied law, and was admitted to the bar in 1845. In 1850 he was elected Attorney-General of Delaware and held the office five years. In 1859 he was elected a United States Senator, and was subsequently re-elected for a second term, which will end in 1871.

BENJAMIN F. RICE was born at East Otto, Cattaraugus County, New York, May 28th, 1828. Having adopted the profession of law, he removed to Kentucky. He served in the Legislature of that State in 1855-56, and was elected a presidential elector for the Sixth Congressional District in 1856. He removed to Minnesota in 1860. On the breaking out of the Rebellion he entered the Union army as a private, and was promoted to Captain in the Third Minnesota Infantry Volunteers, and served three years. In 1864 he settled in Little Rock, Arkansas, and practiced law. He took an active part in organizing the Republican party in Arkansas, and served as Chairman of the State Central Committee. In April, 1868, he was elected to the United States Senate for a term ending in 1873.

ALEXANDER RAMSEY was born near Harrisburg, Pennsylvania, September 8th, 1815. In 1841 he was elected Clerk of the House of Representatives of Pennsylvania. From 1843 to 1847 he was a Representative in Congress from Pennsylvania. In 1849 he was appointed by President Taylor the first Territorial Governor of Minnesota, and held that office until 1853. During his term of office he negotiated a number of important Indian treaties. In 1858 he was elected Governor of the State of Minnesota, continuing in that office until 1862. In 1863 he was elected a United States Senator, and was re-elected for a second term ending in 1875.

THOMAS C. McCREERY was born in Kentucky, in 1817. He studied law, but, instead of practicing the profession, turned his attention to agricultural pursuits. He was a presidential elector in 1852. He was a member of the Board of Visitors to the West Point Military Academy in 1858. On the resignation of James Guthrie as Senator in Congress for Kentucky, in 1868, he was elected for the unexpired term ending in 1871.

FREDERICK A. SAWYER.

FREDERICK A. SAWYER, was born in Bolton, Worcester County, Massachusetts, December 12, 1822. He graduated at Harvard University in 1844, and subsequently occupied several years in teaching. In April, 1859, he accepted an invitation to become Principal of a State Normal School, for girls, in Charleston, South Carolina. This position he held until September, 1864, when his persistent loyalty rendered him so obnoxious to the Rebels that they gave him a passport for himself and family through the lines to the post of Port Royal, then in the possession of the Federal forces. In May, 1865, he was appointed Collector of Internal Revenue for the Second District of South Carolina, the first civil appointment made in the State after the rebellion. He was elected a member of the State Constitutional Convention, but was not able to participate in the proceedings of that body. He was elected to the Senate of the United States July 16, 1868, and took his seat immediately for the term ending in 1873.

SCHUYLER COLFAX,

**SPEAKER OF THE HOUSE OF REPRESENTATIVES,
VICE-PRESIDENT ELECT.**

THE name of Colfax appears in Revolutionary history. General William Colfax, grandfather of the Speaker of the House of Representatives, commanded the life-guards of General Washington during the Revolutionary war. Subsequently to the war he was one of Washington's most intimate personal friends. The wife of General Colfax was a cousin of General Philip Schuyler.

Schuyler Colfax, son of General Colfax, and father of the Statesman, resided in New York, where he held an office in one of the city banks. He died soon after his marriage, and before the birth of his son.

Hon. Schuyler Colfax was born in the city of New York March 23, 1823. He attended the common schools of the city until he was ten years old. At this early age his school training terminated, and he launched into active life to acquire learning and make his way as best he could. The boy served three years as clerk in a store, and at the end of that time removed with his mother and stepfather, Mr. Matthews, to Indiana. They could have found no more attractive region in all the West than the place they chose for settlement—the beautiful region of prairies and groves bordering the River "St. Joseph of the Lakes."

For four years following his removal to the West, the youth was employed as a clerk in a village store. At the age of seventeen, having been appointed deputy auditor, he removed to South Bend, the county town which ever since has been his residence. He frequently wrote for the local newspaper of the town, and attracted attention by the perspicuity and correctness with which he expressed his views. During several sessions of the Legislature he was employed in reporting its proceedings for the Indianapolis Journal.

In 1845 Mr. Colfax became proprietor and editor of the "St. Joseph Valley Register," the local newspaper of South Bend. At the outset he had but two hundred and fifty subscribers, and at the end of the first year he found himself fourteen hundred dollars in debt. Being possessed of tact, energy, and ability, he pushed bravely forward in his laborious profession, and soon had the satisfaction of seeing his paper a success. A few years later his newspaper office was burned, without insurance, and the editor had to begin his fortune again at the foundation. Mr. Colfax applied himself with renewed industry to his work, and in a few years made the St. Joseph Valley Register the most influential paper in that portion of the State.

Mr. Colfax was, in 1848, a delegate and secretary to the Whig National Convention which nominated General Taylor. Although his district was opposed to his political party, his personal popularity was so great that in 1849 he was elected a member of the Convention to revise the Constitution of Indiana. He was soon after offered a nomination to the State Senate, which he declined on account of the demands of his private business.

Mr. Colfax received his first nomination as a candidate for Congress in 1851, and was beaten by a majority of only two hundred votes in a district strongly opposed to him in politics. In 1852 he was a delegate to the Whig National Convention which nominated General Scott. He declined to be a candidate for Congress in the subsequent election, which went against his party by a majority of one thousand votes.

The succeeding Congress signalized itself by passing the Nebraska bill, which wrought a great change in public opinion throughout the North. The Representative from Mr. Colfax's district voted for this odious act. He came home and took the stump as a candidate for re-election. Mr. Colfax was put forward as his opponent, and the two candidates traversed their district together, debating before the same audiences the great question which agitated the public mind. The unfortunate member strove in vain to justify his vote, and render the Nebraska act acceptable to the people. He who had gained the previous election by one thousand votes now lost it by a majority of two thousand.

The Thirty-Fourth Congress, to which Mr. Colfax was then elected, convened December 3, 1855. At that time occurred the memorable contest for the Speakership which lasted two months, and resulted in the election of Mr. Banks. At one stage in the contest, an adroit attempt to foist Mr. Orr, of South Carolina, upon the House as Speaker, was defeated by an opportune proposition made by Mr. Colfax, by which the question was deferred and the result avoided.

On the 21st of June, 1856, Mr. Colfax delivered a memorable speech on the "Laws" of Kansas, which fell with decided effect upon Congress and the country, as a plain and truthful showing of the great legislative enormity of the day. During the Presidential campaign of that year, half a million copies of this speech were distributed among the voters of the United States.

While in Washington, Mr. Colfax was nominated for re-election, and, after a laborious canvass, carried his district, although the Presidential election went against his party. To each succeeding Congress Mr. Colfax has been regularly nominated and re-elected.

In the Thirty-Sixth Congress, Mr. Colfax was Chairman of the Committee on Post-Offices and Post-Roads—a position in which he did good service for the country, by securing the extension of mail facilities to the newly-settled regions of the far West.

The nomination of Abraham Lincoln, in 1860, was eminently satisfactory to Mr. Colfax, who entered with great spirit into the canvass, and did much to aid in carrying Indiana for the Republican party. During Mr. Lincoln's entire term, down to the day of his assassination, he regarded Mr. Colfax as one of his wisest and most faithful friends, whom he often consulted on grave matters of public policy.

At the opening of the Thirty-eighth Congress, December, 1863, Mr. Colfax was elected Speaker of the House of Representatives. He has since been twice re-elected to this important office, on each occasion by a larger majority than before. He has displayed signal ability in performing the duties of an office of great difficulty and responsibility. His remarkable tact, unvarying good temper, exhaustless patience, cool presence of mind, and familiarity with parliamentary law, all combine to render him, as a Speaker of the House, second to none who have ever occupied its Chair.

In April, 1865, Mr. Colfax went with a party of friends on a journey across the continent, to San Francisco. The evening before his departure he called at the White House to take leave of President Lincoln. An hour after he grasped his hand with a cheerful and cordial good-bye, he was startled with the intelligence that the beloved President was assassinated. Before leaving for the Pacific, Mr. Colfax delivered a eulogy on the murdered President at Chicago, and afterward, by invitation, repeated it in Colorado, at Salt Lake City, and in California.

On his way westward, Mr. Colfax spent a few days among the Mormons at Salt Lake City, studying their organization with the eye of a statesman. "I have had a theory for years past," he said, in explaining the motives of his journey, "that it is the duty of men in public life, charged with a participation in the government of a great country like ours, to know as much as possible of the interests, developments, and resources of the country whose destiny, comparatively, has been committed to their hands." Brigham Young, inquiring of him what the Government intended to do about the question of polygamy, Mr. Colfax shrewdly replied that he hoped the prophet would have a new revelation on that subject, which would relieve all embarrassment.

The reception of Mr. Colfax along his route and on the Pacific coast was an ovation which revealed his great popularity. On his return, Mr. Colfax, by urgent solicitation, delivered in various cities and before vast audiences, an eloquent and instructive lecture describing adventures, scenes, and reflections, incident to his journey "Across the Continent." The proceeds of the delivery of this lecture were generally given to the widows and children of soldiers who had fallen in the war, and to other objects of benevolence.

On the 20th of May, 1868, the National Republican Convention assembled in Chicago. After unanimously nominating General U. S. Grant for President, the Convention nominated Hon. Schuyler Colfax for Vice-President, receiving on the first formal ballot a majority over all the distinguished gentlemen who had been named as candidates. This nomination was made unanimous amid unbounded enthusiasm.

On the day following his nomination, Mr. Colfax received the congratulations of his friends in Washington, and in the course of a brief speech on that occasion, uttered the following noble sentiments: "Defying all prejudices, we are for uplifting the lowly, and protecting the oppressed. History records, to the immortal honor of our organization, that it saved the nation and emancipated the race. We struck the fetter from the limb of the slave, and lifted millions into the glorious sunlight of liberty. We placed the emancipated slave on his feet as a man, and put into his right hand the ballot to protect his manhood and his rights. We staked our political existence on the reconstruction of the revolted States, on the sure and eternal corner-stone of loyalty, and we shall triumph."

No public party ever made more popular nominations. Both candidates added special and peculiar elements of strength to the Republican ticket.

After one of the most important and exciting political campaigns in the history of the country, Mr. Colfax was, on the 3d of November, elected Vice-President of the United States, receiving, with the illustrious candidate for the Presidency, a large majority of both the electoral and popular votes.

Mr. Colfax was first married at the age of twenty-one to an early playmate of his childhood. After being for a long time an invalid, she died several years ago, leaving him childless. His mother and sister have since presided at his receptions, which, if not the most brilliant, have been the most popular of any given at the Capital. On the 18th of November, a fortnight after his election to the Vice-Presidency, Mr. Colfax was married to Miss Ella M. Wade, of Andover, Ohio. She is a niece of Hon. Benjamin F. Wade, and is a lady whose virtues and accomplishments fit her to cheer the private life, and grace the public career of her distinguished husband.

Mr. Colfax is of medium stature and compact frame, with a fair complexion, a mild, blue eye, and a large mouth, upon which a smile habitually plays. He has a melodious voice, a rapid utterance, and smooth and graceful elocution. Consistent in politics, agreeable in manners, and pure in morals, he has all the elements of lasting popularity.

JOHN A. BINGHAM.

JOHN A. BINGHAM is a native of Pennsylvania, and was born in 1815. After studying at an academy, he spent two years in a printing office, and then entered Franklin College, Ohio, but poor health prevented him from advancing to graduation. He entered upon the study of law in 1838, and at the end of two years was admitted to the bar. From 1840 to 1854, he diligently and successfully practiced the profession in which he attained distinguished eminence. In the latter year he was elected a Representative in Congress, and has been a member of every subsequent Congress except the Thirty-eighth.

In 1864, Mr. Bingham was appointed a Judge-Advocate in the Army, serving six months in that capacity. He was subsequently appointed, by President Lincoln, Solicitor in the Court of Claims, and held the office until March 4, 1865, when he became a member of the Thirty-ninth Congress.

Mr. Bingham served as Special Judge-Advocate in the great trial of the assassination conspirators. Immense labor devolved upon him during this difficult and protracted trial. For six weeks Mr. Bingham's arduous duties allowed him but brief intervals for rest. He occupied nine hours in the delivery of the closing argument, in which he ably elucidated the testimony, and conclusively proved the guilt of the conspirators.

Mr. Bingham's success in this great trial attracted general attention, and awakened a wide-spread curiosity to know his history. Soon after the close of the trial, a correspondent of the Philadelphia *Press* having expressed the deep interest he had felt in arriving at a well-founded conclusion as to "the guilt of the prisoners and the constitutionality of the court," proceeded:

"Grant me space in your columns to give expression to my most unqualified admiration of the great arguments, on these two main points, presented to the Court by the Special Judge-Advocate-General, John A. Bingham. In the entire range of my reading, I have known of no productions that have so literally led me captive.

"For careful analysis, logical argumentation, profound and most extensive research; for overwhelming unravelment of complications that would have involved an ordinary mind only with inextricable bewilderment, and for a literal rending to tatters of all the metaphysical subtleties of the array of legal talent engaged on the other side, I know of no two productions in the English language superior to these. They are literally, as the spear of Ithuriel, dissolving the hardest substances at their touch; as the thread of Dædalus, leading out of labyrinths of error, no matter how thick and mazy. Not Locke or Bacon were more profound; not Daniel Webster was clearer and more penetrating; not Chillingworth was more logical.

"I feel sure that the author of these two unrivaled papers must possess a legal mind unrivaled in America, and must be, too, one of our rising statesmen. But who *is* John A. Bingham, who, by his industry and learning displayed on this wonderful trial, has placed the country under such a heavy debt of obligation? He may be well known to others moving in a public sphere, like yourself, but to *me*, so absorbed in a different line of duty, he has appeared so suddenly, and yet with such vividness, that I long to know *some*, at least, of his antecedents."

Upon which the Editor remarked: "The question of our esteemed correspondent is natural to one who has not, probably, watched the individual actors on the great stage of public affairs with the interest of the historical and political student. We are not surprised that the arguments of Mr. Bingham before the Military Commission should have filled him with delight. It was worthy of the great subject confided to that accomplished statesman by the Government, and of his own fame.

"When the assassins of Mr. Lincoln were sent for trial before the Military Court by President Johnson, the Government wisely left the whole management to Judge Holt and his eloquent associate, Mr. Bingham; and to the latter was committed the stupendous labor of sifting the mass of evidence, of replying to the corps of lawyers for the defense, of setting forth the guilt of the accused, and of vindicating the policy and the duty of the Executive in an exigency so novel and so full of tragic solemnity. The crime was so enormous, and the trial of those who committed it so important in all its issues, immediate, contingent, and remote, as to awaken an excitement that embraced all nations. The murder itself was almost forgotten by those who wished to screen the murderers, and the most wicked theories were broached and sown broadcast by men who, under cloak of reverence for what they called the law, toiled with herculean energy to weaken the arm of the Government, extended, in time of war, to save the servants of the people from being slaughtered by assassins in public places, and tracked even to their own firesides by the agents and fiends of Slavery. These poisons of plausibility, blunting the sharpest horrors of any age, and sanctifying the most hellish offenses, required an antidote as swift to cure. Mr. Bingham's two great arguments, alluded to by our correspondent, have supplied the remedy. They are monuments of reflection, research, and argumentation; and they are presented in the language of a scholar, and with the fervor of an orator. In the great volume of proof and counter-proof, rhetoric and controversy, that for ever preserves the record of this great trial, the efforts of Mr. Bingham will ever remain to be first studied with an eager and admiring interest. That they came after all that has and can be said against the Government, is rather an inducement to their more satisfactory and critical consideration. For from that study the American student and citizen must, more than ever, realize how irresistible is Truth when in conflict with Falsehood, and how poor and puerile are all the professional tricks of the lawyer when opposed to the moral power of the patriot."

In Congress, Mr. Bingham has had a distinguished career, marked by important services to the country. In the Thirty-seventh Congress he was earnest and successful in advocating many important measures to promote the vigorous prosecution of the war, which had just begun. Returning to Congress in 1865, after an absence of two years, he at once took a prominent position. Upon the formation of the Joint Committee on Reconstruction, December 14, 1865, he was appointed one of the nine members on the part of the House. He was active in advocating the great measures of Reconstruction which were proposed and passed in the Thirty-ninth and Fortieth Congresses. The House of Representatives having resolved that Andrew Johnson should be impeached for "high crimes and misdemeanors," Mr. Bingham was appointed on the Committee to which was intrusted the important duty of drawing up the Articles of Impeachment. This work having been done to the satisfaction of the House, Mr. Bingham was elected Chairman of the Managers to conduct the Impeachment of the President before the Senate. On him devolved the duty of making the closing argument. His speech on this occasion ranks among the greatest forensic efforts of any age. He began the delivery of his argument on Monday, May 4th, and occupied the attention of the Senate and a vast auditory on the floor and in the galleries during three successive days. At the close of his argument, the immense audience in the galleries, wrought up to the highest pitch of enthusiasm, gave vent to such an unanimous and continued outburst of applause as had never before been heard in the Capitol. Ladies and gentlemen, who could not have been induced deliberately to trespass on the decorum of the Senate, by whose courtesy they were admitted to the galleries, overcome by their feelings, joined in the utterance of applause, knowing that for so doing the Sergeant-at-Arms would be required to expel them from the galleries. The history of the country records no similar tribute to the oratorial efforts of the ablest advocates or statesmen.

ELIHU B. WASHBURNE.

ELIHU B. WASHBURNE was born in Livermore, Maine, September 23, 1816. He served an apprenticeship as a printer in the office of "The Kennebec Journal," and studied law at Harvard University. Removing to Illinois he settled at Galena, in the practice of his profession. He was elected as a Whig to the Thirty-third Congress, and was eight times re-elected. In the Thirty-eighth Congress he became the "Father of the House" by reason of having served a longer continuous period than any other member. He acted with the Republican party from its organization, voting always for freedom, from his vote against the Kansas bill to his vote for the Constitutional Amendment extending suffrage without distinction of color. He was Chairman of the Committee on Commerce in each Congress from the Thirty-fifth to the Thirty-ninth. At the death of Thaddeus Stevens, he became Chairman of the Committee on Appropriations. He has been the distinguished champion of economy in the House, opposing every subsidy, and doing his best to expose, if he could not defeat, every game of plunder.

Perhaps his most distinguished service to the country is that of having been the first to bring the genius of General Grant to public notice and official recognition. Mr. Grant had resided several years at Galena before Mr. Washburne knew him. The latter was then the leading man in his District, owned and resided in one of the most elegant residences in the city, while Grant was a clerk in his father's leather store, and occupied a little two-story cottage.

At the first war-meeting held at Galena to muster volunteers, Washburne offered resolutions and managed the meeting, and Rawlings made a speech. Grant was present, but took no conspicuous part. The first company raised elected one Chetlain captain. Jesse Grant's partner, Mr. Collins, a Peace Democrat, said to Mr. Washburne, "A pretty set of fellows your soldiers are, to elect Chetlain for captain!" "Why not?" "They were foolish to take him when they could get such a man as Grant." "What is Grant's history?" "He was educated at West Point, served in the army eleven years, and came out with the very best reputation." Washburne immediately called upon Grant and invited him to go to Springfield. He did so, and was employed to assist in Governor Yates's office, and in mustering in regiments. Governor Yates at length appointed Grant colonel of a regiment, but he was indebted for his next promotion to Washburne. President Lincoln sent a circular to each of the Illinois Senators and Representatives, asking them to nominate four brigadiers. Washburne pressed the claims of Grant, on the ground that his section of the State had raised a good many men, and was entitled to a brigadier. Grant, Hurlburt, Prentiss, and McClernand were appointed. When Grant heard of his promotion he said, "It never came from any request of mine. It must be some of Washburne's work." In October, 1861, while Grant was in command at Cairo, Washburne made him a visit, and then for the first time became impressed that he was "the coming man" of the war.

After the battle of Fort Donelson, Grant no longer needed Washburne's kind offices to secure his promotion. Nevertheless, Washburne found frequent opportunities to give his influence and arguments in refutation of unjust criticisms of Grant's soldierly qualities. He framed the bill to revive the grade of Lieutenant-General which had been previously conferred only on Washington, and was an efficient leader in every movement to further Grant's progress toward the chief command of the armies.

Upon General Grant's accession to the Presidency he appointed Mr. Washburne Secretary of State. He held this office but a few days, however, when he was appointed United States Minister to France.

Mr. Washburne is a man of marked peculiarities—vigorous in body, bluff in manner, vehement in oratory, making no display of learning nor show of profundity in argument, carrying his point rather by strong blows than by rhetorical art.

SIDNEY CLARKE.

SIDNEY CLARKE was born at Southbridge, Worcester County, Massachusetts, October 16, 1831. His ancestors were among the earliest settlers of New England, and were numbered among the stanch loyalists of the Revolution. His grandfather was an officer under General Gates at the battle of Stillwater, and was present at the surrender of the British Army under General Burgoyne, at Saratoga. His father served in the war of 1812, and was a well known and prominent citizen of the county in which he resided. His mother was a woman of fine mind, great energy of character, and of devoted piety, and the mother of seven children, of whom the subject of this sketch was the youngest.

Mr. Clarke did not enjoy the advantages of a liberal education. At eighteen years of age, he left the farm and district school, to engage in mercantile pursuits at Worcester, Massachusetts. While thus employed, he commenced to write for the press, and soon obtained recognition as a versatile and forcible contributor.

It was at this time he became an active member of a literary society, whose members were young men who, in the main, were denied by their circumstances the advantages of a liberal education, but who, by means of the opportunities enjoyed in this and similar organizations, acquired compensating attainments. In debate, as well as in other exercises, Mr. Clarke soon occupied a prominent position.

In 1854, he returned to his native town, and became the editor and proprietor of the *Southbridge Press*, a weekly newspaper, which he continued for five years to edit and publish. During this time he took an active part in politics, identifying himself with the Free Soil party. His first vote was cast for Hale and Julian, in the election of 1852. In 1856 he was a warm supporter of Gen. Fremont, and rendered efficient service both as editor and speaker throughout that memorable campaign. In the spring of 1858, in accordance with the advice of his physicians, he sought the more genial climate of Kansas, visiting the settled portions of the territory, and becoming ardently interested in the future of that historic community. The following year he fulfilled his purpose of making Kansas his home, and settled at Lawrence, in Douglas County. During the first two years of his residence in Kansas, Mr. Clarke became actively engaged in political affairs, and warmly espoused the cause of the "Radical wing" of the Free State party.

In 1862, he was elected to the State Legislature, where he at once took front rank among the many able men who composed that body. In 1863, he was appointed Assistant Adjutant-General of Volunteers, by Mr. Lincoln, and was at once assigned to duty in the Bureau of the Provost-Marshal General as Acting Assistant Provost-Marshal General for the District of Kansas, Nebraska, Colorado, and Dakota, with headquarters at Leavenworth, Kansas. In this line of duty he at once obtained recognition as an efficient and popular administrative officer. In the strict enforcement of the provisions of the Enrollment Act, and the superintending of the volunteer recruiting service, his office in a widely-extended district was a model of perfect organization and efficiency.

At the Republican State Convention, in the autumn of 1863, Mr. Clarke was chosen Chairman of the Republican State Central Committee, a position previously held by the ablest of the old Free State leaders. From this time forward, his record has been one of ceaseless activity and constantly enlarging influence in the political affairs of his State. So long as General Jas. H. Lane remained the advocate and exponent of Radical ideas, he heartily sympathized with and supported him. When the Legislature of 1864 irregularly elected Gov. Thomas Carney United States Senator, to supplant General Lane, Mr Clarke went at once before the people, promptly denouncing the election as fraudulent and illegal, and the fruit of a conspiracy. The campaign fully established his reputation for ability and political sagacity, and the action of the Legislature was overwhelmingly repudiated. On the opening of the Presidential campaign of 1864, Mr. Clarke canvassed the State in favor of Mr. Lincoln's re-election; and by the State Convention of his party, on the 8th of September, 1864, was nominated as a candidate for the Thirty-ninth Congress.

Although bitterly opposed by malcontents, who coalesced with the Democrats to secure his defeat, he was triumphantly elected over his competitor, General Albert L. Lee, by more than fifteen-hundred majority. He was renominated for the Fortieth Congress by acclamation, and was elected by a majority of more than eleven thousand. For the third time renominated, he has again been re-elected, receiving the handsome indorsement of a majority of about seventeen thousand.

As a member of Congress, Mr. Clarke has worked with great industry for the interests of his constituents, and enjoys the reputation of an able, zealous, and faithful representative. As a member of the House Committee of Indian Affairs and the Pacific Railroad Committee, while representing a new State, extensive in territory, with diversified local interests, and rapidly developing its vast resources, he has secured the confidence of his constituents by steadfast devotion to the rights and interests of the great mass of the people. His first speech in Congress was on behalf of unqualified impartial suffrage in the District of Columbia, and he has always advocated and voted for the legislation which represents the advanced ideas of the Republican organization. He has participated in all the leading conflicts which have made the policy of Congress memorable during the six years last passed, while assiduously laboring for local measures, looking toward the material development of the State he represents. Mr. Clarke possesses an active, nervous temperament, but is endowed with remarkable powers of endurance, physically as well as mentally. In one of his political campaigns in Kansas, in less than thirty days he made nearly seventy speeches, traveling in an open carriage at the same time above twelve hundred miles, visiting the most remote sections of the State, and concluding his labors apparently unaffected by fatigue.

Mr. Clarke has devoted himself with great assiduity and sagacity to the development of the material interests of his rapidly-growing State: more especially to the protection of its people against the growth of those land and other monopolies, which in all Western States have had to be struggled against. In doing this, however, he has wisely and liberally aided all reasonable efforts to promote public and private improvements.

W. B. STOKES,
REPRESENTATIVE FROM TENNESSEE.

WILLIAM B. STOKES.

WILLIAM B. STOKES was born in Chatham County, North Carolina, on the 9th day of September, 1814. In the month of March, 1818, his father started with his family to the new State of Tennessee. On his way thither he was killed by the passage of a wagon over his person. The care of a large family now devolved upon the mother, who, with limited means, was unable to educate, beyond the rudiments of an English education, the elder members of the family. Young William was an active, spirited boy. He married early, and betook himself to the pursuit of agriculture. He was an active, enterprising farmer, and possessed the good-will of his neighbors from his warm-hearted generosity, his candor and integrity of character.

He has held a number of posts of honor and trust, by the choice of his fellow-citizens.

In 1849 he was first elected to the lower branch of the Tennessee Legislature; in 1851 he was re-elected. In 1855 he was chosen to represent his District in the State Senate.

Mr. Stokes was always a Whig in politics, and devoted to the great leader of that party, Mr. Clay. In 1836 he voted for Hon. Hugh L. White for President; in 1840, for Gen. Harrison; 1844, for Henry Clay; 1848, for Gen. Taylor; 1852, for Gen. Scott; 1856, for Millard Fillmore; 1860, for John Bell; 1864, he was elector for Lincoln and Johnson.

In 1859 he was chosen to represent his District in the Thirty-sixth Congress, carrying the District by a majority of five hundred over Col. Savage, who had carried the District in previous elections, by a majority of fifteen hundred. In the Thirty-sixth Congress he voted generally with the Republicans.

Gen. Stokes was always a bold opponent of rebellion, in all its forms and disguised names. He exerted all his power and influence to dissuade his fellow-citizens from entering the rebellion in 1861.

As soon as the Federal army appeared in Tennessee he hastened to join it, and was commissioned by Gov. Andrew Johnson to raise a regiment of cavalry, which he led gallantly through the war. It is justice to the brave men in this regiment to say that they did invaluable service to the Government on many a well-fought field.

At the close of the war Col. Stokes was honorably discharged, and was breveted, by President Johnson, Brigadier-General for his gallant services.

He was one of the leading Unionists that sought to reorganize the new State government.

In August, 1865, Mr. Stokes was elected a member of the Thirty-ninth Congress, but, with the remainder of the Tennessee delegation, was not admitted until July, 1866.

He was constantly a bold and unyielding advocate of the Congressional plan of reconstruction. He demanded that the Government of the rebel States should be placed in the hands of loyal people, whether white or black. He was an early advocate of equal rights for all men, regardless of race or color.

When it was proposed to modify the test oath, so that it could be taken by David F. Patterson, who had been elected a United States Senator from Tennessee, Mr. Stokes opposed the proposition with all his influence and eloquence. "On the night of the 22d of February last," said Mr. Stokes, "I delivered a speech in Nashville, and there and then declared, if admitted as a member of this House, I would freeze to my seat before I would vote to repeal the test oath. [Long continued applause on the floor and in the galleries.] I have made the same declaration in many speeches since then.

"Sir, I regard the test oath passed by the United States Congress as the salvation of the Union men of the South as well as of the

North. I regard it as sacred as the flaming sword which the Creator placed in the tree of life to guard it, forbidding any one from partaking of the fruit thereof who was not pure in heart. Sir, this is no light question. Repeal the test oath and you permit men to come into Congress and take seats who have taken an oath to the Confederate Government, and who have aided and assisted in carrying out its administration and laws. That is what we are now asked to do. Look back to the 14th of August, 1861, the memorable day of the proclamation issued by Jefferson Davis, ordering every man within the lines of the Confederacy who still held allegiance to the Federal Government to leave within forty-eight hours. That order compelled many to seek for hiding-places who could not take the oath of allegiance to the Confederate Government. When the rebel authorities said to our noble Governor of Tennessee, 'We will throw wide open the prison doors and let you out, if you will swear allegiance to our Government,' what was his reply? 'You may sever my head from my body, but I will never take the oath to the Confederate Government.'"

In the summer of 1867, Mr. Stokes was re-elected to Congress by a majority of 6,440.

The character of Mr. Stokes is thus drawn by Hon. J. S. Fowler, Senator from Tennessee:

"Gen. Stokes possesses by nature a constitution of the finest quality, combining great activity and power of endurance. No man possesses greater quickness of apprehension, nor can any one devote himself more ardently to study. His time is always employed. During his canvasses he studies all his own and his adversary's points by day and by night.

"He early espoused the cause of loyal enfranchisement, and advocated with great force and power all the questions involved in the principle settled in Tennessee as the basis of reconstruction. No more earnest and effective advocate of the principle that loyal men, without distinction of race, should govern the Nation and the States, has been found. His speeches are numerous, and had great effect on public opinion, not only in Tennessee, but throughout the country. He has a restless anxiety for the success of every measure he espouses until he has secured his point. As a debater he is open, bold, and ardent, and presses with force every argument and point in his case. He is a man of great skill, and seldom fails to take advantage of any unguarded point in the defenses of his opponent. Whoever makes a canvass with him must look well to his facts, or he will be overthrown.

"Gen. Stokes has been the architect of his own fortune. From humble circumstances he has made himself one of the favored children of the Republic. He has attained this position by honest industry, devotion to his country, and fidelity to his principles."

HENRY VAN AERNAM.

HENRY VAN AERNAM was born in Marcellus, New York, March 11, 1819. In his infancy, his parents removed to Cattaraugus County. This portion of New York, then known as the "Holland Purchase," was at that time almost an unbroken forest. Educational facilities were very few, and Henry Van Aernam enjoyed but rare opportunities of attending common school. His parents being poor, with a large family dependent on them, he early learned to rely on his own resources, and after the age of fourteen he received no pecuniary assistance from any one.

By serving as clerk in a country store he earned money to pay his expenses during a short course of study at an academy. He afterward studied medicine with Dr. Levi Goldsborough. He graduated in 1845, and settled in Franklinville for the practice of medicine and surgery. In the same year he was married to Miss A. M. Etheridge of Mansfield. In 1858 he served in the New York Assembly.

Soon after the breaking out of the Rebellion, Dr. Van Aernam entered the army as a regimental surgeon. He was successively promoted to be Brigade-Surgeon, and "Surgeon-in-Chief" of the Second Division, Eleventh Army Corps. He served on the "Operating Staff" at the battles of Chancellorsville, Gettysburg, Wauhatchie, Chattanooga, Ringgold, Rocky-faced Ridge, Resacca, Dallas, New Hope Church, Kenesaw Mountain, Peach Tree Creek, and Atlanta.

These arduous labors impaired his health to such a degree that he was compelled to resign and quit the service. In 1864, while still in the field, Dr. Van Aernam was elected a Representative from New York to the Thirty-ninth Congress, and was re-elected as a Republican to the Fortieth Congress. He was appointed to the Committee on Pensions, and did much valuable service in liberalizing and improving the Pension laws.

His ability as a legislator, while recognized by the country at large, was more apparent to the Representatives themselves, by whom his advice on important measures was frequently sought and followed. He invariably gave his voice and vote in favor of extreme radical measures. In an important speech delivered on the 9th of June, 1866, he advocated equal civil and political rights for all men, taking ground far in advance of his party. "The black man in the war," said he, "has shown that he has an intelligence not to be deceived, a virtue not to be seduced, and a valor not to be daunted. In what quality of manliness does the negro race fall below the degraded whites of the South? Yet these men are and have been voters always. Is there no danger in intrusting the ballot to so many ignorant blacks? I answer frankly, there is. But the danger is far greater of intrusting it to the ignorant and disloyal whites alone. Loyal ignorance, whether white or black, is beyond comparison less dangerous than disloyal ignorance. * * Worst and most perilous of all is disloyal intelligence. This, in the persons of such men as Calhoun and Rhett, Breckinridge and Jeff. Davis, has brought upon us the awful perils through which we have just passed and are now passing. If the negro is below the whites of the South in mental strength and culture, is he not infinitely above a large majority of them in all the instincts of loyalty and devotion to liberty? He at least has always been true and faithful to his country, which has repaid him with injustice, oppression and stripes. He has always obeyed the laws of the land, paid taxes without a murmur, and yielded his body a willing sacrifice whenever perils dawned upon the nation; and by his singularly good conduct in the trying situation of the last five years he has earned this boon of suffrage, if it were not his by right, and has given ample evidence that he will make a proper use of it."

Soon after the inauguration of President Grant Mr. Van Aernam was nominated and confirmed as Commissioner of Pensions, an office for which he is well qualified by his military and Congressional services, as well as by his general ability.

JOHN COVODE.

MORE than a hundred and thirty years ago a child was stolen in Amsterdam by a sea-captain, who gave him the name of Garrett Covode. The boy was brought to Philadelphia and sold into bondage, in which he continued till twenty-eight years old. At this age he was unable to read a word. He afterwards attended General Washington in the capacity of a servant, and died in 1826, at the advanced age of ninety-four.

His grandson, John Covode, was born in Westmoreland County, Pennsylvania, March 17, 1808. The mother of John Covode was of Quaker descent, her ancestors being among those early pioneers who came over with William Penn; two of whom, and a third by the name of Wood, wrote the protest against Penn's decision in favor of human bondage, which was said to have been the first anti-slavery document written on this continent.

John Covode's opportunities for early education were limited. He was brought up on a farm, and afterward learned the trade of woollen manufacturing, which business he has now conducted for about forty years. At the same time, he was a man too energetic and progressive to devote all his attention to a woollen mill. When the State canal was building, he was one of the first to give it encouragement. After its completion he engaged in the transportation business, and commanded the first section boat that went over it from Philadelphia to the Ohio. When the Pennsylvania Railroad was contemplated, he gave to that great enterprise his time, his influence, and his means. He was in partnership with the company in the transportation business, until the completion of their road through to Pittsburg. He then organized the Westmoreland Coal Company, and commenced shipping gas coal to the Eastern markets. Of this company he was President until his duties in Congress compelled him to resign, and this enterprise, which he organized, and which he managed for several years, is, like most of his undertakings, a complete success.

Mr. Covode was first a candidate for office in 1845, when he was the Whig nominee for the State Senate in a district strongly Democratic. At his second nomination he came within so few votes of being elected, that the opposing party became alarmed at his growing popularity and changed the district. He was then taken up and elected by his party to the Thirty-fourth, Thirty-fifth, Thirty-sixth, and Thirty-seventh Congresses, during which time he was Chairman of the celebrated Investigating Committee, which did so much to show up and bring to light the enormous frauds and corrupt practices of certain parties at that time associated with the Government.

On the breaking out of the rebellion Mr. Covode was one of the first to urge bold, decisive measures. He sent three sons into the army, the youngest of whom was only fifteen years old. They joined the Fourth Pennsylvania Cavalry, one of the most gallant and meritorious regiments in the service. His eldest son, George Covode, became Colonel of the regiment, and was killed while gallantly leading his regiment at St. Mary's Church, near Richmond. The youngest suffered the miseries and torments of Andersonville for a year and a half, from the effects of which he will never recover. The second son returned at the expiration of his term of enlistment.

In Congress Mr. Covode was placed upon the Joint Committee on the conduct of the war. After the close of the war he was sent South by the President, to aid the Government in working out its Reconstruction policy. His views, however, failing to harmonize with those of Mr. Johnson, he declined any further connection with his administration.

For the Thirty-eighth and Thirty-ninth Congresses Mr. Covode was not a candidate, and his district was carried by the Democrats. At the earnest solicitation of the Republican party he consented to be nominated for the Fortieth Congress, and was elected by a majority of three hundred votes.

JOHN F. DRIGGS.

BOTH the grandfathers of John F. Driggs were soldiers of the Revolution. His ancestors were residents of Connecticut, whence his parents removed to Kinderhook, New York. Here John F. Driggs was born March 8, 1814.

In the year 1817 his father emigrated to the banks of the Susquehanna river; and after a brief residence there, moved to Fort Montgomery in the Highlands of the Hudson, near West Point. Here he resided until his son was fourteen years of age, when he again moved to the village of Tarrytown; and after remaining there two years, he settled in New York City. Here the father and mother both died, leaving a large family of sons and daughters, who inherited nothing except a moral and religious training, and limited education.

At the age of sixteen John F. Driggs was apprenticed to learn the sash, blind, and door-making business. Having finished his apprenticeship, and worked as a journeyman for two years, he commenced business as a master mechanic.

Mr. Driggs received strong anti-slavery convictions at a very early period of his life. When a boy, residing among the Highlands of New York, he had for neighbors many of the men who had been soldiers during the Revolution, and from them he frequently heard the story of the war. Such influences, together with the teachings of religious and patriotic parents, implanted within him a hatred of oppression and slavery which has been his cardinal principle of action in every phase of life.

After his removal to New York, he became vice-president of an anti-slavery society, organized among the young men attached to

JOHN F. DRIGGS.

the Bedford-Street Methodist Episcopal Church. This infant organization was strongly opposed by the old and leading members of the church, who considered it their duty to stop all anti-slavery agitation. Extreme measures were resorted to by the church authorities. To show how utterly futile would be their efforts to stifle the liberty of speech and the dictates of conscience, Mr. Driggs wrote the following lines:

> While life's blood circles through my veins,
> And of the man one drop remains,
> My voice shall aid to part the chains
>   That bind the slave.
> While Southern tyrants wield the rod
> O'er half-starved images of God,
> And Northern dupes obey each nod
>   They choose to give;
>
> I neither seek nor ask applause
> From men engaged in such a cause;
> I'd rather suffer by their laws
>   Than have their praise.
> Go kiss the feet of tyranny,
> Ye cowards, bend the trembling knee,
> Nor dare on bleeding Liberty
>   Your eyes to raise.
>
> With fiendish passions uncontrolled,
> The man who man as slave would hold,
> Would buy and sell his God for gold
>   Had he the power.
> So would the man in Christian guise
> Who feels no pangs, nor pity rise,
> Where fetter'd slaves, with pleading eyes,
>   Trembling cower.
>
> So would the man who claims to be
> The friend of human liberty,
> Yet for the wrongs of slavery
>   Will find excuse.
> So Northern dupes and Southern knaves,
> Who are yourselves the meanest slaves,
> No fairer title merit craves
>   Than your abuse.

Opposition to slavery is no new thing with Mr. Driggs, but has been a deeply felt and openly avowed conviction from his early years.

Mr. Driggs, being an ardent admirer of Jefferson and the Declaration of Independence, was a Democrat, but took no part in politics, except to vote, until 1844, when he actively participated in the reform movement by which James Harper was elected mayor of New York. Mr. Driggs was appointed by the Common Council Superintendent of the Blackwell's Island Penitentiary, and held the office two years, discharging its duties with fidelity and to the satisfaction of the people.

In 1856 Mr. Driggs removed to East Saginaw, in the State of Michigan, where he now resides. On his removal to the West, he immediately identified himself with the Republican party just organizing. Two years after his settlement in Michigan, he was elected President of the Village of East Saginaw, by a large majority over an old resident and popular Democratic lawyer.

In 1859 he was elected a member of the Michigan Legislature, receiving three hundred and twenty-seven majority out of five hundred votes cast in his village, and thirty-one majority in the district, which gave three hundred Democratic majority on the remainder of the ticket.

Upon the accession of Mr. Lincoln to the Presidency, Mr. Driggs was appointed Register of the United States Land Office for the Saginaw District.

In 1862 Mr. Driggs received the Republican nomination for Representative to the Thirty-eighth Congress from the Sixth District of Michigan. This district is very large, embracing all the Upper Peninsula, including the entire Lake Superior region, with its vast copper, iron, salt, and lumber interests. In this district, which was claimed by the Democrats, and regarded by the Republicans as doubtful, Mr. Driggs received a majority of eight hundred and fifty-seven votes. He has since been twice re-elected, receiving in 1864 a majority of eighteen hundred and fifty-six, and in 1866 a majority of four thousand and forty-six.

Soon after the commencement of the war, Mr. Driggs aided his eldest son in raising a company of volunteers for the first regiment of sharpshooters, which he commanded, and which did gallant service until the close of the rebellion.

During the war, Mr. Driggs devoted all his time, when not in Congress, to the work of raising men for the army. When he returned home from the long session of 1864, he met Governor Blair in Detroit, who requested him to raise one of the six regiments allotted to his State under the last call for three hundred thousand men. Mr. Driggs replied that he had been absent from his family for eight months, and could not undertake the work. "If we do not save our country," replied the Governor, "what will become of our families?" Mr. Driggs promptly responded, "I will try." He went immediately to work, and in sixty days the Twenty-ninth Regiment of Michigan infantry was ready for the field.

While in Washington, Mr. Driggs was untiring in his attentions to sick and wounded soldiers in the hospital. When an Indian lieutenant in his son's company, and his uncle, a former chief, died of their wounds in the hospital, Mr. Driggs had their bodies embalmed and sent home to their friends at his own expense.

In Congress, Mr. Driggs has been laborious and faithful to the country at large and to the interests of his widely-extended district. He has been very successful in securing grants of assistance to public improvements, greatly needed in his new and undeveloped district.

Since he took his seat in Congress he has never been absent at the commencement or close of any session. He has laboriously and faithfully served on the Committees of Public Lands, Pensions, and Mines and Mining, rarely missing a meeting of his committees or a vote in the House.

READER W. CLARKE.

READER WRIGHT CLARKE was born in Bethel, Clermont County, Ohio, on the 18th of May, 1812. His father was a native of Yorkshire, England, and his mother was of Scotch-Irish descent, born in Surry County, North Carolina. He was raised in a village, but employed in his youth in farming. His education was obtained by attending school in the winter, and private instruction at home by his father, who was a man of liberal education. He learned the art of printing, and at eighteen years of age established a paper at Rockville, Parke County, Indiana, called the "Wabash Herald," the first paper ever printed in that county. In 1833 he was married, and in May of that year located at Shawneetown, Illinois, where he published the "Illinois Journal." In consequence of the ill-health of his family, he removed in 1834 to Ohio, where he engaged in mercantile pursuits, in the meantime reading law. His business proved disastrous, and he was completely prostrated, financially. He struggled along as best he could, with little or no means, and managed to keep up his law reading, buying his own books, and reading without a preceptor, until April, 1836, when he was admitted to the bar of his native county. About the same time he engaged in the newspaper business, and with A. M. Gest established the "Clermont Courier," a radical Whig paper, that started out in the support of General Harrison for the Presidency. With that paper he has been connected, as publisher, editor, or correspondent, for more than thirty years. In 1838 he was a candidate for Prosecuting Attorney of his county, and although his party was in the minority over five hundred votes, he only fell thirty-six votes short of election. In 1840 he was a candidate for the Legislature, was elected by a large majority, and re-elected in 1841, when he declined further to be a candidate. In the Legislature he was a leading member, and Chairman of the Committee on Public Printing. His report in that capacity attracted much attention, and drew down upon him the wrath of the opposition press, and especially that of Samuel Medary, then public printer of the State. In 1844 he was a delegate to the Baltimore Convention, and candidate for elector on the Whig ticket that year, and aided in casting the electoral vote of Ohio for Henry Clay. In 1846 he was appointed Clerk of the Common Pleas and Supreme Courts of his county, which position he held until 1852, when the new Constitution went into effect and the office became elective, and he was not a candidate for the place.

In 1858 he was the Republican candidate for Congress, in a District with over fifteen hundred opposition majority. He was beaten about eight hundred, carrying his own county by seven majority, when the Democratic majority was over five hundred—Mr. Howard, his competitor, residing in the same county with him. In 1860 he was a delegate to the Chicago Convention, and was one of the Ohio delegation most zealous for the nomination of Mr. Lincoln. In 1864 he was the Republican nominee for Congress for the 6th District of Ohio, and elected by a large majority over Chilton A. White, the then sitting member. He was re-elected in 1866 over Mr. Howard by a decided majority, and in 1868 was defeated in convention by a whisky ring, to which he refused to surrender. At the close of his Congressional term, in 1869, he was appointed Third Auditor of the Treasury of the United States, which office he now holds.

In Congress he was always found acting with the Radical Republicans. His speeches in the House, which are carefully prepared and read from manuscript, will compare favorably with the best. A practical economist all his life, in Congress he uniformly voted against all measures of extravagance and prodigality. His private character, and his integrity and uprightness are unquestioned.

ABNER C. HARDING.

ABNER C. HARDING was born in East Hampton, Connecticut, February 10, 1807. He studied and commenced the practice of law in the State of New York, but subsequently removed to Warren Co., Illinois, where he has since resided, engaged in the practice of his profession, in extensive farming operations, and in railroad management. He was a member of the State Constitutional Convention of 1848, and subsequently of the Legislature.

In 1862 he enlisted as a private in the Eighty-third Regiment of Illinois Infantry, and was commissioned as Colonel. His military service is chiefly noted for his gallant and successful defence of Fort Donelson, Tennessee, February 3, 1863. The army of Rosecrans was awaiting reinforcements and supplies, which must come by the Cumberland river. The rebels appreciating the situation determined to cut off the line of the Cumberland by re-taking Fort Donelson. For this purpose they organized a force of eight thousand men, and thirteen pieces of artillery, under Generals Wheeler, Forrest, and Wharton. This force quietly moved north, between the Tennessee and Cumberland rivers, flanking General Rosecrans, and on the morning of February 3, were within seven miles of Fort Donelson, when a colored man brought to Colonel Harding the first intelligence of their approach. Colonel Harding immediately prepared to defend his position. His whole effective force did not exceed eight hunded men, with four six-pounder rifled guns, and one thirty-two pounder. He sent all the women and refugees on board a small steamer — the "Wild Cat," with orders to drop down the river. Forrest's command surged up the hill in repeated charges, only to be repulsed with terrible slaughter everywhere around the lines. The rebels, maddened by the unexpected resistance from this handful of heroes, charged with fiendish yells until their dead and wounded strewed the hill-sides. They gained a strong position between the Union forces and the river, thus cutting them off from water; but Colonel Harding leading a charge in person, speedily dislodged them at the point of the bayonet. It was now growing dark; the unequal contest had been maintained for more than six hours. The Union forces had suffered considerable loss, and were much fatigued by their constant fighting and rapid movements from one part of the line to the other. Soon after dark a rebel officer came in with a flag of truce and peremptorily demanded a surrender. To this Colonel Harding returned a prompt and positive refusal. The rebel emissary affected great amazement at this response, but no sooner had he rejoined his forces than they began to withdraw. In a few moments after their departure the hoarse cough of gun-boats was heard as they rounded the bend of the river two miles below, followed by the shriek of the shell which they threw into the timber back of the fort. The steamer "Wild Cat" had gone down the river until she had met Captain Fitch, with a fleet of gun-boats, conveying a large number of transports with sixteen thousand men, and immense stores for the army of the Cumberland. As soon as informed of the state of things, Captain Fitch signalled the gun-boats to put on all steam and started to the rescue.

In this battle the rebels lost more men in killed, wounded, and prisoners, than Colonel Harding had in his command. The latter lost about one hundred men. The importance of the result of this engagement is not easily over-estimated. Had Wheeler succeeded in capturing or driving out Colonel Harding, he would have immediately occupied Fort Donelson. From that position he could have checked the gun-boats, prevented reinforcements from reaching Rosecrans, and perhaps compelled him to retire from his advanced position at Murfreesboro. Thus the work of two grand armies for a year would have been lost.

Colonel Harding was promptly promoted Brigadier-General, and had the high compliment of being confirmed by the Senate without reference to a committee. He was subsequently stationed at Murfreesboro for a short period, from whence he was transferred by the people to the House of Representatives at Washington. Taking his seat as a Representative for Illinois in the Thirty-ninth Congress, he served on the Committees on Manufactures and the Militia. He was re-elected to the Fortieth Congress and served on the Committees on Union Prisoners, Claims, and Militia.

RALPH P. BUCKLAND.

OUR recent civil war, the war of 1812, and that of the American Revolution, are all associated with the history of the subject of this sketch and his immediate ancestors. His grandfather was a captain of artillery in the Revolutionary War, from East Hartford, Connecticut. He was taken prisoner by the British, and died in the Jersey prison-ship, near New York. His father went from Massachusetts to Portage County, Ohio, as a surveyor, in 1811. He enlisted as a volunteer in Hull's army, was surrendered at Detroit, and died at Ravenna, Ohio, a few months after his return home, from disease contracted in the service.

Ralph Pomeroy Buckland was born in Leyden, Massachusetts, January 20, 1812. His father, a short time before his death, had conveyed his family to the West, and settled them in the wilderness of Ohio. His premature death left them in dependent circumstances.

Ralph was dependent upon the exertions of his mother and the kindness of friends for support until he was old enough to earn a living by his own labor. He had the advantage of attending the common schools of the country during the winter, and attended the academy at Talmadge during the summer of 1830. In the following autumn he went down the Mississippi River, stopping a few months at Natchez, where he found employment as a clerk. In the spring of 1831 he was sent by his employers to New Orleans in charge of two flat-boats loaded with flour. He remained at New Orleans as clerk of the cotton house of Harris, Wright & Co. until the summer of 1834, when he returned to Ohio, spent a year at Kenyon College, studied law with Gregory Powers at Middlebury, and Whitlessey &

Newton at Canfield, and was admitted to the bar in the spring of 1837. During the time he was at New Orleans his leisure moments were occupied in prosecuting his studies and in learning the French language. In the summer of 1837 he commenced the practice of his profession at Fremont, Ohio, where he now resides.

In January, 1838, he was married to Miss Charlotte Boughton, of Canfield, Ohio. In 1855 he was elected to the State Senate, and re-elected in 1857, serving four years.

In October, 1861, he began to organize the Seventy-second Regiment of Ohio Volunteer Infantry, which in three months was fully equipped and ready for the field. Soon after entering upon active service, Colonel Buckland was assigned to the command of the Fourth Brigade of Sherman's Division.

On the 7th of March, 1862, he moved up the Tennessee River, and on the 17th encamped at Pittsburg Landing—the left of his brigade resting at Shiloh Church. On the 3d of April he made a reconnoissance with his brigade four miles to the front, and on the 4th he participated in a skirmish with some of the enemy's advanced forces. On the morning of the 6th, Colonel Buckland's brigade was in line full one hour before the hard fighting began. He advanced his lines about two hundred yards on the left and about four hundred yards on the right, and met the enemy. The fighting was desperate for two hours. During this time the colonel was riding along the line encouraging his men by word and example, the rebels being repeatedly driven back. Colonel Buckland's brigade maintained its ground until ordered back by General Sherman. He was heavily engaged during the second day, and was continually in the saddle.

On one occasion, being ordered to advance his brigade under a very severe fire of artillery and musketry from the enemy, one of his color-bearers hesitated to advance. Colonel Buckland rode to the front, seized the colors, and planted them at the desired point. His brigade instantly advanced, with cheers.

General Lew. Wallace remarked on Tuesday morning, while riding over the ground which the brigade had occupied, that, "judging from the dead bodies, here seems to have been the best and the hardest fighting."

Colonel Buckland continued in command of the brigade during the advance on Corinth until about the middle of May, when he was succeeded by General J. W. Denver. At Memphis, Tennessee, he was assigned to the command of a brigade in General Lauman's division, and formed part of the Tallahatchie Expedition.

As soon as the news reached General Grant that General Van Dorn had taken Holly Springs, General Buckland was sent with his brigade to retake the place. This having been accomplished, he was sent to drive Forrest from his camp at Dresden, West Tennessee.

On the 20th of March he joined General Sherman's corps in front of Vicksburg, and participated in the series of battles which occurred in the movement to the rear of that place. During the siege he was always active and vigilant, and at times much exposed. On the 22d of May he led his brigade down the grave-yard road, marching on foot to support the assault on the enemy's works, exposed to a murderous fire of artillery and musketry. Although General Buckland was constantly exposed until all his regiments were in position, and his men were shot down around him in great numbers, he escaped unhurt.

General Buckland remained with his command in the rear of Vicksburg after the surrender until the 1st of October, when his right arm was broken by the falling of his horse. By this injury he was incapacitated for active field service, but continued to command his brigade, except for a short time, until on the 26th of January, 1864, he was assigned to the command of the District of Memphis, where his administrative abilities were exemplified and his integrity of character was clearly manifested.

At the time of the Forrest raid into the city, General C. C. Washburne commanded that department, with his headquarters at Memphis. General Buckland had command of the troops in the city. Most of the troops had been sent in pursuit of Forrest under command of General A. J. Smith. Forrest eluded Smith near Oxford, Mississippi, made a rapid march to Memphis, captured the cavalry patrol, rushed over the infantry pickets, and was in Memphis before daylight, took possession of General Washburne's headquarters, capturing his staff officers, clerks, and guards—the General escaping to the fort below the city. When General Buckland was awakened by the sentinel at the door, the rebels were in possession of a considerable part of the city, and on all sides of General Buckland's headquarters. General Buckland rallied about one hundred and fifty men quartered near him, caused a small alarm-gun to be rapidly fired, and instantly attacked the rebels at General Washburne's headquarters, although they out-numbered him four to one. General Buckland very soon concentrated all his forces, which were stationed in different parts of the city, and followed up his attack so rapidly and with such spirit that in less than an hour he had driven every rebel out of the city, and attacked General Forrest's main force just outside; and after a sharp fight of about one hour General Forrest was in full retreat, having entirely failed in the object of his attack on Memphis. But for General Buckland, Forrest would have held the city and captured immense stores of Government property.

General Buckland remained in command of the post at Memphis until December 24, 1864, when he resigned his commission.

Without having sought or expected political favor, he had been nominated for Representative in the Thirty-ninth Congress while still serving in the army. Without having gone home to further his interests, he had been elected by the people of the Ninth District of Ohio. In obedience to their wishes he left the military for the civil service of the country. During the Thirty-ninth Congress he served on the Committee on Banking and Currency and on the Militia. In 1866 he was re-elected to Congress, in which he is now giving his country and constituents the same conscientious faithful service which marked his military career.

WILLIAM H. ROBERTSON.

WILLIAM H. ROBERTSON was born in the town of Bedford, Westchester County, New York, October 10, 1823. The summers of his boyhood, with few exceptions, were spent upon his father's farm. His education was obtained in the common school and at Union Academy, then a flourishing literary institution in northern Westchester. After leaving the academy, he taught a district school for two years. He subsequently studied law, and in September, 1847, was admitted to practice in all the courts of his native State.

In 1848, he was elected Member of Assembly on the Whig ticket, and served two terms. He gave a vigorous support to the bill, which became a law, for the establishment of Free Schools throughout the State. His motto was "Education for all, Liberty for all."

In 1853, he was elected Senator on the Whig ticket, although the district gave the Democratic State ticket at that election about three thousand majority. As Chairman of the Committee on Literature, he reported and carried through a bill separating the office of State Superintendent of Common Schools from that of Secretary of State, and establishing a distinct and independent bureau for the educational interests of the State. He also introduced and carried through a bill for the protection of mechanics and laborers in the erection of buildings in his county, which has never been repealed. Every bill introduced by him during his legislative career, passed that branch of the Legislature of which, at the time, he was a member. During the period of his service in the House and Senate, there were passed at least fifty local bills affecting the section he represented.

WILLIAM H. ROBERTSON.

At that time Know-Nothingism was at its flood. Mr. Robertson introduced in the Senate a series of concurrent resolutions, which were adopted by the Legislature of 1855, which demanded the repeal of the Fugitive Slave Act and the enactment of a law declaring that slavery shall not exist except where it is established by the local laws of the State; declared that New York would never consent to the admission into the Union of any State that may be formed out of the Territory of Kansas and Nebraska, unless its constitution shall prohibit the existence of slavery within its limits; and that every attempt to control, by the dictation of secret political societies, or by the imposition of oaths or kindred obligations, the political action of any citizen, is at war with the true theory of our Government, destructive of personal independence, hostile to the rights of the great body of the people, and detrimental to the public welfare.

In 1855, he was elected County-Judge of Westchester County, on the Republican ticket, was re-elected in 1859, and again in 1863, although the County was at each of these elections largely Democratic. In 1860, he was a Presidential Elector, and voted in the Electoral College for Lincoln and Hamlin. He was Chairman of the Senate Committee appointed by Governor Morgan, in 1862, to raise volunteers in the Seventh Senate District of New York, which sent many soldiers to the front, and especially the Sixth New York Heavy Artillery. In 1864, he was a delegate to the Baltimore Convention, and favored the nomination of Lincoln and Johnson.

In 1866, he was elected on the Republican ticket a Representative to the Fortieth Congress, from the Tenth Congressional District of New York, by a majority exceeding two thousand. He was appointed a member of the Committees on Commerce and Revolutionary Claims. He favored the Impeachment of Andrew Johnson, and voted uniformly against his vetoes. Mr. Robertson declined a re-nomination for Representative, in order that he might devote himself exclusively to his profession.

CALVIN T. HULBURD.

THE immediate ancestors of Calvin T. Hulburd were of New England birth and Welsh descent. They emigrated to St. Lawrence County, New York, when that portion of the State was a wilderness. Here Calvin T. Hulburd was born, June 5, 1809.

Having enjoyed the limited advantages which the common schools of his neighborhood afforded, at the age of fifteen he entered an academy for the purpose of preparing for college. He finished his preparatory studies, and entered Middlebury College, Vermont, in 1825. During his four years' continuance there, he was known as a ready debater—one of the best Belles Lettres students of his class, and an easy and graceful writer. Though not allowed by the college regulations to be very prominent in politics, yet, during his college course, he was more than once left in editorial charge of the only Democratic paper then published in the vicinity of the college.

In 1830, Mr. Hulburd commenced the study of law with the venerable Abraham Van Vechten, of Albany. The following year he spent at the law school connected with Yale College, and after another year in law offices of Troy and Albany, he was admitted to the New York bar. During the three years above named Mr. Hulburd not merely read but studied law; and Judge Daggett, the then accomplished principal of the New Haven Law School, is known to have said that he made, while there, the best proficiency of any student ever connected with the institution.

All his friends anticipated for Mr. Hulburd a professional career of usefulness and honor. But when his professional studies entitled him to apply for admission to practice, his close application to books had seriously impaired a strong constitution. He found, on repeated trials, that he could not bear the drudgery and close confinement of the office, and thus, at the very entrance to his chosen profession, he was constrained to turn anew to a more active business.

In 1839, associated with an enterprising brother, Mr. Hulburd purchased a few hundred acres of unimproved land, embracing a portion of the bed and banks of the St. Regis river, in the boundaries of the town of Brasher. In the development of the resources of the town, and especially the improvement of its water-power, the brothers soon built up quite a manufacturing village, and gave to it the name of *Brasher Falls*—which it still retains.

In 1842, Mr. Hulburd was elected, on the Democratic ticket, to the State Legislature, where, in the first month of the session, he so defined his own position and that of his county, in the financial crisis of the State, as ever afterwards to be heard with respect and attention. In the Assembly of 1843, he was placed at the head of the Committee on Canals—also that on Colleges, Academies, and Common Schools. As Chairman of the latter Committee, he made a Report setting forth the necessity of retaining in the School system of New York the office of County Superintendent, and suggesting various amendments in the laws; all of which were adopted. In 1844, he was again returned to the Assembly; and as Chairman of the Educational Committee, he was required once more to examine and review the whole educational system of the State, expose its deficiencies, and suggest remedies. In his labors and investigations pertaining to this important commission, Mr. Hulburd proved himself greatly efficient, and as already possessed of those liberal and enlightened views respecting the true theory of Public Schools which are doubtless destined to universal prevalence in the country. In his Report to the Assembly, he asks: "Is it too Utopian a hope to be indulged, that even in our day we shall be permitted to see education free— free in the district school, free in the academy, and free in the college—every advantage, every facility, free to all? Would not this be indeed Democratic?"

By order of the Assembly, Mr. Hulburd was directed to visit Massachusetts for the purpose of examining the workings of the Normal schools established there. Returning, he made a Report comprising the result of his observations and investigations. In this Report, he traced, in a clear and succinct manner, the origin, progress, and results of the establishment of teachers' seminaries in Europe, and in Massachusetts, so far as they had been tried there, and concluded by recommending the establishment of such an institution in the State of New York, and the introduction of a Bill accordingly. This Bill, though encountering much opposition, was sustained by arguments so able and conclusive by Mr. Hulburd, and others, that it became a law by a large majority.

After several years of voluntary retirement, in the fall of 1861 Mr. Hulburd was again elected to the Assembly, and was placed at the head of the Committee of Ways and Means, then as now the post of honor, and in the war exigences of the times, a position of peculiar responsibility. Early in the session he introduced important Resolutions, looking toward the adoption and maintenance of a sound financial system for the country.

In the State legislature, Mr. Hulburd had the reputation of being a clear and vigorous thinker and an effective debater. In these particulars he was classed with such men as Allen of Oswego, Bosworth of New York, Hoffman of Herkimer, Sampson of Rochester, and Seymour of Utica. It was remarked of him by Mr. Hoffman, that he was the ablest man—Silas Wright excepted—ever sent to Albany from St. Lawrence County.

In 1862, Mr. Hulburd was elected to the Thirty-eighth Congress from what is familiarly known as the St. Lawrence District, and one of the most Radical in the State. He was made Chairman of the Committee on Public Expenditures, and a member of the Committee on Agriculture. During the first session he delivered his maiden speech on the President's Emancipation Proclamation. Of this speech it was well said, that "had an older member with a recognized position uttered that speech, it would have attracted more attention than it received for the soundness and sagacity of its views. It will, whenever and wherever read, be regarded as a complete, scholarly, and convincing argument—remarkable for the positions taken, and yet more remarkable that subsequent events have fully confirmed its correctness."

But chiefly was Mr. Hulburd conspicuous in the Thirty-eighth Congress for his examination and fearless exposure, in a Report to the House, of abuses and corrupt practices existing in connection with the New York Custom House.

Re-elected to the Thirty-ninth Congress, Mr. Hulburd was continued at the head of the Committee on Public Expenditures, and placed also on the Joint Committee on the Library. During this session, he spoke on the finances, Niagara ship canal enterprise, and other subjects. But his efforts were mainly directed to a continuance of the New York Custom-House investigation. By order of the House, he spent some time in Boston, examining the so-called Williams wine cases; and his report of these cases settled not only their legal status, but the moral status of several officials implicated. The report resulting from the New York investigation, while it exposed other flagrant abuses, brought out clearly the corrupt purposes and practices of the Collector of that port, so that a resolution was passed by a more than two-thirds vote, declaring that the Collector ought to be removed. The publication of this report produced a great sensation, not only in New York, but in the country generally, and is considered as one of the most fearless and masterly documents that ever emanated from the American Congress.

Mr. Hulburd, having been elected to the Fortieth Congress, was still continued Chairman of the Committee on Public Expenditures. He has also served on the Reconstruction Committee, occasionally speaking on subjects emanating from that committee. He also delivered a brief speech on the question of the Presidential impeachment.

Mr. Hulburd, though a Radical, has never been regarded as an extremist. On all subjects, his views have been characterized by liberality, comprehensiveness, and practical common sense.

SHELBY M. CULLOM.

SHELBY M. CULLOM was born in Wayne County, Kentucky, November 22, 1829. His father moved from Kentucky with his family when the subject of this sketch was scarcely a year old, and settled in Tazewell County, Illinois, where he now resides.

Young Cullom remained with his father until nineteen years of age, working upon the farm in summer, and attending a neighboring school in the winter. He, however, taught school about ten months of the time above named. At the age of nineteen, he left home and entered school at Mt. Morris University, but was obliged to leave at the close of the second year, on account of his health.

Having returned home, he remained there until his health was restored, when he entered the office of Messrs. Stewart & Edwards, at Springfield, Ill., and commenced the study of law. He was in a short time admitted to practice, and was immediately elected City Attorney, which office he held during one year.

The presidential campaign of 1856 then came on, and Mr. Cullom was placed upon the electoral ticket for Fillmore. He was also nominated for the State legislature by the Fillmore and Fremont parties uniting together, and was elected. At the meeting of the legislature, he was voted for by the Fillmore men for Speaker of the House. In 1860 he was again elected to the legislature from Sangamon County, and this time was chosen Speaker.

In 1862, Mr. Cullom was appointed by President Lincoln on a commission with Gov. Boutwell, of Massachusetts, and Charles A. Dana—afterward Assistant Secretary of War—to proceed to Cairo,

SHELBY M. CULLOM.

Illinois, for the purpose of examining into the accounts and transactions of quartermasters and commissary officers, and pass upon claims allowed by them against the Government. He was afterward a candidate for the State Senate, and for a seat in the Constitutional Convention, in a Democratic District, and was defeated.

In 1864, Mr. Cullom was nominated by the Union party of his District for Congress; and although the District, at the last previous election, had been Democratic by about fifteen hundred majority, yet he was elected by a majority of seventeen hundred—thus defeating the Hon. John T. Stewart, with whom he had read law.

The first speech made by Mr. Cullom in Congress, was in answer to Mr. Harding, of Kentucky; who had made a bitter speech against the Union party of the country, and among other things, had said that "it was time a little posting was done." We give here an extract or two from Mr. Cullom's response:

"But, sir, as the gentleman proclaimed to this House and the country that it was time a little posting was done, I thought with him; and let me tell the gentleman and his political friends that the great Union party which has stood by the nation's flag and borne it aloft amid the fierce storm of war, is always willing that the books should be posted; and the great measures of the party, for the support of which they have received the unmeasured abuse of traitors and their sympathizers, held up to the inspection of the patriotic millions of this land.

"We are not the men, sir, to shun such an examination. The party which has shaped the policy of this nation since the election to the Presidency of the great martyr to the cause of liberty, and which has never turned its back upon the Government in its contest with treason and rebellion, and which has procured the recognition of the great principles of freedom throughout the land, has no cause for alarm when it is proposed to spread before the world its political record.

"Sir, we are willing that the items of the account shall be called over, the long columns added together, a balance-sheet struck, so that the people may see at a glance how the matter stands. And may I call upon the loyal people to hold to strict accountability the party who is the debtor, as appears from a posting since the beginning of the accursed rebellion."

At the close of this speech, after posting the books and discussing Reconstruction at some length, Mr. Cullom said:

"I do not desire to deal harshly with these States or any fallen enemy. Rather would I turn from the scenes of rebellion and barbarity which have been enacted by those engaged in the attempt to overthrow the Republic, and look upon a brighter, better scene, as we commence the great work of rebuilding upon the scattered ruins of those once prosperous States. I shall not be guided in my action as a legislator by malice or revenge. But, sir, I cannot forget the thousands of brave and gallant men who laid down their lives in the terrible struggle that the nation might live. I cannot forget that four long years were required to crush out the causeless, wicked rebellion against the best Government in the world.

"Sir, I cannot forget that night in April last when that great man, so fitly styled the saviour of his country, was murdered by a fiend pushed on by the maddened exasperation of a dying rebellion.

"Sir, I perhaps feel as keenly the result of that last tragic act as any man upon this floor. Abraham Lincoln, a martyr for the cause of liberty and patriotism, murdered by traitors, now sleeps in the bosom of my own State and city; the patriotic sons of the Prairie State will closely guard his honored remains. And as we proceed in the performance of our responsible duties, let us stand by that old maxim, 'Let justice be done though the heavens shall fall.'"

Mr. Cullom was renominated by the Union party of his District, in 1866, and was elected by more than double his first majority. In the doings and deliberations of the Fortieth Congress, to which he was thus elected, Mr. Cullom took an active part.

On one occasion, in participating in a discussion on a measure for the protection of American citizens abroad, Mr. Cullom said:

"To-day there are about two million people in our country from the German States, and about the same number from Ireland, that land of persecution. During the fiscal year ending June 30, 1866, there were three hundred and thirty thousand seven hundred and five emigrants came to this country; and during the last fiscal year ending June 30, 1867, there were three hundred and ten thousand one hundred and fourteen. Sir, they are coming—they are coming with brave hearts and stout hands; they are coming with souls panting for liberty; they are coming as it were with the eye of faith fixed and gazing upon the tree of liberty planted in American soil, enriched with patriots' blood; and as they come, full of hope and courage, they expect soon, to gather beneath its protecting branches, and enjoy the blessings of a free Government. Shall this nation, as in days past, still say, Come? Shall our consuls and emigrant agents abroad still continue to point out to those oppressed millions the advantages and glories of this country, its lands, its institutions, its Government? Shall we continue our naturalization laws upon our statute-books? Shall we invite men—honest men—to take an oath to support the Constitution of the United States, and renounce all allegiance to the sovereign over the land of their nativity? Sir, the answer to these questions depends upon the action of the Government in protecting or failing to protect its people.

"Our duty is plain, sir. It is to declare the position of the American Government, and see that the Government stands by and maintains that position, in the protection of the rights of naturalized citizens whom we have invited to our shores, and who have sworn allegiance to our country.

"Mr. Speaker, one of the chief glories of a nation is in its disposition and courage to protect the rights of its people; and the nation that will not strive at least to do that deserves to be blotted from the face of the earth. I do not fear, sir, either a lack of disposition, courage, or ability to do justice to all our citizens in the present struggle. All that is needed is that the American nation shall demand the right, and it will be yielded."

DEMAS BARNES.

COMMERCE as well as politics has representatives in the Fortieth Congress. Prominent among these is Demas Barnes, who was born in Gorham Township, Ontario County, New York, April 4, 1827. Left an orphan while yet in infancy, his life, even as a child, was full of industry and sacrifice.

At the age of fourteen he went forth into the world penniless and alone. With all his worldly possessions in his hand, he worked his way towards New York City, where, after weeks of labor and travel, he arrived without money to buy a breakfast. He immediately went to work and earned his first meal by noon. Soon after, as country boys are apt to do, he conceived a desire to visit a theater. Arriving in front of the Park Theater, fascinated by the bill and the music, he took account of his cash, but had not enough to enter the cheapest amphitheater. Where that theater then stood, is now one of the finest warehouses in America, owned by our youthful hero, and worth not less than one hundred thousand dollars.

Business being depressed, he again drifted into the country, worked upon a farm, and attended district school as he could. At eighteen we find him a clerk in a store; at twenty a country merchant; at twenty-two commencing a small business in the city of New York. The dependence of a widowed mother, and half brothers and sisters by her subsequent marriage, surrounded him with responsibilities and inspirited him with energy, frugality, and ambition. Depriving himself of luxuries, he applied himself to business with untiring assiduity and with signal success.

He soon became the leading merchant in his department of business in the world, his principal house being in New York, with branches in San Francisco, New Orleans, and Montreal.

While accumulating wealth by extraordinary exertions, he was ever alive to his want of literary culture, and applied himself at all times to the collection of useful information. A close observer of near and remote events, and a patron of benevolent institutions, his lectures before agricultural societies, and contributions to the press, called him into public notice, and obtained for him, from one of the Universities, the title of LL.D.

Mr. Barnes early became a prominent member of the Chamber of Commerce in the city of New York, a director in insurance companies, and a trustee in benevolent institutions.

Having invested largely in the mineral lodes of the Western States, and being president of several mining companies, he felt it his duty to inspect them in person, and in 1865 he undertook the arduous task. He crossed the continent to the Pacific Ocean in a wagon, visiting the mines of Colorado, Utah, Nevada, and California. While making this trip, he contributed to the journals a series of letters replete with interesting narratives of personal adventure and practical observations.

These letters were subsequently published by Van Nostrand as a book, entitled, "From the Atlantic to the Pacific."

In politics Mr. Barnes was first a Whig, and an ardent admirer of Clay and Webster. Opposed to oppression and inclined to progress, he entered the Republican party at its organization, and as a private citizen resisted the extension of slavery into the Territories.

Deeming the Republican party to be drifting into sectionalism, in 1860 he declined to go as a delegate to the Chicago National Convention, saying, " I am a citizen—not a politician."

Being convinced that the nomination of Lincoln and Hamlin would prove the initial point in a future war, he immediately coined his political theories into commercial accounts, and on the 16th of June, 1860, closed his business with the Cotton States. He was the first

merchant in America who refused to do business except for cash.
When the war came, it found him financially prepared.

In 1864 he was nominated for Congress, but declined in favor of
another representative of his own political faith. In 1866 he was
again nominated, and elected by the largest majority ever obtained
in his district.

In Congress he was placed upon the important Committees of
Banking and Currency and of Education and Labor.

He was from the first opposed to the inflation of the currency.
But this measure having been forced upon the country, and its results
becoming incorporated into our financial system, he saw disaster in a
too rapid contraction, and in an elaborate and exhaustive speech, delivered January 11, 1868, said:

'The currency of a country is like the center of a wheel, the value
of property resting upon it being the circumference. We can follow
its expansive centrifugal force without danger; but when the motion
is reversed, and it acts with contracting centripetal power, it checks
the momentum of the financial world. Remove the center, and the
circumference crumbles with the slightest touch. The conditions of
society accommodate themselves to an expanding currency without
interruption. They cannot do so when contraction takes place, for
the reason *that one side of the account becomes fixed and immovable.*
As money disappears, values shrink with unequal rapidity, *but debts
remain at their full face.* A large proportion of our property is represented by credits or debts which no legislation can reduce. We
have $21,000,000,000 of property represented by $700,000,000 of
circulating medium; or three per cent. of money to ninety-seven per
cent. of confidence and credit. We have a national, state, municipal,
and personal indebtedness of over $6,200,000,000. To contract our
currency $100,000,000, reduces the total value of our property oneseventh, or $3,000,000,000. To contract $300,000,000, as is proposed, would extinguish one-half the values of our property, and
leave our indebtedness wholly unaffected, the end of which is bankruptcy to the citizen and repudiation by the Government. We have

inflated the balloon; we have landed upon a barren island. Instead of undertaking to swim to the mainland against tides, against winds and currents, I would wait for the friendly craft to insure our safe deliverance. We must now wait for the increase of wealth and population to overtake our changed condition, and restore us to the specie standard of the world."

Mr. Barnes opposed the Impeachment of the President, in a speech delivered in the House, characterizing it as a party measure fraught with mischief to the country, as merging the Executive and Legislative Departments into one, inciting the spirit of retaliation, involving the stability of our national bonds, and possibly leading to civil war. He closed his argument with the following words: "I ask, gentlemen, what is to be the effect of their hurrying this nation into the jaws of a revolution, the end of which no man can foretell? * * I beseech you to pause in these high-handed, these useless, these dangerous measures. Behold the stagnation, destruction, sorrow and death, which have already followed as the result of your legislation. Retaliation is an element of human nature. Long pent-up rage strikes with mighty force when its chains are broken. Your zealous, enthusiastic, ambitious, and dangerous men, control the action of unthinking good men. The history of the past admonishes you—the uncertainty of the future warns you of what may follow. You are certainly sowing the seeds of anarchy, destroying national credit, and disheartening our already despondent people. Be wise, be just, be humane while yet you can. The memories of the past, the hopes of the future, our own liberties, the liberties and prosperity of our children and of our children's children, are involved in the vote you this day give. As for me, if you this day impeach the President of the United States upon the *evidence now before us*, I shall consider our liberties less secure, properties less valuable, our national honor tarnished, our country disgraced, our rights invaded, and the future full of woe and untold disaster."

JOHN LYNCH.

JOHN LYNCH was born of poor but respectable parents, in the city of Portland, Maine, February 15, 1825. Having been left an orphan at the age of seven years, he was apprenticed to a house carpenter, with the condition that he should attend school until fourteen, and then serve his apprenticeship of seven years. His master, soon changing his occupation to that of a retail grocer, took him into the store as "boy of all work."

Young Lynch was favored with good opportunities of elementary instruction, and graduated at the Portland Latin High School at the age of sixteen. He soon after became clerk in a wholesale grocery and commission house, where he remained until 1848, when he commenced the same business on his own account. This, with the importing business, he has continued until the present time, with very satisfactory success.

Mr. Lynch became an Abolitionist as soon as he was capable of forming an opinion upon moral and political questions. On becoming a voter, he identified himself with the Free-Soil party, and continued to act with it until the formation of the Republican party, of which he has been an active member from the first.

He was elected a member of the Maine Legislature in 1861, and was re-elected two years after. He did valuable service to the State on the important committees of "Frontier and Coast Defenses," "Banks and Banking," and "Finance."

In 1862 he was appointed Commandant of Camp Abraham Lincoln, with the rank of Colonel, and organized the Regiments of Maine Volunteers that rendezvoused there.

In 1864, Mr. Lynch was elected to the Thirty-ninth Congress, over

Hon. L. D. M. Sweat, Democratic member of the Thirty-eighth Congress, by fifteen hundred majority.

Two years after, he was re-elected over the same competitor by a majority of about four thousand. His native city, where both candidates reside, gave Mr. Lynch more majority than all the votes she gave his competitor.

In the Thirty-ninth Congress, Mr. Lynch served on the Committee of Banking and Currency, and on the Special Committee to form a Bankrupt Law. One of the first bills passed by the Thirty-ninth Congress, was that introduced by him to prevent the return and register of those American vessels which deserted the flag during the rebellion. In advocating this measure, Mr. Lynch said:

"The question arises whether it is right to allow vessels to come back in this way by an evasion of the spirit of the laws; whether it is just to those owners of vessels who have refused to desert the flag of their country in her hour of peril? It is a cowardly argument to offer in behalf of these ship-owners, to say the country could not protect them. On the same principle the whole population might leave with their property and place themselves under foreign protection. It is for the people to protect the country in time of war; they are part of the country, and ought not to desert her when in danger. It would certainly be dangerous policy for a nation to offer inducements for its citizens to desert with their property, and identify their interests with its enemies in time of war.

In July, 1866, Mr. Lynch obtained the passage of a law exempting from duty materials to be used in building up that portion of Portland destroyed by the great fire.

In March, 1866, he made a speech on the Loan Bill, and against the contraction of the currency.

"In regard to our finances," said he on this occasion, "we have received and believed in the old and long-established precedents of the nations of Europe. Because it took Great Britain many years to return to specie payments after an exhausting war, the theory has been accepted almost without question that we cannot do otherwise. Sir, the experiences of the country for the last five years have exploded many false theories and falsified many sanguine predictions. It was positively asserted by our foreign foes that the South could not be conquered; that it never yet had been that a free people of the numbers, resources, and territory of the Southern people were defeated and compelled to submit to the will of a conqueror; that we could not raise armies sufficient for the work; that we had no money of our own, and could borrow none in Europe; that the armies, even if raised, would, upon a return to civil life, so disorganize society that Government would be upheaved and civil order destroyed.

"Well, sir, we have seen the result of all these predictions; we have astonished the civilized world by setting at naught the most profound theories of these modern sages; we have overturned the accepted notions and ideas of past centuries, and in their stead we have hewn out our own destiny in our own way, until we stand on ground where we may safely bid defiance to the assaults of the combined physical and moral Powers of Europe.

"In view of all these facts, so grandly and imperishably carved in our history, why should we follow the ideas of Europe in regard to our financial, any more than we did in regard to our military, administration? Because the London *Times* raises the cry, and our own croakers echo it, that "we must have a financial crisis" in passing from a paper to a specie circulation, is it necessary for us to precipitate one upon the country in order to verify the predictions of these prophets of evil?

"Every day's experience goes to prove that our true financial policy is to go on and provide for the maturing obligations of the Government, without contracting or disturbing the currency of the country, which is the life-blood of its commerce. Let it alone, and it will flow when it is wanted, and find ample field for employment."

On the 4th of February, 1867, Mr. Lynch introduced bills " to provide against undue contraction of the currency," and " to provide for a gradual resumption of specie payments." He introduced the same bills in the succeeding session of Congress, and on the 7th of March,

1868, made an able speech in support of the measures. "Sir," said he, "in my view, it is of the first importance that the currency of the country shall, as soon as practicable, be placed upon a specie basis. That is the only sure foundation for our system of paper money. * * * A resumption of specie payments cannot be secured by any mere arbitrary enactment that it shall take place immediately or on any specified day in the future; not by writing at once over the door of the Treasury, 'Specie payments are resumed,' nor by giving an order that such inscription shall be placed there on the 1st day of January, 1869, nor by attempting the financial impossibility of borrowing $250,000,000 of coin in Europe, where our bonds are now selling at about thirty per cent. discount, and removing it to this country with the expectation of retaining it as the permanent basis of our paper money. If we promise to resume to-morrow, the public know the promise cannot be kept. The margin of forty per cent. existing between gold and paper cannot be extinguished in a day. The chasm between our paper currency and gold cannot be leaped; it must be bridged. If we promise to resume a year hence, with no provision for appreciating, in the meantime, our paper toward a par with gold, and no provision guarding against the otherwise irresistible effect of a sudden panic after the resumption has taken place, the public will not believe that we can perform our promise; and this want of faith insures failure. If we undertake only what the financial world regards as practicable to be accomplished, we shall so inspire confidence as to insure success. To inspire confidence rather than to create distrust, should now be the first aim of our financial policy."

Mr. Lynch was among the first to arrive at the conclusion that the President should be impeached. He voted for Impeachment when the measure was first introduced in the House. When it finally passed on the 24th of February, he made an able and effective speech advocating the taking of the step, which he styled "one of the highest prerogatives of the House."

GLENNI W. SCOFIELD.

GLENNI W. SCOFIELD was born in Chautauqua County, New York, March 11, 1817. In early life he had such educational advantages as are usually furnished in the common schools. When about fourteen years of age, he quit school to learn printing, and worked at this trade about three years. At seventeen he went back to his books, and entered upon a course of classical study. In the fall of 1836, he entered Hamilton College, New York, as a Freshman, and graduated from this institution, with fair rank of scholarship, in 1840. The two years immediately following his graduation, he spent in teaching; the first in Fauquier County, Virginia, and the second in McKean County, Pennsylvania. While teaching, he studied law, and was admitted to the bar in 1842, and at once entered upon the practice of his profession at Warren, Pennsylvania, where he has ever since resided.

Except when interrupted by several terms of service in the State Legislature and the National Congress, his whole time has been devoted to his profession. In 1849, he was elected to the Legislature of his State, and re-elected in 1850. While a member of this body, he was esteemed one of its most effective debaters, and was chairman of the Judiciary Committee. His speech on the elective judiciary was quite widely circulated at the time, and attracted considerable attention throughout the State. Although during this term of service in the Legislature he acted with the Democratic party, as he did some years subsequently, he was always an anti-slavery man. During his college life he was a member of an Abolition society formed by a number of young men in the Institution, and never relinquished his early convictions in hostility to slavery. In accordance with these convictions, and while still acting with the Democratic party, he advocated the Wilmot Proviso, opposed the Fugitive Slave Law, and the repeal of the Missouri Compromise, taking the anti-slavery side of all kindred questions.

When the Republican party was formed in 1856, he immediately severed his old party connections, and in a public address united his political fortunes with the new party of freedom and progress. In the fall of that year he was nominated by the Republicans for the State Senate; and in a district before largely Democratic, was elected by a majority of twelve hundred. He occupied this position three years, and ably sustained the reputation which he had gained as a debater in the lower branch of the Legislature. While in the Senate he introduced and advocated bills to exempt the homestead from sale for debt, and to abrogate the laws excluding witnesses from testifying on account of religious belief. Neither of these bills passed; but Mr. Scofield's speeches in their favor, which were reported and printed, prove that they should have passed. His bills were voted down, but his arguments were not answered. He was more successful in his efforts to procure State aid for the construction of the Philadelphia and Erie Railroad. This aid secured the construction of a line of road which has already worked wonders in the development of that large and previously wild and neglected section of the State in which he resided. For a short time in 1861, he was President Judge of the District composed of the Counties of Mercer, Venango, Clarion, and Jefferson, having been appointed by Governor Curtin to fill a vacancy.

In 1862, he was elected to the Thirty-eighth Congress, and re-elected to the Thirty-ninth, Fortieth, and Forty-first. During his term of Congressional service, he has uniformly acted with the Radical Republicans. As a debater, Mr. Scofield has been much admired for his analytical, terse, and logical style. Without striving to be amusing, he not unfrequently enlivens his argument by pungent

satire and humorous illustrations; but the general character of his
efforts is that of clear statement and close reasoning. He seems to
aim only at conviction. The following extract from a speech delivered in reply to Mr. Brooks of New York, in January, 1865, in the
House of Representatives, is a fair specimen of his style of address
and power of discussion:

"It has been often said of late that history repeats itself. Of course,
it cannot be literally true; but the gentleman reiterates it, and then
proceeds to search for the prototype of the terrible drama now being
enacted on this continent, and affects to find it in the Revolution of
1776. Having settled this point to his own satisfaction, he proceeds
to assign to the living actors their historic parts. The rebels take
the position of the colonial revolutionists; the Government of the
United States re-enacts the part of George III. and his Ministers;
while for himself and the Opposition debaters of this House, he selects the honorable *rôle* of Chatham, Fox, Burke, and other champions of colonial rights in the British Parliament. Let us examine
this. It is true that the colonists rebelled against the Government
of Great Britain, and the slaveholders rebelled against the Government of the United States; but here the likeness ends. Between
the circumstances that might provoke or justify rebellion in the two
cases, there is no resemblance. The Government from which the colonies separated was three thousand miles beyond the seas. They
could not even communicate with it in those days in less than two or
three months. In that Government they had no representation, and
their wants and wishes no authoritative voice. Nor was it the form
of government most acceptable to the colonists. They preferred a
republic. The rapidly-increasing population and the geographical
extent and position of the colonies, demanded nationality. Sooner
or later it must come. The tea tax and other trifling grievances only
hurried on an event that was sure to occur from the influences of
geography and population alone. How is it in these respects with the
present rebellion? The Government against which the slaveholders
rebelled was not a foreign one; it was as much theirs as ours. They

were fully represented in it. There was scarcely a law—indeed I think there was not a single law upon the statute-book, to which they had not given their assent. It was the Government they helped to make, and it was made as they wanted it. They had ever had their share of control and patronage in it, and more than their share, for they boasted with much truth that cotton was king. Nor is there any geographical reasons in their favor. It is conceded even by the rebels themselves that a division of the territory lying compactly between the Lakes and the Gulf, the Atlantic and the Mississippi, into two nations would be a great misfortune to both. If it were the Pacific States demanding separation, bad as that would be, there would be some sense in it; but for this territory, you cannot even find a dividing line. When you attempt to run one, the rivers and mountains cross your purpose. Both the land and the water oppose division. There is no disunion outside the wicked hearts of these disloyal men. I can see no resemblance, then, between our patriot fathers, who toiled through a seven years' war to establish this beneficent Government, and the traitors who drench the land in blood in an attempt—I trust in God a vain one—to destroy it."

250

DANIEL J. MORRELL.

BERWICK, in the State of Maine, is the native place of Daniel J. Morrell, who was born August 8, 1821. He received a common school education, inherited a fine constitution, and grew up amid the invigorating influences of farming labors, and a healthy climate. At sixteen years of age, he left home, and engaged in the mercantile business in the city of Philadelphia. In this business, as clerk and principal, he continued during eighteen years. At the end of this time, his talents and industry had won for him such a position in business, that he was selected to take charge of, and, if possible, to resuscitate the works of the Cambria Iron Company, located at Johnstown, Penn. These works had been erected in 1853, but the company became financially embarrassed before their completion, and the enterprise had proved unprofitable. A lease of the entire property was now made to the firm of "Wood, Morrell & Co.," who not only carried out the original plans of the Cambria Iron Company, but during their lease they greatly enlarged the works, and increased their capacity.

In 1862, the Cambria Iron Company was reorganized with a capital of $1,500,000, Mr. Morrell being retained as superintendent. Since then, it has carried on the business of mining and manufacturing under its charter, and is now the largest manufacturer of railroad iron in the country, and has achieved an almost world-wide reputation for the extensiveness of its operations, the liberality of its management, and the superiority of its products. The company owns about thirty thousand acres of land—mostly mineral land—has four large blast-furnaces, rolling mills, machine shop, foundry, etc., with numerous dwellings for the accommodation of its operatives. The original mill building having been burned in 1857, it was rebuilt in the same year by the lessees. The new edifice is six hundred and twelve feet in length, by one hundred feet wide, with cross wings three hundred and seventy-two feet by seventy-four in width. Then in 1863, an additional mill building was erected, three hundred feet by one hundred, with a connecting wing seventy-four by twenty feet. In 1865, a further extension of the building was made of three hundred by one hundred feet. The production of this immense establishment in 1865 was about one thousand tons per week, while the extensions and improvements have increased its capacity equal to the production of from sixty to seventy thousand tons of finished railroad iron per annum.

Mr. Morrell has proved himself not only a capable and successful business man, but a man of much public spirit and benevolence. His advent at Johnstown was a source of great advantage to that place. He not only raised the bankrupt Cambria Company into life, and carried forward its works to completion, but he inspired on every hand a spirit of enterprise for the improvement and growth of the town. A national bank was established, of which he became the president, and he was for a number of years an active and influential member in the councils of the town.

In 1866, Mr. Morrell was elected as a Republican Representative in the Fortieth Congress, from the 17th District of Pennsylvania, and was re-elected in October, 1868. As might be expected, Mr. Morrell is an active and efficient member of the House. Though a new member, he was honored with the chairmanship of the important Committee on **Manufactures**. This committee, in June, 1868, presented to the House a voluminous and able Report on "Protective Policy," which doubtless was mainly prepared by Mr. Morrell, as chairman of the committee. In this Report it is maintained that the protective policy is sanctioned by public sentiment—that it was the policy of the early statesmen of this country—that it is the policy of all industrial nations—that such policy is justified by experience—that it is indispensable to the existence among us of a diversified industry—that it is requisite to secure a remunerative market for the products of agriculture—and, finally, that it is a benefit, instead of a tax, to consumers.

During the first session, Mr. Morrell introduced a finance bill, which he supported in a speech in which he advocated an American system of industry and finance as the guaranty of national prosperity.

He also introduced a bill to provide for a reserve of gold in the Treasury and national banks, and for other purposes; another bill authorizing the payment of bounties to persons who were rejected as volunteers, and were immediately afterward drafted and held to service.

Mr. Morrell's speech in support of the Finance bill alluded to has attracted much attention, and no little severe criticism from those who differ from its views as to legislative policy on the subject.

On the 7th of July, 1868, Mr. Morrell delivered another interesting speech on the occasion of his reporting a bill for modifying the warehousing system. He concludes this speech as follows:

"It will perhaps be charged that the purpose of this bill is to diminish imports. I admit the charge and defend the purpose. We want less of the products of foreign labor, and more constant employment for our own. We want to bring the aggregate of our imports below the sum of our exports. We have sent abroad during the eleven months of the fiscal year up to May 31, $64,486,258 in gold, besides a shipment, probably of twice that amount, in the interest-bearing bonds of the Government, States, and corporations, in the settlement of trade balances.

"I do not know of the exact shipments of gold for June, but from unofficial reports judge it will be as heavy as in May, when it reached the enormous amount of $10,668,712, or an aggregate of over seventy-five million dollars for the fiscal year ending June 30. The entire estimated annual production of the precious metals in the United States and Territories is thus swept away, while we are still adding to our foreign indebtedness at the rate of perhaps $200,000,000 per annum.

We are constantly talking of a return to specie payments; and there is scarcely a member of this House who has not presented a plan to accomplish that desired end, and yet the price of gold continues to advance, and rules higher now than three years ago.

"The necessities of the country demand some practical legislation in the interest of our own people, and especially such legislation as will tend to check over importations, employ our own labor, and prepare the way to a safe return of specie values. In the absence of a thorough revision of the revenue laws, looking to greater protection, and the suppression of frauds on the Government, the passage of this simple and brief bill will do some good, and I trust there will be no opposition to it."

We have already alluded to the enterprise and efficiency of Mr. Morrell as a member of the House. No man there works harder in the committees; and when he speaks, he is listened to with attention, it being well understood that he is master of the subjects on which he dilates. He affords a most gratifying illustration of the benefit which the public councils may derive from the practical and experienced views of a man actively interested in business affairs.

Mr. Morrell is one of those men who have made their own way in life by the force of a strong and honorable character. His countenance affords a vivid insight into his disposition and purposes, and shows him to be a man who thinks for himself. He is a man whose plans are always the result of reflection and sound practical judgment; and when once adopted, are carried forward and executed with unswerving resolution. Probably in the whole country there is no person with a clearer head for a great business enterprise, and certainly there are none having more general information regarding the iron interest, banking, and the political affairs of the nation. Almost entirely self-taught, he has enriched his mind by the lessons of observation and experience, which have been afforded in his varied career as a merchant, manufacturer, banker, and statesman.

Truly your friend
J. M. Ashley

JAMES M. ASHLEY.

AMES M. ASHLEY is a native of Pennsylvania, and was born November 14, 1824. He left home before attaining his fifteenth year, and for a time was a cabin-boy on Western river steamboats. He subsequently worked in a printing office, and visiting Portsmouth, Ohio, where his father had at one time resided, he connected himself with the press, to which his tastes and inclinations appear to have led him, and presently became one of the editors of the *Dispatch*, and afterwards editor and proprietor of the *Democrat*.

From the editor's sanctum, Mr. Ashley went into the law office of C. O. Tracy, Esq., at that time one of the most distinguished lawyers of Southern Ohio. There he remained three years, and was admitted to the bar in 1849, but never practiced his profession.

He engaged for a time in boat-building, and in 1852 we find him at Toledo, Ohio, engaged in the drug business. Meanwhile he participated actively in politics, and in 1858 was elected to the Thirty-sixth Congress from the Tenth Ohio District.

Without experience in public life, Mr. Ashley entered upon his Congressional career at a time of unusual interest, when the tempest of Southern treason was gathering in the firmament. While many were faltering in the enforcement of the popular demand for the nationalization of freedom, he maintained a uniform consistency, and was among the foremost in demanding this reform. All the great measures which now shed luster and honor upon the record of the Republican party, were advocated by him long before their adoption, and many of them were by him first introduced into

Congress. He prepared and reported to the House the first measure of Reconstruction submitted to Congress, which, though defeated at the time of its first presentation, finally received the overwhelming indorsement of his party, both in and out of Congress. He has presented several propositions which, at the time of their introduction, failed to command the united vote of his party in Congress, but not one of importance which did not finally receive that indorsement.

Mr. Ashley has ever been a most active and reliable friend of the soldier. Every measure for their benefit or relief has received his earnest and active support. During the war very much of his time, when not at his post in Congress, was spent in visiting them in the hospitals and upon the field, and their every want or request met with his hearty response. The greater portion of his salary was expended for their relief, and no demand upon his charity or labor in their behalf failed to meet a generous response at his hands. Since the close of the war he has been ever vigilant in looking after their claims against the Government, and his efforts have been of much service in securing them against tedious delays and the treachery of unscrupulous agents.

Mr. Ashley was the first to move in the House for the impeachment of Andrew Johnson, and made several speeches advocating that measure, and for some time stood comparatively alone.

On the 29th of May he took the lead again in introducing into the House a constitutional amendment, the object of which was to abolish the office of Vice-President, making the presiding officer of the Senate elective by that body, limiting the term of the President to four years, and providing for his election directly by the people.

Mr. Ashley made a speech advocating this amendment, on which a contemporary very properly remarks that "the time has been in our history when reputations for statesmanship were established by speeches of less ability."

"The country," said he in that speech, "has been distracted, and its peace imperiled more than once, because of the existence of the office of Vice-President. The nation would have been spared the terrible ordeal through which it passed in the contest between Jefferson and Burr in 1801 had there been no vice-presidential office. Had there been no such office, we would have been spared the perfidy of a Tyler, the betrayal of a Fillmore, and the baseness and infamy of a Johnson.

* * * * * *

"While each of the candidates for President and Vice-President professes to subscribe to the so-called platform of principles adopted by the conventions which nominate them, they nevertheless represent, as a rule, opposing factions in the party, and often at heart antagonistic ideas, which are only subordinated for the sake of party success. This was the case with Harrison and Tyler, Taylor and Fillmore, Lincoln and Johnson. When each of these Vice-Presidents, on the death of the President-elect, came into the presidential office, he attempted to build up a party which should secure his re-election. For this purpose they did not scruple to betray the great body of men who elected them to the office of Vice-President, nor did they hesitate at the open and shameless use of public patronage for that purpose. The weakest and most dangerous part of our executive system for the personal safety of the President is a defect in the Constitution itself. I find it in that clause of the Constitution which provides that the Vice-President shall, on the death or inability of the President, succeed to his office. The presidential office is thus undefended, and invites temptation. The life of but one man must often stand between the success of unscrupulous ambition, the designs of mercenary cliques, or the fear and hatred of conspirators."

In a recent address, Mr. Ashley paid the following tribute to certain prominent anti-slavery men of the country:

"To the anti-slavery men and women of the United States we owe our political redemption as a nation. They who endured social and political ostracism, the hatred of slave-masters, and the cowardly assaults of Northern mobs, in defense of those who were manacled and dumb, and could not ask for help, were the moral heroes of our great anti-slavery revolution. To them, and to many thousands whose names will never be written on the pages of history, but whose lives were as true, as unselfish, and as consecrated as any, is the nation indebted for its regenerated Constitution, its vindication of the rights of human nature, and its solemn pledge for the future impartial administration of justice. To me these are the men whose lives are the most beautiful and the most valuable. . . . The world is full of men whose pure and unselfish lives ennoble and dignify the human race. My exemplars are the men who in all ages have lived such lives, whether religious reformers like Luther and Wesley, or philosophers and statesmen like Hampden and Sydney, Locke and Bacon, Cobden and Bright and John Stuart Mill; or like our own Washington and Lincoln, Phillips and Garrison, Stevens and Sumner, Greeley and Gerrit Smith. To me the only model statesman is he who secures liberty and impartial justice for all, and protects the weak against the strong. He is the statesman and the benefactor who aids in educating the ignorant, and in lightening the cares of the toiling millions."

For ten years Mr. Ashley held a seat in Congress by successive re-elections. In the fall of 1868, however, the official returns gave the election to the Forty-first Congress to his opponent, but under such circumstances as to cause their accuracy to be questioned. He was nominated by President Grant for Governor of the Territory of Montana, and was confirmed by the Senate.

JOHN T. WILSON.

JOHN THOMAS WILSON was born in Highland County, Ohio, April 16, 1811. His father was in politics a Whig, in religion a Methodist, and by trade a carpenter. He died when his son, the subject of this sketch, was six years old. Highland County was, at that time, in a wilderness, and it was no unusual thing to hear the wolves howling nightly around the log cabins of the settlers.

John commenced business for himself at sixteen years of age. He began with clerking in a store at four dollars a month, and after a short time engaged in teaching school. When nineteen, he went to Tippecanoe County, Indiana, where he spent the winter in splitting rails, at the rate of thirty-seven and a half cents per hundred. In the spring following, Mr. Wilson rented some ground and planted a corn-field. When this was "laid by," he engaged himself as a farm hand at seven dollars per month; and in the succeeding winter, again took to the woods with his ax, to resume, at the same price as before, the manufacture of rails.

He was now in the twenty-first year of his age; and returning to Ohio, he commenced mercantile life in the County of Adams, and continued in that business during the twenty-four succeeding years. He commenced in a humble and modest way—his first stock of goods not being much more than sufficient to load a wheel-barrow. At the commencement of the rebellion, Mr. Wilson was one of the first to respond with means and influence for maintaining the Union. He first gave to his country an only son, a youth of noble intellect and liberal attainments. This young man enlisted in the Thirty-third

JOHN T. WILSON.

Regiment of the Ohio Volunteers, organized at Portsmouth, and commanded by the gallant Colonel Sill. He was appointed Orderly Sergeant of one of the companies, and distinguished himself as one of the most talented and faithful non-commissioned officers of the regiment. But he did not long survive the hardships of a soldier's life, and died by sickness at Louisville, Kentucky, in the following year.

As more men were called for by the country, Mr. Wilson himself soon volunteered his services, and accepted a recruiting commission for the Seventieth Ohio Regiment. He was promptly elected captain of one of the companies of this regiment, and after visiting his dying son at Louisville, he joined his regiment at Paducah. He was in Sherman's Division in the expedition up the Tennessee. Reaching Pittsburg Landing, his regiment had its position in front of Grant's army, near Shiloh meeting-house. He was in the sanguinary battle of Shiloh, where, although his company had never before been under fire, it distinguished itself for coolness and bravery. Among the officers honorably mentioned in the Commanding Officer's Report, none were more highly complimented than Captain Wilson. After the battle, he was violently attacked with disease, and his recovery deemed hopeless. In a state of insensibility he was sent home, and, by careful treatment, he recovered, so as to be able to rejoin his regiment. He continued in the service till forced by disability to resign his command. He was afterwards detailed as Brigade Quartermaster, which post he filled with ability and faithfulness until the commencement of 1863, when he received an honorable discharge from the service.

In 1863, Captain Wilson was elected to the Ohio State Senate, and was re-elected in 1865. In 1866, he was elected to the Fortieth Congress as a Representative from the Eleventh District of Ohio, and was re-elected in 1868.

LEONARD MYERS.

LEONARD MYERS was born near Attleborough, Bucks County, Pennsylvania, Nov. 13, 1827. Here the first ten years of his life were passed, after which his parents removed to Philadelphia. After receiving a liberal education, he entered the profession of the law, became solicitor for two municipal districts of that city, and in 1854, upon the consolidation of the Districts into one municipality, he digested the ordinances applicable to the new government, under authority of City Councils. Previous to this he frequently contributed articles to the magazines of the day, and translated several works from the French. In 1862, he was elected a member of the Thirty-eighth Congress, from the Third District of Pennsylvania, and was re-elected to the Thirty-ninth and Fortieth Congresses. In October, 1868, again unanimously renominated by the Republicans of his District, he was defeated by a small majority which bore such evident marks of being fraudulent, that he at once took the testimony to prove himself legally elected and justly entitled to a seat in the Forty-first Congress.

In June, 1865, Mr. Myers delivered in Philadelphia a memorial address on Abraham Lincoln, which was heard with marked attention, and favorably noticed by the press throughout the country. The following extracts will give some idea of its merits:

"Great occasions call forth the qualities of true greatness. Genius frequently culls opportunities for itself, but adversity is the crucible which tries men; and when the storm comes and the waves run high, and the passengers begin to despair, the quiet faith, and bravery, and skill of him who guides the vessel through in safety, marks him distinguished among his fellow-men.

"Such an one was Abraham Lincoln. His life covering nearly all of the present century, he stands in moral grandeur the foremost man of his time.

"The past four years have been years of sad realities, of almost incredible romance, too. The stride of a century was not expected to do so much. More history has been crowded into them than will be told in tenfold their time.

"Four years ago, American slavery falsified the Declaration of American liberty; to-day that slavery is dead, and waits but the forms of burial. Four years ago, the art of war, known to us in earlier struggles, seemed to have been forgotten; now, the most warlike people of the earth, we again relapse into the pursuits of peace, secured to us by the ordeal of battle.

"Four years ago, civil strife, the cruelest test of a nation, long predicted, long warded off, had not yet fairly burst upon our hitherto fortunate land; but it came in all its fury, and with the world as spectators, some confiding, but more predicting disaster and political destruction; we have passed through the fiery furnace, not unscathed it may be, yet purified and regenerate. Republican institutions have stood the trial. The sovereignty of the people — the right of the majority to rule, asserted in the beginning, has been vindicated to the end, even through rivers of blood. The Flag was the shibboleth; but on its starry folds, in storm and sunshine, still floated 'the Union,'—'the People!'

"And all along this terrible struggle every eye was bent, every thought turned to him who was at the helm—now in doubt or despondency, now in hope and confidence.

"Remembering that a soft answer turneth away wrath, the cavil and the sneer fell harmless at his feet. With thanks for those who approved, he kept steadily onward. True as the needle to the pole, he only sought the salvation of his country, never forgetting the priceless legacy committed to his keeping, never doubting the justice of his cause or its final triumph, never taking a step backwards. And so he won the goal amid the hosannas of his countrymen. * *

"He died in the very fullness of a well-spent life, laid upon the altar of his country; just when a nation's thanks and a nation's love seemed to encircle him; when the sneer had died upon the lip, and a world had learned to know the greatness of his heart and intellect; when he had demonstrated that among freemen there can be no successful appeal from the ballot to the bullet, and accomplished the task which he truly foreshadowed had devolved on none other since the days of Washington.

"The world contains no like record. A whole people stricken in the midst of the joy of victory and peace, to the innermost depths of grief, flags suddenly draped, the song of triumph hushed. Such sorrow never before trembled along the electric wire.

"They took him back to his home in the West, by the route which, but little over four years since, he traversed amid the shouts of a people; they laid him in the great Hall of Independence he so revered, while from the belfry above the solemn dirge floated away into the night; and ever as he was borne onward to his resting-place, through pageants of unutterable woe, millions came quietly out to gaze upon his bier, or catch a glimpse of that dear face; and women laid flowers upon his coffin, and strong men wept like children.

"Time may mellow the grief, but the gratitude of a nation will endure for ever. Those who were dear to him must be cared for by his countrymen. Above all, let his death waken us to a new life, that henceforth treason shall be branded—a crime without a name—never in another generation to disgrace the land; and when public virtue, and unsullied honor, and high principle need a synonym, let us remember Abraham Lincoln."

Mr. Myers has taken an active part in the important measures of the Congresses of which he was a member. On the 24th of March, 1866, he delivered an able speech on the "Acceptance of the Results of the War the true basis of Reconstruction," wherein he gave utterance to views several of which were adopted by the Congressional Committee on Reconstruction, and embodied in their Report. He was prominent in securing the acceptance by the Government of League Island as a naval station, delivering an effective speech on this subject in the House, on the 7th of June, 1866. On the 29th of February, 1868, he ably and eloquently advocated the impeachment of the President, giving a brief and startling review of the wrongs which entitled Andrew Johnson to a prominent position among "instances of men in high places, who in the madness and egotism of their ambition forgot their better days, and only remain as a reproach on the pages of history."

The main reliance of the President's advocates against this impeachment was upon the alleged "construction" which it was generally admitted the First Congress gave to the Constitution in regard to the power of removal by the President, and which it was said the passage of it had reversed. Mr. Myers traced the history of the legislation on this subject, and claimed that the acts of 1789-1792 and 1795, which declare how vacancies in the Departments shall be filled when the President shall remove the principal officers, were in reality *not constructions* of the Constitution, but *legislative grants* of power which could be and *had been repealed*, showing that in that First Congress "the clause was only passed in the House by a close vote, and in the Senate by the casting vote of its presiding officer—all those against it protested such was not the meaning of the Constitution, while sufficient of its supporters to have defended it, placed their vote upon the ground that they desired to confer this authority *by law*."

As a member of the Patent Committee, Mr. Myers has taken a warm interest in the inventors of the country, reporting and advocating several measures which won notice in the scientific world. In the Fortieth Congress he was also appointed on the Committee of Foreign Affairs, from which he reported and caused the passage of a Joint Resolution appealing to Turkey on behalf of the gallant but unfortunate inhabitants of Crete. In this Congress he delivered a speech favoring the purchase of Alaska, which possesses special interest.

RUFUS MALLORY.

RUFUS MALLORY was born June 10, 1831. His birthplace was Coventry, Chenango County, New York. Soon after his birth, his parents emigrated to Alleghany County, where they resided until 1838, when they removed to Steuben County. Young Mallory enjoyed such educational advantages as the common-schools then afforded. His allotment in this respect was that which, to this day, is common with farmers' boys; that is, he attended school in winters, and wrought upon the farm during the remainder of the year. At the age of thirteen, he attended an academy at Alfred Centre during the winter term, returning to labor upon the farm through the summer and fall. After two more terms at the academy, he commenced teaching a district school at the age of sixteen. He continued teaching in winters, laboring upon the farm during the summer, and studying at the academy in the fall, until twenty-one years of age.

He now engaged himself as a clerk in a small store in Andover, Alleghany County, in which capacity he acted for about two years, when he purchased an interest in the store, and became a partner. One of his associates in the firm, J. C. Everett, Esq., was a lawyer of superior attainments, who had been thoroughly educated at one of the Eastern colleges, and had commenced practice at the same bar with Daniel Webster. He had retained his large and well-selected library, and Mallory, under his instruction, commenced the study of law. He continued his studies until 1855, when he left the State of New York, and went to reside in the West, making his home in Henry County, Iowa.

During the three years of his residence in Iowa, Mr. Mallory devoted most of his time to teaching, yet giving all his leisure hours to the diligent prosecution of his law studies. Leaving Iowa in the fall of 1858, he emigrated to Oregon—reaching that territory at New Year, 1859. His first residence here was Roseburg, the capital of Douglas County, where he resumed the business of teaching, which he continued for fifteen months. During this time, through the kindness of Hon. S. F. Chadwick, then the County Judge, he had access to an excellent law library—a privilege of which he eagerly availed himself for the prosecution of legal study.

In the month of March, 1860, at the term of the Circuit Court of the State, held in Douglas County, Mr. Mallory was admitted to practice as an attorney and counsellor-at-law. In June following, he was elected District Attorney of the First Judicial District, in which capacity he served during two years. In June, 1862, he was chosen to represent his county in the lower house of the State legislature, which held its session in the following September. He was there made Chairman of the Judiciary Committee; and after the close of the session, he was appointed, by Gov. Gibbs, District Attorney of the Third Judicial District, in place of Hon. J. G. Wilson, appointed Judge of the Fifth District. In 1864, he was elected to the same office, and continued to fill it during the term of two years, when, in 1866, he was chosen a member of the Fortieth Congress by a majority of about six hundred.

In politics, Mr. Mallory was a Whig, and cast his first vote for Gen. Scott for President, and continued to adhere to the Whig party so long as it had an existence. In 1860, he voted for Stephen A. Douglas; but at the breaking out of the war, he was among the first to advocate the rubbing out of all party lines, and of uniting without regard to former political opinions for the purpose of crushing the rebellion—thus forming the great Union party that swept the State at the June election of 1862. Mr. Mallory was elected as a Union man to the legislature in that year, and has continued to act with the Republican party to the present time.

MARTIN WELKER.

FEW men in this country have a history which illustrates in a more striking manner what can be accomplished by energy, perseverance, and native talent, under the favoring influences of our free institutions, than that of Martin Welker.

He was born in Knox County, Ohio, April 25, 1819. His father, who was of German extraction, was an early settler in Ohio; and having but little means to educate a large family, the subject of this notice was obliged to rely almost exclusively upon his own resources, which did not consist in money, influence, or friends. His educational advantages in youth were limited to a few years' winter instruction in the log-cabin school-houses of the West. At an early period he developed an unusual taste for books and knowledge, and such were his habits of application that he very soon acquired a knowledge of the English branches taught in the schools at that time. At the age of thirteen he left his father's farm, and obtained a situation as clerk in a store, where he remained five years, in the mean time occupying much of his leisure time in studying the higher branches of an English education. At the age of eighteen, having made considerable progress in a general education, he entered a lawyer's office, and commenced the study of a profession in which he has since become distinguished.

While engaged in the study of the law, he occupied a portion of his time in the study of the Latin language and general history. In the literary societies with which he was connected at the time, he soon became noted as an able debater and a vigorous and accomplished writer.

In the political campaign of 1840 he took a very active part for one so young. The editorial department of the paper published in the county in which he resided received many able contributions from his pen.

At twenty-one he was admitted to the bar, and rapidly rose to distinction as a jurist and advocate. After he had been practicing ten years, he was nominated and elected District Judge of the Sixth District in Ohio, and served for a term of five years. At the close of his term he was re-nominated; but on account of much political excitement at the time, he being a Whig in politics and the district largely Democratic, he lost a re-election, though running far ahead of his ticket.

His judicial career was marked by great industry, legal knowledge of a high order, and the strictest impartiality in the administration of justice. By his urbanity of manner, his uprightness of conduct, his discriminating judgment, and his stern inflexible impartiality, he won the respect of his colleagues on the bench, the members of the bar, and his fellow citizens.

Possessed of decided executive ability, and with a great knowledge of men, and of the means of political advancement, Judge Welker has at all times exerted a large influence in the political organization with which he has acted. In a quiet and unobtrusive way, he has contributed much towards shaping the political destinies of his State.

In politics he has been always a firm and unwavering friend of freedom.

In the fall of 1857 he was elected Lieutenant-Governor of Ohio, at the same time that Chief-Justice Chase was elected Governor. He served one term, and declined re-election. As President of the Senate, *ex-officio*, he was distinguished as a model presiding officer; his great self-possession, urbanity of manner, legal knowledge, and executive ability, admirably adapting him to a position of that kind.

At the breaking out of the rebellion, he was appointed a Major on the Staff of General Cox, afterwards Governor of Ohio, and served out the term for which the first soldiers were enlisted. He was then appointed aid-de-camp to the Governor, and assigned to the duties of Judge-Advocate-General of the State, and served until the expiration of the term of Governor Dennison. In this position, by his fine business qualifications, he contributed valuable service in calling out and organizing the Ohio troops.

In 1862, he was appointed Assistant-Adjutant-General of the State of Ohio, and was the State Superintendent of the draft in that year. While on that duty he was nominated for Congress by the Republican party of the Fourteenth Ohio District, but was defeated by a majority of thirty-six votes. In 1864, he was again nominated, and was elected by a large majority to the Thirty-ninth Congress. In 1866, he was re-elected to the Fortieth Congress, serving on the Joint Committee on Retrenchment and on the Committee for the District of Columbia. In October, 1868, he was elected to the Forty-first Congress.

As a representative in Congress, Judge Welker is a working member. When he speaks, he speaks briefly, to the point, and with much force and clearness. Thoroughly Radical in his political views, he has supported with ability all the leading measures of his party.

When the great subject of Reconstruction was under consideration, on the 7th of February, 1866, Judge Welker made a speech in the House of Representatives, from which the following extracts are taken:

"No graver or more responsible duties ever devolved on an American Congress than are now upon us. This is the time and this the occasion to settle for all time in this country the great ideas and principles lying at the foundations of our noble structure of government. Let these foundations now be made strong, that in coming time the winds and storms of rebellion and revolution may beat in vain against the grand fabric erected thereon. Our fathers made this for a free government; one to which the persecuted and downtrodden of the world might fly and find secure asylum and equal rights. In the short period of less than a century, which is but a day in the life of a nation, the grand idea of our fathers was so far forgotten and departed from that we held four millions of God's creatures as the brutes of the field to be sold in the market, and their unrequited toil used to nurture and support a purse-proud and haughty oligarchy of oppressors in the land.

"Let us now make it what our fathers intended it to be, and secure to all their God-given rights, secure equal and exact justice to all men. To accomplish this we must not be in a hurry with the work. In this fast age we are apt to desire the accomplishment of too much in a given time. Let these men so lately engaged in the rebellion have time to satisfy us that they are thoroughly cured of many of the heresies they have heretofore entertained. They can afford to wait after what they have done against the Government, after the great injury they have inflicted upon the country—the deluge of blood, the ravages of war they have caused all over our land, the widows and orphans they have made, the crippled and maimed soldiers they have scattered everywhere among us. There is much for them to do in the way of improvements and reforms in their localities before they are ready to assume all the responsibilities of government. As a matter of law, most of them have forfeited their lives; and if the laws were enforced strictly against them, many of them would be hung for treason. They should remember that during these bloody four years they have caused the sacrifice of millions of precious lives and thousands of millions of treasure in this attempt to disconnect themselves from the Government, and establish for ever the infernal institution of slavery.

"From the first commencement of this unholy war until their final surrender to overpowering force, these rebels never for a moment entertained any love for our Government or regret for what they had done. Now that they are conquered by our arms, they have no right to complain upon the demand of them of conditions and guarantees for the future." * * *

HENRY D. WASHBURN.

HENRY D. WASHBURN was born in Windsor, Vermont, March 28, 1832. In the same year his father removed to Ohio, and Henry, at the age of twelve, was thrown upon his own resources. He was, at thirteen, apprenticed to a tanner, but remained in that occupation only one year; and from fourteen to twenty he was mostly engaged in attending and teaching school. Meanwhile, he commenced the study of law, and at twenty-one he entered the New York State and National Law School, from which he graduated in the same year.

Mr. Washburn then commenced practice of law at Newport, Vermillion County, Indiana. In the following year (1854) he was elected Auditor of Vermillion County, and in 1856 he was re-elected to the same office, in which he served, while continuing his law practice, until 1860, when the latter having become extensive and lucrative, he relinquished the Auditorship, and devoted himself exclusively to his profession.

On the breaking out of hostilities in 1861, Mr. Washburn was among the first in his section of the State to raise a company for service in the army. Of this company he was unanimously elected captain, and was attached to the Eighteenth Regiment of Indiana Volunteers. This regiment was, for gallantry and long and faithful service, second to no other of the many brave regiments of Indiana. August 17, 1861, the regiment left Indianapolis for St. Louis, to join in the Western campaign under General Fremont. Before its departure, however, Captain Washburn was promoted as its Lieutenant-Colonel. This regiment accompanied Fremont in his march to Springfield, and General Hunter on his return march to Otterville. Afterwards it participated with Pope's army in the movement which resulted in the surprise and capture of a rebel camp at Milford, December 18, 1861.

In March following, the regiment took part in the battle of Pea Ridge, a hotly contested fight, in which it performed deeds of great valor, re-capturing several cannon which had been taken by the enemy, and saving an entire brigade from capture. For its gallantry the regiment received, on the battle-field, the high commendations of the general commanding. Shortly after this, Lieutenant-Colonel Washburn was promoted to the Colonelcy of the Eighteenth Regiment, and was presented, by the privates of his regiment, a beautiful sword and silver scabbard. In December, 1864, he was breveted a Brigadier-General for gallant and meritorious conduct; and in July following, was breveted Major-General.

During the war he was under command of the following officers, and participated in the battles fought by them: Gen. Fremont's hundred days campaign; Gen. Pope's Black Water campaign in Missouri; Gen. Curtis in Southwest Missouri and Arkansas, and his famous march from Pea Ridge to the Mississippi River; Gen. Davidson, S. E. Missouri; Gen. Grant's campaign in the rear of Vicksburg, and the siege of the same; Gen. Banks' Teche River and Texas Coast Expedition. He also served under Gen. Butler at Deep Bottom, Va., and under Gen. Sheridan, in the Shenandoah Valley.

In January, 1865, General Washburn was ordered to Savannah, and was assigned to the command of the Southern District of Georgia, consisting of forty-five counties. He remained in command until July 26, 1865, when the war being closed he was mustered out of the service one month afterwards. The 18th Regiment, with which he entered the service, and which he subsequently commanded, was also mustered out, and arriving at Indianapolis, was welcomed home by speeches from General Washburn, Governor Morton, and others. On the discharge of the regiment, General Washburn was the only survivor of its original officers. As a military officer, General Washburn was among the best and most efficient that entered the service from Indiana. Among the first to enter the service of his country to put down armed treason, he was among the last to leave the service; he remained in it until the last rebel laid down his gun, and the flag of the Republic floated in triumph over all the States of the Union. The soldiers he so honorably commanded in so many battles, were among the bravest in the service, and will always cherish his name as a kind, considerate, and gallant officer.

In 1865, while in the field, General Washburn was nominated by the Republicans of the Seventh District as their candidate for Congress in opposition to Hon. D. W. Voorhees. After an exciting canvass, Mr. Voorhees was declared elected. General Washburn, however, contested the election, and having proven that he was defeated by fradulent votes, he was admitted to a seat in the Thirty-ninth Congress. He was appointed on the Committee on Claims, of which he made a most valuable member during the remainder of his term.

As a member of this Committee he took an active part in opposition to what was known as the "Iron Clad Bill," which had already passed the Senate. This bill appropriated several millions of dollars to the projectors and builders of iron-clad vessels used in the navy during the late war. When the Special Committee of Five to examine into the condition of Southern military railroads was raised, he was appointed one of its members, and as such traversed many of the Southern States in search of facts and evidence. Before the close of the session he prepared and introduced a most elaborate and thoroughly digested bill for the reconstruction of the Southern States on a sound loyal basis, giving the loyal people of these States the power to form State governments, but subjecting all their legislation to the approval of Congress. He took a deep interest in all legislation affecting the interests of soldiers of the late war.

In the spring of 1866, General Washburn was re-nominated by the Republicans of his District for the Fortieth Congress, and was elected by a majority of 513 votes. In this Congress he was continued on the Committee on Military Railroads, and, in addition, placed on the Committee on Military Affairs and the Committee on Pensions for the Soldiers of the War of 1812. Early in the session, as a member of the Pension Committee, he introduced "a bill granting pensions from date of discharge," also, "a bill providing for paying pensions in coin." March 19, 1867, he introduced a resolution declaring that in any future system of funding our national securities, the right to tax for municipal and State purposes should be directly granted.

In July of the same year he moved the appointment of a special committee on bounties. The committee was raised, and he was made its chairman. Since then he has made the subject of bounties a specialty, and has introduced many reforms in the payment of the same.

In March, as Chairman of the Sub-Committee on Military Affairs, he reported to said committee, and afterwards to the House, a general bounty bill, granting to all soldiers eight and one-third dollars per month for every month served, deducting all bounties previously paid. As a member of the Committee on Pensions he assisted in framing, and was instrumental in securing the passage through the House of a bill granting bounties to the soldiers of the war of 1812.

Besides these legislative labors, General Washburn has made several speeches in Congress which have given him reputation as a skillful debater. He is a popular orator on the stump, and has participated in the political campaign of several States with much acceptance and success. Of a recent speech of his at Keene, N. H., a Boston paper said:

"General Washburn held the undivided attention of the crowded assembly for nearly three hours, in a speech full of interesting matter, sound reasoning, and thrilling eloquence. It was one of the best specimens of Western oratory, and universally pronounced to be the most powerful speech which has been made in Keene during the present political campaign. Gentlemanly in his address and language, he wields a weapon keen as a Damascus blade. He was well known by the Boys in Blue as a brave and efficient commander on the field of battle during the rebellion, and he is equally efficient in the forum as in the field."

CHESTER D. HUBBARD.

CHESTER D. HUBBARD was born in Hamden, Connecticut, Nov. 25, 1814. In the following year, his father removed to Western Pennsylvania, and, in 1819, to Wheeling, Virginia. Here young Hubbard prepared for college, and then entered the Wesleyan University at Middletown, Conn., where he graduated in 1840. He then returned to Wheeling, and engaged in business pursuits. He was interested in the manufacture of lumber and iron, and was for several years President of the Bank of Wheeling.

Mr. Hubbard was a Whig in politics, and, in 1852, was elected to the lower house of the Virginia Legislature, where he won esteem and confidence for a devotion to principle which was to bring him forward, in due time, to a wider field of usefulness.

During the stormy period which preceded the rebellion in Virginia, and when it not unfrequently cost a man his life to proclaim his adherence to the General Government, Mr. Hubbard was clear and outspoken. In 1861, he was elected a delegate to the Richmond Convention, which passed the ordinance of secession. To the inquiries propounded to him as to his views, and the course he would pursue in that Convention, he published a letter in the *Wheeling Intelligencer*, of which the following is an extract:

"I realize that in the present condition of affairs much will depend on the course Virginia shall adopt. If she be found faithful—and who can doubt it?—to herself and the Union, all may be saved. If she wavers, and turns her back on the work of her own hands, all is lost; and the dial of human progress goes backward, and the hopes of humanity are blasted for untold ages. Therefore, the necessity—

CHESTER D. HUBBARD.

West Virginia has been acknowledged as a State by the executive department of the Government in all its branches. Her name has been entered on the roll of States by the Supreme Court of the United States—no Justice on that bench, so far as I know, dissenting therefrom. She has fulfilled all her constitutional obligations as a State since her admission. She furnished her full quota of soldiers for the defense of the Union—all volunteers, no drafted men among them. Can the gentleman's district say as much? She has paid her share of the direct tax, and stands as ready to-day to sustain a preserved Union as she did to defend it in its time of danger and peril.

"I know she is not a State by the consent of rebels or rebel sympathizers. I know her name is not called in Democratic convention, that it is not enrolled on Democratic banners, for she does not muster in that camp; and I am not surprised that the gentleman's ire is excited by seeing her Representatives on this floor. But I am surprised at the bitterness of invective with which she is assailed, and especially that it should come from a Representative from the State of Ohio —a State which, of all others, (I speak it in no spirit of boasting), has most reason to thank God for the loyalty of West Virginia. For four long years of fire and death, West Virginia stood between the citizens of Ohio and the destroyer. We were her wall of defense; while our fields were laid waste and desolated, theirs were rich with fruitful harvests; while our homes were left without a roof-tree by the ruthless hand of war, theirs were the abodes of peace and plenty; and yet a government and recognition among the States of the Union, secured by such earnest devotion, and won by such heroic sacrifices, must be branded as 'illegitimate,' 'conceived in sin and born in iniquity,' and that by a Representative of the people who have been most benefited by that devotion and that sacrifice. O shame, where is thy blush?"

WILLIAM A. PILE.

WILLIAM A. PILE was born near Indianapolis, Indiana, February 11, 1829. He received an academic education, studied theology, and became a clergyman of the Methodist Episcopal Church, and a member of the Missouri Conference.

In May, 1861, he joined the First Missouri Infantry, as Chaplain, and was with General Nathaniel Lyon in his campaign embracing the battles of Boonville and Wilson's Creek. After the battle of Boonville, Chaplain Pile was sent out with a party of five men to look after the dead and wounded. Believing in the Scripture doctrine, "Let the dead bury their dead," he went after the living rebels and captured twenty-six of them with their arms, and several teams and wagons, which were of great value in pursuing the campaign; on account of his gallantry in this action, he was called the "fighting parson."

In September, 1861, he was commissioned Captain of a battery in the First Missouri Artillery. It was his battery of Parrott guns of which General Pope made such favorable mention during the siege of Corinth. In August, 1862, he was promoted to the Lieutenant-Colonelcy of the Thirty-third Missouri Infantry. In December, 1862, he was promoted to the Colonelcy of the regiment stationed at Helena, Arkansas, where he was placed in charge of the construction of the fortifications of that post.

In September, 1863, he was promoted to be Brigadier-General of Volunteers, and placed in charge of the organization of colored troops in the department of Missouri. In a few months, under great difficulties, he enlisted, armed, equipped, and sent into the field over seven thousand colored troops, who rendered efficient service on several hard-fought fields. From Missouri he was ordered to an important command in Texas, and stationed at Brazos, Santiago, where he remained until the commencement of the Mobile campaign, in which he distinguished himself in command of his brigade, at Fort Blakely, being among the very first to enter the Fort, in the charge which resulted in its capture.

For his gallantry on that occasion he was breveted Major-General. He was not allowed to retire to private life on being mustered out of the army. His course during the war had made for him warm friends among the loyal men of Missouri, who pressed him into service as their candidate for Congress in the First District, against John Hogan, a Democrat.

In this contest he made many friends and admirers by his sterling qualities of both head and heart, and secured his election as member of the Fortieth Congress.

Mr. Pile has proved himself an able and efficient member of the House of Representatives. His career in life having placed him in contact with the various classes of society, from which stand-point he studied the people and their wants, his speeches are more noted for their plain common-sense view taken of pending questions, than for beauty of style or finished eloquence, although for these qualities they compare favorably with those of his peers in the House.

They evince his sterling patriotism and his concern for the welfare of the country in all its varied interests, urging "the largest freedom for all classes of people, not because of claims of peculiar races, but because freedom is the normal condition of all men. Therefore all would be benefited in proportion as any other class is benefited."

His speech pending the question of the impeachment of President Johnson may be considered as a fair sample of his forensic efforts, and from this we present two or three brief extracts:

"The President," said Mr. Pile, "has violated the plainest terms of the law solemnly enacted by the Congress of the people, according to and in pursuance of the provisions of the Constitution. Amid the momentous and multiform duties of this body arising from the condition of the country emerging from a great war, with industrial pursuits deranged, business depressed, trade stagnant, values disturbed, the people overburdened with taxes, capital timid and withdrawn from business, and the public mind feverish and unsettled, every man going to his chamber at night with an undefined, and therefore all the more disturbing, conviction that ere he wakes in the morning some new danger may threaten the peace or life of his nation—amid all this, the highest officer known to the Constitution and the laws startles the nation, from the shores of the Atlantic, 'where the sons of the Republic keep watch at the rising of the sun,' to the golden shores of the Pacific, 'where they keep watch at the going down of the same;' has startled and moved the public mind and heart to its profoundest depths by a violation of law at once so flagrant and assumptive as to leave him without excuse, and to make his defenders on this floor morally participants in his crime. * * * What insolent and brazen effrontery is it for his friends on this floor to claim for him innocent intentions and pacific motives! It will be difficult to find, in the annals of all the past, so many acts of a single tyrant disclosing the same wicked purposes, and exhibiting the same criminal intentions, as are found in this record of infamy made by Mr. Johnson. * * *

"The violated supremacy and outraged majesty of the law demand the impeachment of the President of the United States for high crimes and misdemeanors. I urge and press his impeachment in the name and for the sake of the toiling millions of my countrymen, who are wearied and exhausted by the long and fearful struggle of the past, and the unsettled and deranged condition of the present. In the interest of the industrial pursuits of the country, unsettled and depressed as they are; in the interest of stagnated trade and commerce, and deranged and fluctuating finance; and for the sake and in the name of the humanity and civilization of the age, I ask that the official career of this man shall be speedily and for ever terminated, in order that the country may have rest, quiet, and prosperity, and that the nation may continue in its high career of progress and civilization.

"In the name of the half-million of brave men whose ghastly corpses lie beneath the green sward of the South, and who died for liberty and loyalty, I demand the impeachment and removal of this man, who, in the exercise of the great power of his high office, seeks to betray into the hands of its enemies the country for **which** they fought and died."

In March, 1869, Mr. **Pile was nominated by** President Grant for United States Minister to Brazil, **but failed to be** confirmed by the Senate. He was **subsequently appointed Governor of the** Territory of New Mexico.

www.ingramcontent.com/pod-product-compliance
Lightning Source LLC
Chambersburg PA
CBHW022122290426
44112CB00008B/779